CUSTOMER EDUCATION

WHY **SMART COMPANIES** PROFIT BY MAKING **CUSTOMERS SMARTER**

ADAM AVRAMESCU

ISBN 978-1791729-8-8-2

Special thanks to:

Dave Derington, Jesse Evans, Gordon Mak, Alessandra Marinetti, Daniel Quick, Linda Schwaber-Cohen, Christine Souza, Yeesheen Yang, and Jennifer Murnane-Rainey.

And of course, Fabiola Contreras, who tolerated me throughout this entire process.

Contents

Introduction   1

   Filling a leaky bucket   5

   Customers don't care about your product   7

   Customer Education drives healthier businesses   9

   Defining Customer Education   13

Building the Case for Customer Education   16

   You're looking at the wrong mountain   18

   Customer Education in a cloudy world   25

   Why call it "Customer Education"?   26

   Are you ready for Customer Education?   28

Customer Education through the Customer Journey   33

Awareness: Customer Education as a Marketing Demand Generator   35

   How does Customer Education support demand generation efforts? 36

   Ungated documentation: your SEO savior   38

   Developer documentation as a marketing tool   43

   Training as a marketing tool   44

   Certification and Community as marketing tools   47

   Brand power   48

Evaluation: Customer Education as a Pre-Sales Differentiator   49

   The end of solution sales and the beginning of the helping sale 50

   Provide talking points and a demo   51

   Appeal to the head: Statistics and data points show impact 52

   Appeal to the heart: Quote me on this   54

   The power of the preview   55

   Sales-humans are humans too!   56

Onboarding: Customer Education is your scale engine to drive product adoption 56

   Customer Education boosts your onboarding maturity   61

   Onboarding for higher scale   62

   Onboarding for higher stakes   67

   Onboarding during a free trial   72

   Single-sourcing and repurposing content   74

Retention and Growth: Customer Education increases customers' desire to renew and reduces friction   76

    Self-service documentation is key, even in the enterprise   78

Training and maturity models: A perfect pair   81

    Customer Education in the QBR process   83

    Certification programs drive value over time   84

    Community grows over time   85

    Bring it all back to attribution   86

Where does Customer Education sit in an organization?   88

    Customer Success   88

    Professional Services   89

    Marketing   90

    Product   91

    Human Resources or Sales Enablement   91

The Customer Education Technology Stack   95

Your "On-the-Job" Stack   98

    Knowledge Bases and Help Centers   98

    In-Product Education   106

Your "Social Learning" Stack   114

Your "Formal Learning" Stack   117

    LMS   118

    Virtual Classroom & Live Labs   128

    E-learning authoring tools   131

    Certifications & Assessment Platforms   133

Supplementing Your Stack   135

    Customization & Design   135

    Designing for Data & Integrations   137

    Build vs. Buy   140

Better Content Bootcamp   143

Where content goes wrong   145

    Dismantling "Sage on the Stage"   148

    Dismantling "Spray and Pray"   150

    Take a Bite out of BITE   152

    Everything is 80/20   157

    Boosting your signal   160

Removing noise   172
Creating Courses that Boost Signal and Reduce Noise   174

Building better content   **189**
Getting it Write   190
Vim, vigor, and video   195
Improved In-Product Education   197
Keeping content agile   206

Meet Your Metrics   215

Operational metrics   **217**
Knowledge Base metrics   219
Training metrics   229
Community metrics   237
In-Product Education metrics   240

Value metrics   **242**
Rollup metrics   244
Measuring Return on Investment   246

From Here to Eternity   257

Crawl   **259**
Escape from Ad-Hoc-atraz   260
Test, learn, iterate   263
Team: No one learns until you do   265

Walk   **268**
Your first few quarters of Customer Education   268
Creating your two-year roadmap   273
Team: Finding good partners and letting them run   277

Run   **284**
Into the Future   284
Embracing trends and avoiding fads   286
Pricing and services   287
Team: Building your tribe   292
A Culture of Education   294

INTRODUCTION

INTRODUCTION

You could have the most beautifully designed piece of software in the world—each element of the interface perfectly calibrated for user engagement, each line of code more artful than the last—but it won't matter if your customers don't use it. Let's face it: In the current world of software, where every day is part of your renewal cycle, you won't succeed unless your customers succeed at gaining value from your product.

So, what do most companies do to capture long-term value from customers? From an early stage, they invest in Customer Support reps to answer questions from users. Ask an early customer what their favorite feature of the product is, and they may very well respond, "My Support rep!" Then companies invest in a Customer Success Manager or Account Manager to help insure the relationship after the sale.

In your first few years of life as a company, this is how you forge the path forward. Your small band of customer-facing employees becomes a larger band of product experts. Your early accounts have matured along with your company, and now they're asking about more complicated issues. You've released some new features, and those old support articles you wrote are long out-of-date. New team members come on, and they don't have the same knowledge stuffed into their head as your earliest successful employees. Those early accounts that once seemed solid have reached the end of their contract terms, and your renewals are hard-fought. Your small accounts have "landed and expanded" into enterprise contracts. Your tens of accounts have become thousands of accounts.

Before you know it, your company's org chart rolls several-hundred deep, and you haven't scaled your business to keep your accounts healthy. What went wrong?

Unfortunately, many startups neglect the activities that can truly help them scale and differentiate themselves until it's too late—and they're no longer startups. Because they were able to delight their early users with highly knowledgeable employees and personalized service, they miss the warning signs that those techniques, at some point, are no longer scalable.

Many companies miss a crucial distinction: Growth and scale are not the same thing. To grow, obviously, is to get larger. To scale is to grow proportionally and profitably. You can scale something to any size without losing fidelity.

To grow without scale, you must continue to invest in more humans and cross your fingers that they can meet your customers' needs. You'll possibly develop account planning frameworks, playbooks, and other tools to support all these individual humans. But most account plans and playbooks either help you *monitor* or *react* to what customers are doing. They don't actively help your accounts grow, nor do they inspire your product's users. Without help, your customers end up with skill gaps. And without the right skills, they won't fully adopt your product or derive value.

Instead, the work of actively driving product adoption is left to Customer Success Managers and Support reps to figure out: They each forge their own path through training and guiding customers. Beyond a certain size, relying on individual CSMs to educate customers is like managing customers out of a spread-sheet instead of a CRM (Customer Relationship Management) tool. It's possible to do, but it requires a tremendous amount of effort and creates additional risk that your customers will slip through the cracks.

To serve thousands of accounts or millions of users with the same quality at which you served hundreds, you can't afford to manage your accounts haphazardly. You need Customer Educa-tion to be your scale engine for customer growth.

When companies start to scale, they bring in tools and processes to help them do it. That's why they use CRM platforms instead of spreadsheets, and service desk tools instead of answering support tickets by email. Each of these activities takes some of the guesswork and manual labor out of account management, so that customer-facing teams can focus on more important things.

Increasingly, growth-stage companies are turning to Customer Education as a new "secret weapon" to help them scale quickly and differentiate them in the market.

For many companies, the most valuable accounts with the highest lifetime value (LTV) are the ones who are educated—not just about product features, but about key workflows, advanced skills, emerging trends and techniques, and maturity in the broader industry.

To quote Lincoln Murphy, Customer Success expert and co-author of *Customer Success: How Innovative Companies are Reducing Churn and Growing Recurring Revenue*, "We have to educate people on not just how to use our product, but quite frankly, that they need the product. And what they'd even do without a product."

Yet many businesses don't invest in ongoing, scalable education *programs*; they do some training and documentation *activities* and call it a day.

If you recognize your own business in this story, the pages ahead will help you define your Customer Education strategy and grow your function to deliver ongoing value for your customers.

I know that this story isn't universal: consumer products differ from B2B products, and hardware differs from software. My experience lies within B2B software products, and that's what I'll be discussing for most of this book. Specifically, the first sections of this book walk through how you might approach starting a brand-new Customer Education function, which many B2B software companies are now doing. I intend the later sections to serve as more of a handbook for new Customer Education leaders to make their first hires, create killer content, implement the right systems, and measure the success of their programs.

FILLING A LEAKY BUCKET

You know the classic tech company founding story: A couple of people in a bedroom or garage (or, if they're lucky, a startup incubator) hack away, get their first few accounts, and then see explosive growth. By the time they've raised a few rounds of funding, acquire thousands of accounts, and hire hundreds of employees, their early success seemed predestined.

What's overlooked is the amount of drive, grit, and sheer effort that went into building the company to get it to that size. When the company's employees number in the tens, the company probably has a Sales-human or two, but nobody tasked with protecting existing account revenue. Makes sense, right? There aren't many existing accounts whose revenue you need to protect, and you are able to develop personal, one-on-one relationships with them.

Your first users are *early adopters*, in the parlance of Geoffrey Moore's *Crossing the Chasm*. Early adopters already know what problem your product is supposed to solve. They already see the value; they just need a product to help them get things done. So, the company hires its first "service" person—usually a generalist who handles support questions, custom solutions, and the occasional trainings. The company provides "white-glove" service to its customers and does whatever they need to help them be successful. They use drive, grit, sheer effort.

Fast-forward a year later… the company has fifty employees and a few hundred accounts. Last year's contracts are coming up for renewal, and more new accounts are coming on board. The generalists are quickly becoming overwhelmed with onboarding new accounts, renewing the existing ones, and answering a deluge of support questions.

The company realizes that it needed Customer Success, like, yesterday. So now there are Customer Success Managers. They get thrown a heavy portfolio of accounts and are asked to catch up on the context for each account. Assume that these CSMs' portfolios will be reshuffled and re-segmented at least once a year.

These new customers aren't as enthusiastic about using the product as the early adopters, and they need a little more help getting up and running. Their CSMs are now supposed to handle all the renewals, onboard new accounts, and re-onboard existing accounts when they add new users. (Not to mention the other new initiatives they're tasked with each week: "We forgot to announce this new feature!" "The customer's site is down!" "We're starting a customer advisory board and need six of your accounts to participate!")

Flash forward another year. The company is still successful by most outward indicators: It has over a hundred employees, accounts now number in the thousands, and revenue growth is meteoric! The fledgling Customer Success team has built itself up, adding new friendly faces to provide delightful, white-glove service.

But trouble is brewing.

The early adopters are less engaged than they used to be, or they feel neglected because they're getting less personal attention than they used to get from the jack-of-all-trades—and you never re-negotiated their contracts. Now they cost the company more to support them than they're paying. The newer customers don't feel like they're getting value from the product and are threatening to leave unless they get deep discounts. The newest users have so many questions about the product that it seems like they might never get up to speed.

How do you get them up to speed? Not easily: Your CSMs struggle to provide a consistent training experience, and there is no standard of excellence for how they train customers or what they train them on. Everyone has determined their own best way to get customers onboarded, and no one has the time to look at the program holistically and evaluate what's working and what's not.

All of this is compounded by significant turnover in your customer-side points of contact, even among your healthiest accounts. Months into a relationship, you find yourself in perpetual user onboarding, where the success of a single individual may determine the health of an entire account.

Now, accounts are starting to churn (for those of you who aren't in the Software-as-a-Service world, *churn* means *cancel* or *downgrade*). The company can continue to bring in new business, but that business is far more expensive to acquire. The company's board becomes obsessed with "CAC/LTV" ratio—that's the Cost to Acquire the Customer vs. the customer's Lifetime Value.

In other words, if new accounts don't stay long enough to make up the cost it took to acquire them, then it's like pouring water into a leaky bucket: You have to fill bucket fast enough, or you're in trouble.

The reason that many companies' boards want to know about their Customer Success strategy is that, without a strategy to protect revenue, they will eventually run out of new accounts to sell. Without a strategy to grow accounts *at scale*, existing accounts will leave (or slash their contract values) and won't give positive references in the market.

Here's what's troubling: the actions that most Customer Success teams take in this situation don't qualify as a strategy. When companies focus too heavily on hiring more CSMs and providing delightful, white-glove service, they end up in a position where they simply *can't* scale to keep up with growth.

CUSTOMERS DON'T CARE ABOUT YOUR PRODUCT

Growth and churn aren't simply Customer Success metrics; in the world of subscription software, they are existential issues for companies to solve. Every leader in the company must align around a strategy to retain and grow existing accounts.

Many companies try to retain their existing accounts by churn-fighting. They create customer health dashboards, monitor unhealthy accounts, and put in *more* manual effort to get them to adopt the product. CSMs have monetary incentives to prevent accounts from churning, and they must constantly stay ahead of accounts who are about to renew (or not).

But churn itself isn't the problem. Churn is a symptom of a deeper problem: Customers churn because they don't get value from your product. After doing all the hard work to attract a customer, many companies set themselves up for failure by leaving their product in the hands of people who don't care about it.

If you have a consumer (B2C) product, you typically run advertisements and promotions to get new customers. You can attract them with free trials, send them email campaigns to help them get value, and answer their support questions. You usually have a short window of time to pique their interest and get them to care. After they enter their credit card information, your job is to ensure that they find your product valuable enough to keep renewing.

In the B2B (business-to-business) world, however, there's a disconnect between the user and the buyer. Traditionally, you had a buyer with a fancy title, and you could take them out for a few rounds of golf and a gin martini (this is what I imagine happened, anyway). Then you sign a multi-year contract with hefty implementation fees, and it doesn't really matter if the product sits on the shelf for the next few years, because the software was purchased, and that's that.

In the world of Software-as-a-Service (SaaS), you can't do that. No matter how many rounds of golf are played, or gin martinis consumed, the software buyer is only one piece of the puzzle. Now, with renewals as a more continuous activity, it's the end-users of your software who will make or break your success. Just like some shark species need to keep swimming to live, your users must keep using your software. One problem, though—you didn't take all those end-users out for golf and gin martinis.

Put simply, to prevent your accounts from churning, the users need to get value from your product. To get value from your product, they must adopt it—and keep adopting it. Your buyer, now tuckered out from a day of golf and martinis, can help you drive adoption, but you need to make sure that their team succeeds. That means that you've got to help your product's power users get powerful levels of value, and you've got to make it easy for the end-users to use your product.

You'll see these results in your bottom line. According to Gallup research, only 29% of B2B accounts are engaged. But those engaged accounts helped achieve 50% higher revenue, 34% higher profitability, and 55% higher share of wallet.

Here's the problem, though... most users don't actually care about your product. They didn't buy it. The product that *someone else* bought will determine if *they* are successful in their jobs.

Think about your users—picture their faces if you can—and ask yourself why they care about using your product. Are they intrinsically motivated to because they're super fans? I bet you can think of a few who fit that category. But what about the rest of them?

More likely, they care about doing their jobs well. Or at the very least they care about getting around those little nagging product bugs that cause them frustration.

Customer Education done well provides your users with the inspiration to use your product to get better at their jobs. It even helps your customer accounts drive productive changes in their business.

CUSTOMER EDUCATION DRIVES HEALTHIER BUSINESSES

In 2016, Mark Kilens, the leader of HubSpot Academy, reported that his team delivered more than 70,000 certifications to customers and prospects. That's 70,000 more people in the world who know how to do inbound marketing—and how to use HubSpot as their tool of choice!

Similarly, if you went to Salesforce's annual Dreamforce conference in the past few years, you may have seen that the branding revolves around colorful mascots from Trailhead—Salesforce's online education site. In case you missed it, that's a multi-billion-dollar software juggernaut whose conference attendees take over an already conference-prone downtown San Francisco, using its *education program* as its annual conference theme.

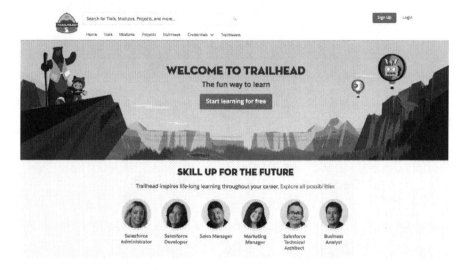

Salesforce Trailhead [https://trailhead.salesforce.com]

In the time I worked at Optimizely, the world's leading digital experimentation company, our Optiverse education brand contributed over a million dollars in annual multi-touch attribution while slicing support case volume by two thirds in its first year, while In-Product Education efforts were tripling the adoption of key features.

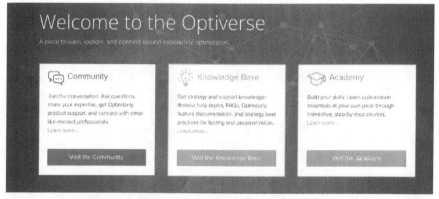

Optimizely's Optiverse site [https://optiverse.com]

According to research by the Technology Services Industry Association (TSIA), some member organizations found that their trained customers would renew at rates 12% above those who don't. This increase alone can improve your profitability, as you can expand your current accounts instead of scrambling for new business to fill the leaky bucket.

These examples point to a new way of thinking about Customer Education. Instead of treating it like a pure cost-recovery service or an ad hoc activity, these companies made big bets on Customer Education, treating it more like a product than a service—one that would take some time to develop, but that would deliver more ongoing value for the business.

Like any big investment, you should have a reasonable idea of how it will pay out. In the next section, I'll go into a more detailed ROI argument, but at its simplest, here's where I believe Customer Education gives your business a distinct advantage:

It makes customers successful, at scale.

I often say that "Customer Education is your scale engine for Customer Success." I don't just mean the department called Customer Success—I mean your customers' success.

According to learning industry analyst John Leh, "In a world where customer success increasingly determines overall business success, customer education has become an imperative."

Put simply, your business won't grow if your customers don't. And your customers won't grow if you don't help them find ongoing value in your product. There's a part of this growth that can be done scalably—by providing customer training, help documentation, certifications, community, and so on. Customer Education helps you drive this aspect of growth predictably.

There's also the part that doesn't scale: Especially in B2B companies that serve enterprise clients, CSMs work deeply with each account to understand how it gets value and achieves ROI with your product. How does Customer Education play a role? It contributes to a healthy account plan, where CSMs partner with Customer Education to create custom training plans based on their customers' needs.

More importantly, however, the scalable aspects of Customer Education will buy CSMs and Support reps more time to focus on working deeply with each account, instead of spending that time running trainings or answering support questions.

Customer Education also positions your company as a market leader. When you invest in Customer Education, you're not just teaching current users how to use your product; you're helping raise the bar of your broader industry. By investing in Customer Education that drives industry best practices, not just product knowledge, you show that you know your space better than any of your competitors. You show that you have a unique point of view. You become a "thought leader."

If you want to learn about customer relationship management—not just how to use a CRM tool—you go to Salesforce. If you want to learn about inbound marketing, you go to Hubspot. If you want to learn about experimentation, you go to Optimizely. Becoming the top education provider in your space creates an sustainable competitive advantage for your company.

The ad-buying platform The Trade Desk, through its Trading Academy, offers training and certification on difficult subject matter, breaking it down through videos hosted by industry experts and executives such as its CEO.

According to its press release,

> "Many understand the 'how' of programmatic [ad buying], but few can fully grasp the 'why.' The Trading Academy exists to change that and by filling the marketplace with better, more relevant ads, we aim to keep the advertising ecosystem healthy for years to come."

Even providing good customer care can differentiate you in the market. According to Linda Schwaber-Cohen, Senior Manager of Training at Skilljar:

> "Today's customers expect you to make them successful, and showing them early and often that you have programmatically addressed their success with give them confidence that their investment will be worthwhile."

DEFINING CUSTOMER EDUCATION

As of the writing of this book, if you search Google for "What is Customer Education?" you get this definition:

"Customer education refers to a company's role in providing consumers with the information, skills, and abilities needed to become a more informed buyer."

Not bad. That means Customer Education can include helpful marketing materials like buying guides, frequently asked questions, how-to videos, and similar tools. But in the world of Software-as-a-Service (SaaS), business-to-business (B2B) companies, and the increasing availability of information online, Customer Education can be more. It's not just about becoming a more informed buyer; it's about becoming a more loyal customer that sees more value in a product over time.

When I talk about Customer Education for B2B companies in this book, I'll propose a simple definition, then expand on it:

A Customer Education function strategically accelerates account and user growth by changing behaviors, reducing barriers to value, and improving the way people work.

Let's break the definition down:

> Customer Education is a strategic **function**, not an activity. It's not just "doing training"; it's a portfolio of programs that must be strategically managed.

Customer Education serves both **accounts** and **users**. We must educate both before and after the sale. We educate people who are involved with the buying decision, as well as those who will actually use the product.

Customer Education must **accelerate growth** throughout the customer journey. A comprehensive strategy drives customer maturity throughout their journey. We have to know what they want to achieve and show them the path to get there.

Customer education changes **behaviors, reduces barriers, and improves the way they work.** If you ask the average person in your business what the goal of education is, they would probably say "knowledge." If they have a training background, they also might include "skills." I propose that Customer Education delivers that in service of helping customers find value. To grow an account, each member of the team needs the right skills. They need to overcome hurdles to value. And perhaps most importantly, they should become better at what they do. What could be more valuable than that?

By this definition, what does Customer Education do for your business? If done right, Customer Education drives customer lifetime value and maturity, differentiates your brand as a category leader, and increases self-service efficiency.

Customer Acquisition Cost (CAC): Customer Education can reduce the number of questions your Sales-humans answer repeatedly, and it can help you convert trials to paid plans effectively.

Customer Lifetime Value (CLTV): The longer an account stays with you and the more they buy from you over time, the more value you derive. Customer Education helps to instill customer loyalty by building trust and accelerating value.

Customer Maturity: Closely linked to CLTV is maturity, where customers can see the path to ongoing value over time. Many companies use maturity models to diagnose the customer's current state and set a path to a future state.

Customer Sentiment or Loyalty: Typically measured with

Net Promoter Score (NPS), those 0-10 "Would you recommend this product?" surveys, customers are more likely to renew and expand over time if they're strong advocates of your product. Customer Education helps customers become loyal advocates by empowering them and connecting them with others.

Product Adoption: The path to getting meaningful usage of a product is similar to how you would form any habit, like brushing your teeth. Customer Education helps users understand *why* they should do it and then build a habit around it.

Brand Differentiation: If you are the "education leader" in your category, your brand will be seen as the expert. This makes buying decisions easier, and also increases customer loyalty. It's much harder to win in your category without being able to prove that you know the space better than anyone else.

Customer Self-Service Efficiency: Customers don't like calling in to ask for support. Helping users self-serve not only decreases your support costs, but it also decreases users' frustration.

Scale: I include "scale" as an outcome because I think that Customer Education must be able to do these things at scale, even if some offerings (like in-person training) don't scale as easily. As accounts become more geographically diverse and technology improves, you need a strategy that scales with your company's growth.

Note that my definition doesn't include which programs are included in your portfolio—that's intentional. Customer Education departments can use different programs and strategies to achieve the end goal, and no two are exactly alike.

Customer Education departments now tend to be more comprehensive than pure "training" or "documentation" teams. To get the results I discussed above, we can't be focused just on the activities we do with accounts (e.g. sending them to training, having them read docs) or the content they need to learn (usually a list of product features). Instead, Customer Education teams need the latitude to solve problems based on the *actions* that your customers' teams should perform and the *outcomes* they want to achieve.

Maybe you've heard the phrase, "When all you have is a hammer, every problem starts to look like a nail." When all you have is a training program, every problem starts to look like a training problem. But there are many problems that actually require something different, like change management, reference docs, in-product assistance, and more.

That's why most Customer Education functions include at least a few of the following efforts:

> Documentation (Knowledge Bases, Help Centers, developer documentation)
>
> Instructor-Led Training (In-classroom or virtual)
>
> Self-Paced Training (Usually e-learning and videos)
>
> Certifications (High-stakes assessments or lower-stakes courses)
>
> Communities (Online forums or in-person meetups)
>
> In-Product Education (Contextual help or user guidance)

I'll dig deeper into each of these throughout the book.

Building the Case for Customer Education

In Simon Sinek's famous TED Talk-turned-book, *Start with Why*, he proposes that we can't define *what* a company does or *how* the business operates without first defining *why* the business exists—or, in other words, what core belief it fulfills.

This is true for Customer Education teams too. The *why* of customer education should be at the forefront of all endeavors. One of the biggest mistakes I see businesses make is that they stumble backwards into Customer Education. It looks something like this:

Sandra is a great CSM, and she really loves training new

users. Maybe we should give her more special training projects, and it can eventually be her full-time job once we have enough trainings to do.

Amber really likes writing Knowledge Base articles. She's written most of the ones we have today. Let's make that her full-time job.

Our CSMs do a lot of training during onboarding. Let's redistribute Parvati's book of business and make her an onboarding specialist.

CompetitorCorp has a certification program, and they just leveraged their certifications to beat us out in a lucrative deal! Hold the phone—we need a certification program TODAY!

Those aren't bad things to do, *per se*. But all they do is define the *what* of Customer Education. They miss the *why*.

If you think of Customer Education as "doing trainings," then you're just going to keep doing trainings without a Customer Education purpose or strategy. You'll measure how many trainings you do. You'll measure how happy participants were with the trainings. Maybe eventually, you'll put a price tag on the trainings. And when your users continue not to adopt the product, you'll be confused because you trained them, after all!

If you define your Customer Education scope as "writing Knowledge Base articles," then you're going to keep writing articles. You'll incentivize your team based on how many articles they write. Maybe you'll improve the articles based on user feedback. And you won't understand why those users continue to call your Support team, even though you wrote all those articles.

Some companies don't think they even need Customer Education. They assume that "our product's design is so intuitive that there's no need for education," or "users will just seek out help content if they need it." For many consumer products, this may be true. But the logic doesn't hold up in B2B. If you don't think you need a Customer Education function because your product is so intuitive, then you shouldn't have any adoption or churn problems to begin with, right?

Start with a realistic idea of *why* Customer Education should exist in your organization, and what problem it solves.

YOU'RE LOOKING AT THE WRONG MOUNTAIN

There's a scene in *The Simpsons* where Homer is supposed to climb a mountain called the Murderhorn as part of a promotional campaign for a powerbar. He's looking at the mountain, mouth agape, and then one of his corporate sponsors points out, "Uh, no, that's it over there." The camera pans over to reveal a bigger mountain next to the original one. Homer gasps. The sponsor reassuringly grabs Homer's face, tilting it further to the right. "Yeah, that's it," he says, "Just to the right of the one you're looking at." The camera pans even further to the right, revealing yet another, comically larger, mountain. *That* one is the Murderhorn. Homer lets out a whimper. Bart gives a thumbs up.

This, I think, is a good metaphor for setting your Customer Education goals.

When we developed trainings on how to run A/B tests at Optimizely, one technique we taught our customers was that they shouldn't lose sight of the *global maximum* while pursuing a *local maximum*. A local maximum is some metric that you can optimize (usually something like, "Let's increase the number of people who click this "Contact Us" button by 20%!"), but without some exploration, you may be missing the bigger picture—a global maximum that yields better results overall (maybe something like, "Let's get a 20% higher average sales price from the customers who contact us").

Companies do this all the time with their Customer Education strategies. Unless they can define a clear path to revenue generation by selling trainings, they won't invest in Customer Education.

Don't get me wrong: It's great for your Customer Education programs to bring in revenue, especially as a way to create more perceived value around your educational offerings and to recover costs for your team. It's also common for Education Services teams to set cost-recovery targets for themselves. In particular, if your organization values ACV (Annual Contract Values) above customer retention, then you'll want to explore revenue-generating education.

But I don't think that training revenue is where you should start, nor is that where Customer Education generates the biggest impact on the customer.

Danielle Tomlinson, VP of Education Services for Plex Systems (a cloud-based enterprise resource planning platform), shares:

"With a SaaS-based model, it's much less expensive to renew a customer than acquire one. And the rise of customer retention models/measures have spotlighted that churn is a real problem. Which is why many companies like Plex have shifted their focus from how many customers they can sell training to, to how well we can train our customers to build and reinforce their loyalty."

The trend from generating *training* revenue to optimizing *company* revenue is pervasive. In July 2018, Oracle announced its new free digital learning platform, Oracle LaunchPad. Explaining the rationale in a blog post, Oracle wrote:

"For decades, vendors have offered product information to help their customers learn to properly leverage the solutions they've purchased. More often than not, though, vendors charged customers for the information. After all, the vendor had made a considerable investment to create and deliver material, so they felt that they'd want to recoup the costs (and maybe even squeak out some profit in the process)."

But, recognizing that revenue was an obstacle to helping some customers achieve their outcomes, Oracle needed to create free online options as well. In discussing its Voice of Customer programs the company described, "customers told us that fee-based education, on even the most introductory level courses, was slowing their teams' ability to adopt solutions."

Education revenue is typically a drop in the bucket compared to overall product license fees and recurring revenue (I've heard it estimated around 2%). If you're only looking at revenue-generating programs without thinking about your customer base as a whole, you may be optimizing for the local maximum while missing the global maximum. The best thing you can do for a SaaS business, especially in the earlier stages of maturity, is help increase Customer Lifetime Value (CLTV, or simply LTV).

Let's walk through the business rationale for Customer Education as a driver of CLTV:

In a software business, your Customer Lifetime Value has to outweigh your Customer Acquisition Cost (CAC). In other words, you have to keep your accounts long enough, at a high enough contract value, that you make more money from them than you spent bringing them in the door.

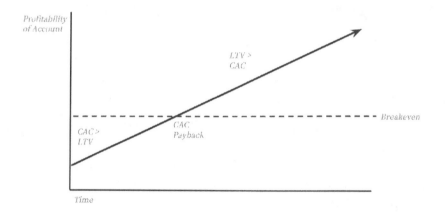

You don't profit from an account until LTV exceeds CAC

What drives LTV? Your best accounts are the ones who receive ongoing, meaningful value from your product. They keep renewing, and even expanding, with you. Conversely:

Your customers don't get value if they're not using the product—so adoption is a strong leading indicator of success.

Your customers don't get value if they never *start* using the product—so getting your accounts to a moment of "first value," or initial success with your product, is a strong leading indicator of ultimate success.

Your customers don't get value if they *stop* using the product—so you must continually help new users adopt your product.

Thus, it's a simple equation. Ultimately a customer's success with your product *is equal to* their **desire** to use your product *minus* the **friction** they experience while using it. In other words, **success = desire - friction.**

Some teams are more adept at increasing a buyer or user's desire to use the product—Marketing comes to mind. Your Marketing team develops value propositions for your products and features and runs campaigns to engage prospects and current customers to use your product.

Some teams are better at removing friction. Your Support team, for instance, does everything they can to quickly remove roadblocks on the user's path.

Customer Education can increase desire to use the product and remove friction, at scale. But you need to start with a charter for *why* Customer Education exists in your business. Let's look at a few common ones.

Customer Education helps scale Customer Success

Under this charter, the focus is on scaling the work that Customer Success and Support teams do, by making their repetitive work more consistent and manageable. I see teams start with this charter quite often.

Up to a certain size, you can have CSMs run every training and have Support reps answer all your support tickets without much trouble. Past a certain point, you need a way to do this at scale if you don't want to eat into your profitability by hiring endless swaths of CSMs and Support reps. Customer Education allows you to automate these repetitive activities in a way that is customer-friendly, and it frees up your individual agents to have more strategic, less transactional interactions with customers.

Teams under this charter typically optimize for *reach*, by making the majority of education programs free for customers and attempting to drive as much education consumption as possible. These teams also focus on measuring the impact that Customer Education has on product adoption and support ticket deflection.

Customer Education drives predictable product adoption and renewal

In SaaS, short-term adoption metrics only matter if they lead to long-term value for an account. This requires that users are not only able to use your product (i.e. "trained") but also motivated to use the product. Customer Education is one of only a few functions that can scale to build motivation *and* skills.

Under this charter, Customer Education programs don't just focus on scaling things that CSMs or Support reps already do—they also focus on driving better user onboarding through techniques like In-Product Education and email campaigns. These programs consider what education customers may need beyond onboarding, and how they can improve the overall maturity of the account.

These programs typically don't charge for education that helps customers onboard or adopt the product, but will charge for custom and on-site trainings (or anything else that requires custom work), certifications, and sometimes subscriptions to premium education content that focuses on job skills. For example, a project management company may give away their basic software training, but charge for courses on advanced project management techniques.

Customer Education drives change management

Often, new products require that companies adopt new processes and new behaviors. Because change is often painful, Customer Education can help drive widespread change management in large organizations. The role of Customer Education here is to make new products less scary and easier to adopt, as well as to show the ways that a new product can help teams do their jobs better.

In a typical "land and expand" strategy, a company will sell into one business unit within a larger organization. That business unit starts to use the product and change their processes, but now the challenge is to help other business units do the same. Each team will have their own small customizations and challenges to overcome.

Customer Education teams with a charter for change management often develop a combination of scalable and customized education options. The scalable components (such as certifications and on-demand learning) help large teams get on the same page about basic concepts and functionality, and then champions from each business unit are responsible for helping drive adoption.

Under this charter, Customer Education is often given a price tag but discounted to support the "land and expand" strategy. For example, custom trainings may still carry a higher price tag because they require hard costs to customize and deliver, but certification bundles may be heavily discounted, allowing certification to be required as part of a business unit's onboarding plan.

Customer Education is a service that drives revenue

Before Software-as-a-Service existed, this was the most common charter for Customer Education. Alongside other paid services like implementation, consulting, and change management, education services acted as an insurance policy for customers as they adopted costly new products. Typically, Education Services teams would sell days-long classroom training sessions and measure the bookings, margin, and revenue generated from selling these trainings.

Today, Education Services teams have adapted to newer technology, focusing not just on selling classroom trainings but also online training subscriptions and other services.

Customer Education differentiates us in the market

Under this charter, Customer Education drives new leads and positions a brand as an industry thought leader, superior to its competitors. Often, Customer Education under this category focuses less on the specifics of how to use the product, and more on industry skills. As an example, Gainsight's Customer Success University teaches you both how to use Gainsight and how to be a great Customer Success Manager.

Without thought leadership, you limit your ability to stand out in a market. This is especially important in crowded markets like project management tools or CRMs; thus, companies need to be able to differentiate themselves by showing that they're innovative and experts in their fields.

This charter also benefits companies who are trying to create new categories (as Optimizely was with its experimentation software, Marketo with Marketing Automation software, or HubSpot with Inbound Marketing software). These companies need to educate their customers on how to use the software as well as how to perform new skills in the market.

Under this charter, Customer Education often focuses entirely on reach over revenue. It becomes a driver to reduce Customer Acquisition Cost and convert prospects into customers. Online courses and guides may be protected behind a lead generation form but rarely comes at a cost. Instead, the focus is on driving consumption of education by prospects *and* customers. Certification programs and learning paths are often completely free, and commonly generate tens of thousands of certificates or badges.

These Customer Education programs may also tie closely into customer communities by offering training sessions at live events, conferences, and roadshows.

All of the charters I've listed can be reasonable, depending on your company's business model, but you likely can't do all of them at once. Be intentional about which one you want to start with, and you'll be able to expand over time.

CUSTOMER EDUCATION IN A CLOUDY WORLD

Not so long ago, the term "Customer Education" wasn't commonly used. Some of us were called Technical Trainers. Others were called Instructional Designers or Training Content Developers. There were some Technical Writers and Knowledge Managers working on documentation, manuals, and Knowledge Bases. There were Training or Education Services teams going on-site to lead week-long classroom trainings for the shiny new on-premise software that had just been implemented at great cost and lengthy contract duration.

When customers were being trained, it was as a paid (but often discounted) service. Often times, training was an *amuse bouche* before a user conference. It happened at a set time, in a set location, in a classroom where presumably lots of people fell asleep listening to boring lecturers. When customers were getting documentation, it came along with a scheduled revision of the software.

Then Software-as-a-Service (SaaS) happened. The Cloud rolled in like fog on a summer day in San Francisco, ushering in continuous updates and freer access to information. Around the early 2010s, Customer Success, Customer Marketing, and Demand Generation experienced explosive growth as companies rushed to acquire and retain customers in new digital channels.

The Cloud didn't just change how people used software; it changed the way people learned. Instead of getting trained in classrooms, customers' learning experience could align to their product experience through single sign-on (SSO). Customers could be trained through online academies and earn certificates. Not only could individual learners use online learning platforms like Coursera and Udacity, but interactive and engaging training could be delivered directly to customers through sites like Hubspot Academy, Salesforce Trailhead, or Optiverse.

The Cloud has created entire categories of software devoted to Customer Education and enablement.

Cloud-based Learning Management Systems, virtual software labs, and webinar-style platforms became more cost-effective ways to conduct trainings for broader audiences.

Documentation was housed in online Help Center software, making it easily searchable and accessible, instead of getting buried in PDFs and quarantined to the digital trash heap.

With the rise of online community forums, passionate users could exchange creative techniques and answer each other's support questions.

Most recently, in-product engagement tools (also known as Digital Adoption Platforms) offer just-in-time, on-demand walkthroughs and support to users.

A modern Customer Education function comprises some combination of these programs—usually along with a healthy dose of old-fashioned classroom training. But *what* Customer Education comprises is less important than *why* it's being adopted by more businesses every year: to make customers successful and differentiate your brand in the market.

WHY CALL IT "CUSTOMER EDUCATION"?

Whether you eat a hazelnut or a filbert, you're eating the same nut. Customer Education is kind of like that—whether you call it Customer Enablement, Training, Education Services, or some other creative option, it's largely the same function. I'm choosing "Customer Education" for this book not only because it's the term I've used in past writings, but because I think it best describes the type of efforts that support a company in driving customer growth, lifetime value, and scale.

"Customer Education" implies that you'll be helping your customers develop higher-order skills that they'll carry with them for a long time. It's not just a training you go to, nor is it just knowledge you absorb. It's an exciting, long-term journey, and isn't that what you want your customer relationships to be like?

Increasingly, older titles and department names like "Training Services," "Instructional Designer," and "Training Coordinators" are evolving with the emergence of Customer Success. Now we have Learning Consultants, Customer Education Specialists, and Learning Experience Designers.

As Danielle Campbell, Head of Americas Digital Learning Services at Adobe, notes, "The focus is outward toward the customer, and while the customer may be familiar with the traditional titles, the emergence of these new titles focuses on elevating the impact, skills required, and our focus on their success."

All that said, there are other names that people use for Customer Education functions. Let's run through some of the alternatives and where they lead.

Education Services

Education Services (or Training Services) teams emerged from their companies' Services department, where training and change management are services offered along with implementation, consulting, or custom development. This title honestly doesn't seem that far off from Customer Education. It's just a bit more limiting—it implies that everything you do is a service. This might subconsciously discourage you from taking on anything that isn't a traditional service—like documentation, In-Product Education, and so on. "Training Services" limits the department scope even further.

Customer Enablement

These days, the person who trains your Sales team is known as a "Sales Enablement" professional. Occasionally, this function also becomes responsible for Customer Education, and thus is known as Customer Enablement. Just like Sales Enablement makes sure that your sales-humans are enabled to sell the product, customer enablement makes sure that customers are enabled to use the product. Not a bad analogy, really. This is a pretty common alternative name to "Customer Education." My quibble with this title is that "enablement" also has a secondary, negative connotation. When you enable someone's *bad* behavior, they become reliant on you. You're an "enabler."

Customer Learning

This one isn't bad, either. There's a subtle connotation that what you're doing is similar to a Learning and Development function in HR. Moving on.

Training

The first time I ever sat on a customer-facing training team was at a company called BancVue, and we were simply the "Training team." Eventually, as the team started to run more change management and coaching initiatives, it shifted its name to "Retail Experience," as the primary training audience was the retail side of banks and credit unions. Even to this day, the team doesn't play a large role in documentation, community, In-Product Education, or other areas where Customer Education can make a big impact.

ARE YOU READY FOR CUSTOMER EDUCATION?

Salesforce, HubSpot, and Optimizely all have relatively mature, innovative Customer Education functions that drive strong value for their overall businesses. But scroll back on the timeline for each of those companies, and you'll find that these functions all have something in common: they began as experiments.

At Hubspot, Kilens described his early efforts to build ten recurring training webinars as an experiment. Before Salesforce Trailhead was influencing company direction, it was a much smaller developer training curriculum. And you had better bet that Optimizely, as an experimentation business, launched its programs through a collection of experiments.

Before you know where you're going, you must know where you are. Even if you don't have a formal Customer Education department, you probably have ad hoc education activities happening around the business.

Try answering the following questions about your business. Give yourself one point for each "Yes."

Do you have anyone in a dedicated Customer Education, Training, or Documentation role (i.e. that is their job title and description, not just a side activity for a CSM or Support agent)?

Do you have an online Knowledge Base or Help Center for customers?

Is more than 50% of the knowledge up to date?

Is 80% of your product's functionality documented?

Does your Knowledge Base include any strategic guidance for the customer's industry (instead of just support articles)?

Do your Support agents write help articles with a consistent, user-friendly tone?

Do all your customers get trained during onboarding?

Do you have an onboarding methodology that you clearly explain to managed customers when they launch?

Is onboarding training consistent across your customer segments (vs. every CSM making their own versions)?

Do you track whether the customer actually did what you trained them to do?

Do you have an online academy?

Does it have any interactive content (vs. just being a series of short articles)?

Does it have any videos?

Does it teach industry-focused content (vs. just product tutorials)?

Do you educate your customers in-product?

Do you contextually answer support issues that they are likely to have?

Do you offer any tutorials or walkthroughs on advanced

features (vs. just a quick onboarding tour)?

Can customers return to tutorial content after they have dismissed it the first time?

Do you have a customer or user community, or customer advocacy program, where your users can generate and share content?

Do you have a certification program for customers?

Of those 20 questions, most early-stage companies can probably answer "Yes" to five or fewer. This means that you haven't begun to use Customer Education as a tool to scale.

Let's look at where Customer Education benefits you in each stage of your customer journey.

CUSTOMER EDUCATION THROUGH THE CUSTOMER JOURNEY

CUSTOMER EDUCATION THROUGH THE CUSTOMER JOURNEY

Once you've made some early decisions about Customer Education and where it fits into your overall business strategy, you'll probably end up with some rudimentary content and measurement targets. To get beyond that phase, it's best to know where your strategy will come into play throughout your customer journey. In this section, we'll follow a typical SaaS product customer's journey.

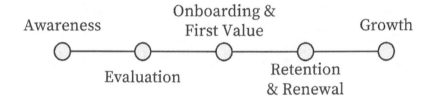

The SaaS customer journey

Awareness: Typically owned by Marketing, this is where potential customers ("leads") become aware of your solution.

Evaluation: Typically owned by Sales, this is where potential customers ("prospects") evaluate your solution for a good fit.

Onboarding/First Value: Typically owned by Customer Success and/or Services, this is where new customers ramp up to achieve their first level of value with the product.

Retention: Typically owned by Customer Success and/or Support, this is the period where the customer continues to use your product and derive value.

Growth: Although not all customers grow, your most successful customers do grow their accounts over time, resulting in horizontal or vertical expansion. Depending on the type of expansion, this phase may be owned by Sales or Customer Success.

Awareness: Customer Education as a Marketing Demand Generator

If you think about your Customer Education program exclusively as a post-sales tool, then you're not thinking big enough. In reality, great Customer Education will generate awareness and increase your market penetration.

In 2008, the *MIT Sloan Management Review* published a study invalidating the widely held belief that once customers are educated on a certain space, they are more likely to shop around for alternatives. In fact, educated customers often see higher levels of perceived quality and trust in the brands that helped educate them.

According to the study,

> "Efforts to enhance customers' service knowledge had a positive and strong impact on customer trust ... Interestingly, however, there were also some secondary effects of customer education. Specifically, the extent to which service employees provided courteous and attentive service had an even stronger positive effect on trust as customer education initiatives increased."

How does Customer Education fit into your current marketing initiatives? Think about how your marketing programs work today. If your company sells to other businesses, you probably use some combination of online advertising, trade shows, and demand generation—all intended to expose your product to a broader audience and position yourself as a thought leader in the space. Most businesses have content marketers to create ebooks, white papers, web copy, ad copy, and other types of content that generate awareness and help the customer evaluate your solution. Furthermore, this content helps position your company as a thought leader in its space.

If your company sells directly to consumers, you may be less focused on "thought leadership" and more focused on selling benefits and value propositions to enhance your brand value.

Regardless of your customer base, you certainly need good content marketers in your organization, but what if your documentation and education programs could serve as a tool to generate awareness, increase trust, and differentiate your company from competitors?

In this chapter, I'll walk through the ways you can use Customer Education as a marketing tool to increase your brand's value.

HOW DOES CUSTOMER EDUCATION SUPPORT DEMAND GENERATION EFFORTS?

According to research by the Corporate Executive Board in its book, *The Challenger Customer*, "the average B2B customer consults *nearly a dozen* sources of information, spread across all touchpoints on the path to purchase." (Emphasis theirs, but I *emphatically* agree with it.)

This gives you three options for Customer Education content:

1. Hide it behind a login gate so customers don't accidentally find it during their search.

2. Pretend that customer don't begin their evaluation process until they talk to one of your Sales-humans.

3. Recognize that your ungated Customer Education content can create awareness and preference for your brand among prospects.

The first option was what companies used to do before the age of inbound marketing; they assumed that siloing education content would protect it from prying eyes. They buried their education in PDF manuals or in gated, proprietary Knowledge Bases that no one could find.

The second option—pretending that customers don't begin their search until they talk to you—isn't how customers look for products anymore. If you're waiting for your talented sales-humans to properly frame the conversation for customers, you've already waited too long. The customer has already done research—and is probably still doing it while talking to your sales team. Don't lose out to a competitor who embraces education as a competitive edge.

It's true that in the past, there were many good reasons not to use Customer Education as a pre-sales marketing tool. But, as Grandpa Simpson famously said, "I used to be with it, but then they changed what 'it' was, and now what I'm with isn't 'it,' and what's 'it' seems weird and scary to me."

The third option—ungated content—makes information easily available for customers and prospects alike. And in doing so, it shows that your company is a thought leader in its space. This grabs the attention of prospective and current customers and creates trust from a company that knows what it's talking about and isn't afraid to show it.

According to Suzanne Ferry, SVP Global Training and Enablement at MapR, her team's efforts to create courses and content that ranked highly in organic search yielded SEO value for MapR in their technical space. People searching for information on topics like machine learning or Kubernetes would find her team's content before they were even aware of what MapR's technology did. This led to net-new name acquisition for MapR.

Of course you still want to have good content marketing pieces—your e-books, blog posts, whitepapers, and the like will still get distributed in your customer's organization. Those content marketing efforts are also good opportunities to provide playbooks for your customer-side champion to help drive the deal forward.

But content marketing and Customer Education shouldn't contradict each other; they enhance each other. Content marketing helps to challenge the customer's expectations and deliver key insights that will position your product as the best solution. To do that, you can't just *say* you're a thought leader—you need to show it. Making your Customer Education content available to customers before they've ever talked to your rep does a few things. It provides:

> **Exposure:** Studies have validated that even "mere exposure" increases preference. When people are familiar with something (such as a prospect might be familiar with a brand from having seen the name in multiple places), they develop a preferential bias toward it.

> **Thought Leadership:** Bill Cushard, an industry expert at the training company ServiceRocket, says, "Software companies should aspire to become the leading education provider in their space." Part of being the leader in your space is finding the key issues facing customers, and educating your customers on how to solve them. While marketing creates the expectation, education delivers on the promise.

If you're reading this section and thinking, "Wait, this won't work with my demand generation strategy. Where am I supposed to get my leads?"—Read on!

UNGATED DOCUMENTATION: YOUR SEO SAVIOR

In 2016, the conversational marketing platform Drift decided to get rid of all its gated content. That's right—no more lead forms for customers to fill out just to get access to an e-book, and no more barriers to information.

David Cancel, Drift's CEO, had this to say: "I think we've lost our way. Marketing today has become more about gaming the system and get rich quick schemes."

Instead of writing gated "premium" pieces (like whitepapers and e-books) and writing five or more blog posts a day linking back to those premium pieces, Drift used content as a tool for enhancing its brand's message. From a demand generation standpoint, this is scary. You start to feel like Jack Lemmon's character in *Glengarry Glen Ross*, shouting, "Where are the leads?!"

But from a customer's perspective, it does a world of good. Instead of looking for content and in the process, getting hit by a long, impersonal lead generation form; and then having to ignore a barrage of nurture emails and calls from a sales representative, you immediately get the information you need to make an informed decision about a product.

And what came of Drift's efforts to remove their lead forms? *More* leads—15% more, in fact.

During my time at Optimizely, our Optiverse site (which contained our docs, academy, and community) was the third most-viewed site in the entire company, ranking behind only optimizely.com and the actual Optimizely product. Why is this? Two reasons:

- The Optiverse site is linked prominently throughout the Optimizely product, in welcome tours, tooltips, and error messages.

- All you have to do is type "Optimizely" plus your search term into Google, and chances are that you'll see content from Optiverse first.

As we produced more content on our product, industry-focused strategies, and complementary technologies, our articles would place first in Google's search results.

It's now common practice to *not* hide help content behind a login gate, or bury it beneath so many layers of clunky interfaces that your customers need to conduct a seance to communicate with it.

Why are companies still hiding their content? Let's dissect a couple of common objections I hear.

You hear: "Our content isn't SEO-friendly."
Which translates to: "Google has been around for two decades

and I'm still putting all my information in PDFs."
For most businesses, PDF manuals aren't coming back. Most of our prospects and customers find content in only a handful of ways: organic search, followed by in-product links, followed by direct links. So if you want to drive self-service, you had better make sure that your content is readily available through organic search and in-product links. You simply must meet your customers where they are.

You hear: "I can't track what my customers are doing if this content is ungated."
Which translates to: "All this data isn't going to ignore itself."

Admittedly, it's annoying not to have deep analytics when you want them. But this objection is also a bit of a red herring: Would you rather be able to see exactly what 100 customers are doing, or provide easier access to 1,000 customers?

Yes, you want to design in a way that is measurement-friendly as much as possible, but what are you really doing with all that tracking? And do you need a login gate to do those things? Today, using web analytics tools and personalization software, you can offer personalized experiences and track user paths without a login gate. On a technical level, much of what you might have used a login gate and signup fields for in the past can be accomplished by using cookies or the browser's local storage.

Not to mention, if you're a global organization, then you may be running afoul of laws governing data privacy, like GDPR (General Data Protection Regulation) in the European Union. Similar laws will likely take effect in other regions as well.

Sure, you may not track all your users, but you'll have a ton more users to measure in the first place!

You hear: "I'm worried our competitors will see our knowledge."
Which translates to: "My fear of competitors is greater than my desire to see our product succeed."

If you have a great product, supported by great help content and documentation, you shouldn't be worried about this;

you should be proud. Yes, you may still want to gate certain proprietary information, but this should be no more than 10% of your content. The value of exposing valuable information to prospects and customers should outweigh the risk of publishing 90% of your content.

Your competitors will find a way dig up dirt on you. They will write articles about you on their blog that you can't refute because you haven't published any ungated information. They will have customers dig up information from your gated Knowledge Base right before they churn on you. They will create fake accounts to get into your systems.

Paranoia is rarely a good reason to make decisions. The value of having your help content come up first in organic search outweighs the damage that might be done by competitors trying to take the low road—and the low road is rarely a good look, anyway.

You hear: "We want to make our education a premium service. You shouldn't see it unless you pay for our product."
Which translates to: "I don't think that educated customers make better buying decisions."

In addition to worrying about the competition, sales leaders also used to bristle at the idea that prospects could get their hands on education materials. They didn't like the idea of "giving away the farm" to people who weren't paying for it.

After all, if a customer is evaluating your product, and they hear that once they sign the contract, they'll get access to your *Knowledge Base* and *onboarding trainings*, they'll probably want to fast track the deal, right? Right? Anyone? Please tell me the last time you bought a software product in order to get access to its Knowledge Base or onboarding trainings.

Taking this approach limits the effectiveness of Customer Education, and it also robs you of a channel that customers can use to learn more about your product. Often, I see Customer Education materials used during the evaluation phase, where they help prospects learn more about the product and show the company's commitment to providing high-quality information.

You hear: "Our help content is poorly written, out of date, and an eyesore."
Which translates to: "I don't actually care about helping our customers." or "I don't believe that customers would actually help themselves. Fix your content already!"

No, seriously, invest in your education materials. If they're not good enough to show to the outside world, then you've underinvested in them, and you're probably infuriating your customers when they try to get help using your product.

The unintended value of ungated content

In some cases, when Optimizely wrote about a generic topic, it would even be included in Google's featured content boxes. For example, one of the troubleshooting solutions for Optimizely involved changing the compatibility mode in Google Chrome, and Google was able to scrape our stepwise instructions.

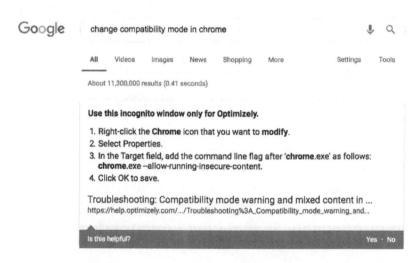

Optimizely appears in Google's featured content boxes.

I'm of two minds about this. On one hand, when you're a growing brand, it's great when your content is easy to find. When you show up in potential customers' search results, you can build their trust in you as a brand. For industry-focused content, like "how to build an optimization roadmap" or "A/B test ideas," the SEO can be a powerful way for customers to discover your brand and build trust in it.

The downside? I imagine this might be a great tactic for B2C (business-to-consumer) companies, who are tasked with bringing in many individual consumer leads. However, for B2B companies, the tradeoff is that a lot of this traffic might be irrelevant. And when you get featured in the actual content box in Google, you don't get to claim those hits on your website, so it artificially distorts your traffic.

DEVELOPER DOCUMENTATION AS A MARKETING TOOL

I once asked a group of technical users, including product managers and software engineers, how they discover new brands. One of them replied, "Good developer documentation is your marketing tool."

Today's market leaders can't just have a clean product interface; they have to focus on effective integrations and creating open platforms that are easy for development. The quality of your API and SDK documentation matters. Look at leaders like Stripe and Twilio: They're proud of their developer documentation, and they know that their prospects' developers will look at it when evaluating which technologies to use. Take a look at Twitter or StackOverflow and see what developers are saying about your company's documentation. Are your docs promoting awareness and enthusiasm for your brand, or potentially crippling your ability to get leads?

For example, the payment processing platform Stripe has set the standard for their API docs, to the delight of developers who attempt to build on top of Stripe's APIs. To quote one comment on Twitter, "@stripe Whomever made your API pages deserves a medal. As a dev, seeing both docs and code in a clear format is amazing!"

A company deciding which payment processing platform to use would be more likely to use Stripe if developers are involved in the decision.

TRAINING AS A MARKETING TOOL

What are companies like Salesforce, Gainsight, Mulesoft, HubSpot, and Hootsuite doing to differentiate themselves in the marketplace? They have robust training and certification programs, in many cases (but not always) offered for free, and centered not just on how to use their product, but how to succeed in their broader industries.

Pardot, the marketing automation company acquired by Salesforce, reported that 80% of respondents in its research cited "authenticity of content" as the main factor affecting whether they would support a brand. This means that if you're pushing out "training" or "articles" that are just thinly veiled advertisements, you're not earning your prospects' trust.

Instead, engage with your customers authentically by helping them do their jobs better. When you go to HubSpot Academy, for instance, you'll have the opportunity to get Inbound Marketing Certified, and you can take their courseware for free. This isn't just a way for HubSpot to get their customers through a launch process; this is a huge source of inbound leads for the company. According to Mark Kilens, Vice President of HubSpot Academy, in 2017 they were awarding more than 8,000 certifications per month!

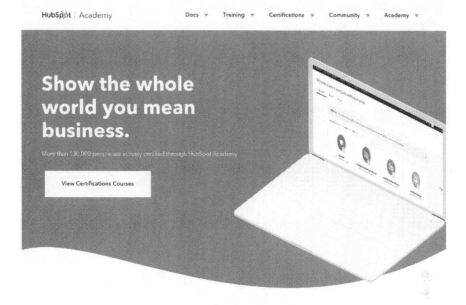

Why Take a Certification?

Get educated.

The business world moves fast. Each certification is loaded with on-demand classes built by inbound experts, ready to get you on the track to success. After all, knowledge is power.

Get connected.

They say you're only as good as your network. Earning certifications through HubSpot Academy opens you up to a network of thousands of other professionals just like you.

Get hired.

You'll learn the skills employers are looking for. Get certified to gain access to exclusive job boards on inbound.org. Your resume will never be the same.

View inbound marketing jobs

HubSpot's free certification courses (https://academy. hubspot.com)

Many software companies are also working with higher-education organizations and universities to teach foundational industry skills: social media for Hootsuite, design for Adobe, marketing automation for Marketo, and so on.

Take a look at how Hootsuite Academy brands itself on its landing page:

Advance your social media skills and career

280,000+	45,000+	880+
STUDENTS EDUCATED	CERTIFIED GRADUATES	SCHOOLS ENROLLED

Academy Courses

Master new social media skills with online classes taught by industry pros.

Hootsuite Academy's landing page [https://education. hootsuite.com]

They prominently display free online courses with the value proposition of leveling up your social media game. That's much different than asking customers to enroll in a two-day classroom training on how to use the Hootsuite platform.

So how do you create training content that works best for marketing?

Make the content industry-focused and and not just about product knowledge: Think about what skills practitioners need to be successful in their jobs, and create content around that.

Put some polish on your content: To be successful as marketing tools, your content is better if it has higher-quality video and copy that sparkles.

Think through your gating strategy: You may not want to put *all* your content outside of a gate so that customers find it in organic search results. After all, it could be confusing to have customers drop in midway through a course; however, you can put your course descriptions outside the gate! Or go bolder, like Salesforce does with Trailhead, and keep your courses ungated until you have it's time for a quiz or some type of interactivity.

Use a combination of self-paced and instructor-led courses: Self-paced content is the most scalable, but companies like Mulesoft use MOOCs (massive open online courses) to deliver content. Outside of course times, the students coach each other, like study groups. If you have really engaging instructors, this can be a selling point for your brand as well.

Tie your content to industry-standard certifications: I'll discuss this in the next section.

CERTIFICATION AND COMMUNITY AS MARKETING TOOLS

In many cases, certification and training programs aren't quite tied together. When you're thinking about how to use Customer Education to drive awareness, they need to be intertwined. In the past, certification was more like a driver's license—it was a necessary, high-stakes step to be able to operate a complex piece of software.

But not all software needs a driver's license. Often, for products that are deceptively simple (such as project management or collaboration tools), the goal isn't protect users against software malpractice, but rather to make sure software gets enthusiastically adopted throughout an organization. Certifications can also be used as low-stakes tools to show proficiency in broader industry skills.

If you're able to create an industry-standard certification verifying that people are proficient in your specific category (like inbound marketing for Hubspot, construction management for Procore, or social media for Hootsuite), then you'll be helping not just your current user base, but your next generation of users, who will go to work for companies where they will hopefully bring your software in with them. Being able to certify customers in your discipline helps to show your thought leadership in that category as well.

Similar to certification, online communities aren't just support forums that customers come to when the product breaks; at their best, they're spaces for practitioners and experts in the field to learn, teach, and share best practices.

As communities grow, they promote active users as "MVPs," "Heroes," or some other title that distinguishes them as power players within the community. Not only can they help other users in the community, but they're also powerful advocates for the brand. As an example, in Salesforce's community, 63% of their MVPs presented at Dreamforce, Salesforce's annual conference, and 69% had a Salesforce administrator certification. This certification makes the product stickier and amplifies the brand. Erica Kuhl, VP of Salesforce's three-million-member Trailblazer Community, reported that the company saw two-times larger deals, two-times more pipeline, and 85% increased propensity for cross-selling and up-selling, from accounts who were active in the community compared to those who were not.

BRAND POWER

According to Lucidpress, when a company's brand is presented consistently, that brand will see an average revenue increase of 23% compared to an inconsistent, confusing brand presentation. That means it's crucial for your education content to have a strong brand—and support your overall brand—like Optiverse for Optimizely or Trailhead for Salesforce.

At Optimizely, we didn't simply have a Knowledge Base, academy, and community. We had "Optiverse." Salesforce doesn't simply have a learning site; they have "Trailhead" with its own brand and logo and hoodies with "Trailhead" emblazoned on them (which incidentally, I see at least once per day on the streets of San Francisco).

Not only should your Customer Education sites be an extension of your corporate brand, but they should also have their own powerful brands. Yes, it's easy to call your learning site "BrandName Academy" or "SubjectMatter University," and no one in marketing will yell at you for doing that. It's safe. But the power of developing a strong brand around Customer Education anchors them in your customers'—and your Sales-humans'—minds. It makes them easier to discuss Customer Education as a value proposition and a differentiator. At Optimizely, most of our competitors had training; none of them had Optiverse.

Evaluation: Customer Education as a Pre-Sales Differentiator

Both the Technology Services Industry Association (TSIA) and ServiceRocket, a training and learning management technology company, oft repeat that "selling doesn't help, but helping sells."

What does "helping sells" mean? It means that Customer Education can be a competitive differentiator for your business during the sales cycle that translates into a sale.

Before I go any further, here's what this chapter is *not*: It is not going to be an explanation of how you sell training services and subscriptions. Instead, I'll focus on how a scalable Customer Education program can support your product's sales process.

THE END OF SOLUTION SALES AND THE BEGINNING OF THE HELPING SALE

In a 2012, the Corporate Executive Board and Google conducted a study of 1,500 B2B leaders in large organizations to attempt to quantify at what point during customers' evaluation of a new solution they actually reached out to someone from a potential supplier. On average, they didn't reach out until the purchase was 57% complete—more than *halfway through an evaluation*, the customer still hadn't talked to any suppliers.

So, by the time your Sales-human enters the picture, the purchase evaluation is already in progress.

Before that 57% mark, the customer has already spent time and effort trying to gain consensus on what the problem is, whether there even is a problem, and what the potential solution would be. That means that, oftentimes by the time the Sales-human starts talking to a company, the stakeholders at the company have already had the opportunity to do plenty of research.

This research was later published by former CEB executives Brent Adamson, Matthew Dixon, Pat Spenner, and Nick Toman, in their book *The Challenger Customer*. The book is a wake-up call for star sales-humans to get into their deals earlier as a coach, and find the right advocates within their prospects' organizations. But I'd argue it's also a wake-up call for Marketing and Customer Education teams. During the 57% of the sales cycle where the supplier isn't even involved, customers are doing their own research.

In their description of "Mobilizers", the people on the customer side who can actually influence decision-making on a purchase, the authors write, "while there's a pretty strong guarantee that your Mobilizer will want to learn, there's no guarantee that they will want to learn from your sales reps."

Potential customers like to share industry reports from research firms like Gartner and Forrester. Often they end up looking at white papers, e-books, blog posts, and other content marketing products from potential suppliers. And, you guessed it—if your Customer Education materials are readily available, your prospects will find those, too.

Here, we come back to the value of making Customer Education materials free and openly accessible. Unlike many content marketing materials, which are hidden behind a lead-generation form, open Customer Education materials can help prospects see the breadth of industry knowledge your company has, and how committed you are to helping your customers succeed.

Of course, this doesn't take away from what your Sales-humans do. They still need to be able to tailor information to customers, challenge their assumptions, and help guide them to insights about how *this* product uniquely meets *this* solution. But Customer Education efforts add support and credibility to the Sales-human's argument; when it's time for her to enter the picture, she'll do so with more wind at her back, thanks to the help your company has already provided in framing the customer's decision.

PROVIDE TALKING POINTS AND A DEMO

If you've built a great scalable Customer Education function, it's more than just an intangible service that can be added to a deal—it's a product in its own right. So how much time do you spend on marketing your education products?

When you think about how your Sales-humans should use your education programs in their deals, think about it like you would any other feature of your product. Create one-pagers, talking points, and other collateral for them to use.

Better yet, create a demo for them to walk the customers through your education materials and highlight the key resources and features. They may not use it for every deal, but it's something that they can certainly highlight for customers who want more education about your product, or want to train their large teams upon implementation. Demoing your education resources can give customers a sense of security; they know that you're committed to enabling them and are a partner in their success.

If you have an internal Knowledge Base or performance support tool for your Sales team, make sure that your information is included and up-to-date in those systems. By linking internal sales enablement content to external Customer Education content, you'll constantly expose your Sales-humans to new information.

The best is when your sales team feels confident enough using your help tools organically during demos. For example, at Optimizely, many of our Sales-humans would take the opportunity, when customers asked questions, to say, "I can answer that question, but let me show you something." They would then type the question into Google, and voila—the search result from our Knowledge Base would show up! Not only were they demoing the ease-of-use for our help content, but they were also helping customers build a habit of self-service before they even became customers.

Knowing that we had a rich base of knowledge around not just our product, but also common industry topics and concepts, instilled trust in our customers.

APPEAL TO THE HEAD: STATISTICS AND DATA POINTS SHOW IMPACT

Your potential customers often want data points to validate their buying decisions—especially when their stakeholders and decision-makers have fancy titles and *don't* have the time to dive into details.

When you're talking about your education programs to prospects, you want to describe how these programs will create immediate or long-term value for them.

But prospects don't care about your vanity metrics. They don't care how many pageviews your Knowledge Base gets, how many members your community has, or how many courses are in your academy—yet these are the first metrics that you often get asked for when someone is preparing the sales pitch deck (if you get asked at all). If you're going to tout those metrics in front of customers, you need to frame them in terms of the value they'll deliver to a customer.

For example, why do Knowledge Base pageviews matter? Well, they matter if they're being used to explain how many customers trust the industry knowledge your company publishes. And they matter if you're explaining how easy it is to resolve any friction your team has using the product. Instead of simply showing the number of articles or pageviews that you have, frame these types of metrics in terms of trustworthiness. For example, how often are you articles audited and updated? Can you guarantee that when customers look for information, it will be up to date? That could be more important to them than the quantity of publications or pageviews.

Why should prospects care how many members your community has? Maybe this is important if you're using the principle of social proof to show that other people use your product. If they're all enjoying your product, maybe your prospect should too. But here, it's less important to show pure metrics and more important to tell the story about how your prospect will be supported in an active, vibrant customer community. Just as you'd show them a current customer list so that they feel like they're in good company as your customer, your community metrics may be able to communicate a similar message.

Why do prospects care how many courses are in your academy? Maybe they don't. Maybe it's more important to show how your academy is different from the mediocre training they got from their previous partner. So instead of showing the number of courses, you might want to present a statistic about your above-average completion rates, which shows that people find your content engaging. Or maybe you can highlight the number of courses you have that cover job skills and industry thought-leadership topics, and not just the courses about your product.

Better yet, show numerically how your education programs will help customers during their journey with you. Do customers who take your training get value from your product sooner? If you use such a "Time to First Value" metric, it's fantastic for communicating the value Customer Education provides. You're talking about Customer Education as a way to protect the customer's investment in your product and help them through the change management that comes with a new product. If you've measured the impact on product adoption metrics for your trained vs. untrained accounts, consider sharing that data with prospects as well. By doing so, you're clearly communicating that you have solutions in place that will contribute to your customers' success.

An important thing to note when communicating value metrics and data points is that they are best delivered in a way that's consumable and comparative. This means:

> **Consumable:** Your data is concise and easy to understand at a glance. "Trained vs. untrained customer product adoption rates" is easy to understand—that's two bar charts. "Statistical regression analysis of renewal propensity" is someone's data science dissertation.

> **Comparative:** Don't just present numbers—compare those numbers to something. For example, show a trend line over time (hopefully going up and to the right) or compare the numbers to a baseline (like trained vs. untrained customer results).

APPEAL TO THE HEART: QUOTE ME ON THIS

Your Customer Education programs should be a competitive differentiator for your business, and that starts with customers loving your programs. For prospects who likely haven't yet seen the magic of your Customer Education, customer quotes are often the most concise way to share the value.

Where do you get these quotes? It depends on whom you want the quote to come from. If you want to show what your actual learners think, try looking for gems in your post-training satisfaction surveys, "was this article helpful?" feedback, and post-onboarding customer surveys. The customer community can also be a great source of testimonials. Just make sure that whatever you're using is approved for sales and marketing use.

Sometimes, though, it's more powerful to have the program leader or executive sponsor on the customer side provide a quote. This shows your prospects' executives that this program will create value for them, too. If you have current customers whom you know are highly involved in your education programs, try reaching out to them for a quote. In many cases, the CSM who owns the account or the Customer Marketing Manager will have a relationship that you can leverage. You'll never know if you don't ask.

THE POWER OF THE PREVIEW

For some customers, no statistic or testimonial will persuade as much as a test drive. This "try-before-you-buy" approach forms the foundation of "freemium" products and 30-day free trials. After all, once you start using a product, you're more likely to get hooked on it.

Using that logic, consider giving prospects access to your learning materials. Sales leaders sometimes object to showing the product too early in the buying journey, because they haven't yet had the opportunity to show the value of the product. The more "Enterprise" your product is, the less impact this tactic has, but for consumer products and down-market B2B products it can be powerful to let your prospect demo the learning materials along with the product, as a way to build trust and drive faster product adoption. If you have great Customer Education programs, letting prospects join in on your foundation-level material can be an effective way to generate engagement and excitement.

If, for example, you have a MOOC (massive open online course), open e-learning courseware, usergroups, or foundational group training, prospects can often learn a lot from these sessions—not just about your software, but about the industry in many cases.

It's especially important for companies with new technologies, or in emerging product categories, to help prospects learn about their industry's emerging trends as they fill skill gaps and make a business case for purchasing new software.

Prospects may not always have time to preview courses, but those who do will often benefit from it, and it can be a signal to the Sales-human that the prospect is engaged.

SALES-HUMANS ARE HUMANS TOO!

We've talked a lot about prospects, but don't forget about your Sales-humans. Across the industry, we often make big investments in sales enablement, but that shouldn't happen in a silo from your Customer Education programs. As part of your sales enablement programs, have your Sales-humans go through the same trainings and resources that your customers use. That's not just so they'll know how to position the education during a sales cycle, but also so they feel more informed and have more expertise on your product. It will make them more capable of answering questions that prospects bring up.

Encourage your Sales team (or work with your sales enablement team) to incorporate your customer-facing training into Sales team onboarding, and make sure that your Sales-humans feel comfortable using your customer Knowledge Base to answer their own product questions as they talk with customers.

Onboarding: Customer Education is your scale engine to drive product adoption

Do you know why your customers are churning?

In 2014, the Preact Customer Success platform released a study showing that the single-biggest predictor of customer churn across all of SaaS was poor onboarding, representing 23% of churn—even more than poor relationship management, product deficiencies, and other likely culprits.

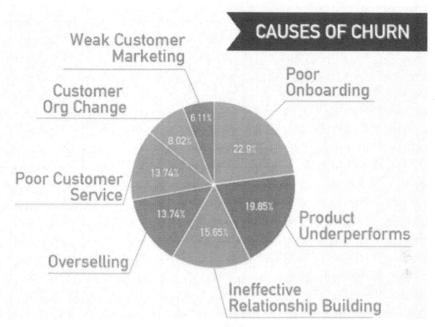

Preact's study of root causes of Churn. Source at https://www.slideshare.net/Preact/causes-of-customer-churn

If we're going to ask our customers to renew with us, we have to make sure they're properly onboarded in the first place. That means we have to focus on their retention and not just on preventing them from churning.

According to Customer Success expert Lincoln Murphy, "Proper onboarding isn't done to prevent churn; it's done to ensure the customer achieves their Desired Outcome. Retention comes from that."

But what is "onboarding," really?

This question often goes unasked at organizations, leaving them without a shared agreement on what the customer onboarding process looks like. Do you truly know what the steps are, and who owns what in the process? It's easy to say you do... and then realize you have no idea.

When you're a young company, you have to onboard every customer somehow. That said, there's not generally an immediate demand for improving your onboarding, so you might keep throwing warm bodies at the process for months or years as long as you don't mind a lot of variance in the quality of your onboarding. Improving onboarding must be a strategic decision that Customer Success teams make as they mature.

The Technology Services Industry Association (TSIA) reports that there is a direct correlation between training and software adoption. As reported in their 2016 poll of 2,800 learners, 68% of customers report using products more after training, 56% use more product features or functions than they would if untrained, and 87% can work more independently (and thus not hammer your CSM and Support teams with basic questions).

Training Drives Adoption

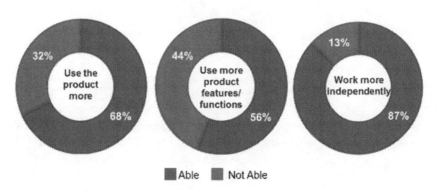

Source: Technology Services Industry Association, Gauging Value: Answering the Training/Adoption Question

Linda Schwaber-Cohen, Senior Manager of Training at Skilljar, a customer training platform, notes the positive impact of Customer Education as she looks across Skilljar's customer base:

> It's no question that customer adoption, engagement and renewal are intertwined. When customers adopt and see value from a product or service, they're inevitably more likely to renew. Skilljar customers have seen time to value drop by

more than 50%, and hours spent on individual consulting and included services drop by 83%.

To gauge how strategic your onboarding program is, and whether Customer Education can help, start by answering some "who/what/when/where" questions. Then try asking them of the Sales, Product, and Customer Success leaders in your company, to see whether you have a shared agreement on the answers.

The "who":

> Which department or team "owns" onboarding? Who defines the onboarding strategy? Who primarily executes onboarding? Does anyone have a high-level success metric tied to it?
>
> Do you have different processes for "account onboarding" where you first sign on an account or business unit and ramp them up, and "user onboarding" where an individual user gets up to speed?
>
> Who, on your customer side, needs to be trained during onboarding?
>
> Who is primarily responsible for making sure customers have the skills they need to use your product? How do you *know* they have those skills?
>
> Do your activities and value metrics change based on your customer segments (such as company size, annual contract value, or geography)?

The "what":

> How do you define onboarding? Do you consider both "account onboarding" and "user onboarding" to be processes, or are you just thinking of them as activities? [For example, you say "onboarding" and it means "an onboarding call" or "the onboarding guiders in the product."]
>
> What are the required activities that occur during onboarding?
>
> What skills do users need to perform by the end of onboarding? How will they gain these skills?

What habits are users supposed to build around using your product?

What's the risk if users aren't onboarded correctly? Will they make critical mistakes, expose sensitive information, cause physical damage, run afoul of legal issues, or otherwise cause mayhem?

How different are the skills needed for different user roles? For example, admins and end-users often need starkly different levels of training.

Which trainings are recommended for customers during onboarding? Do different personas take different trainings?

How do you define "first value" for a customer? How do you know that they've gotten an initial moment of value from your product?

How do you know whether a customer had a "successful" or "failed" onboarding?

The "when and where":

When does onboarding start for a customer? Is it at contract signing? During a trial period? Before the contract is signed? At a kickoff call?

When does onboarding end for a customer? Is it when the customer achieves first value? Is it when the customer hits some sort of adoption milestone? Is it at the first quarterly business review?

When will training happen during onboarding? Is it all at once, in several stages, or on-demand for the customer to take at any pace?

Where will training happen? Is it on-site, online, on-demand, or in-product?

Do you have different processes if the customer came in through a free trial vs. if they signed up as a paying customer from day one?

Answering these questions should give you a sense of how much you know about your own onboarding process and its level of maturity. From these questions, you'll start to form a perspective around how **scalable** your onboarding can be, and how high the **stakes** are for the customer if they fail onboarding.

CUSTOMER EDUCATION BOOSTS YOUR ONBOARDING MATURITY

Earlier, I mentioned that one solution to onboarding is to continue throwing bodies at it. It's the path I see many early-stage companies take, and then they end up wondering why their headcount ratios are out of whack. Or why their revenue model looks like a leaky bucket that they keep trying to fill with new business.

Let's be clear: You need CSMs. They're instrumental in guiding customers along their journey and helping to find new paths to value with your product. CSMs also help increase customers' desire to be successful with your product and remove friction along the way.

But your CSMs can't help your customers realize more value if they're spending all their time doing onboardings and answering basic product questions.

When you have a limited number of CSMs, and a fixed number of onboardings, then one of two things start to happen: either your CSMs spend all their time doing onboardings and can't do much else, or your CSMs start to neglect onboardings because they're busy chasing renewals or putting out fires. You can try to solve this with incentives, but they're both bad outcomes.

Think about this from your customers' point of view. Your customers are busy and using your product isn't their full time job. They don't necessarily want to commit hours to sitting on onboarding calls with you. And what if someone new comes on the team a month later, having missed the onboarding call that your CSM did?

There's another hidden risk to this ad hoc method—when you don't have a repeatable or defined method for delivering onboardings, or standardized materials, then your CSMs will make stuff up and focus on what they think is important. Your best CSMs may tailor the onboarding toward what they believe the customer will find important, but when CSMs are strapped for time, it's hard for them to be at their best. Given that each CSM has a different point of view on what's important, you're creating an inconsistent customer experience.

Instead, what if your CSMs could focus on using their brains? What if they focus more on consulting with the customer and building relationships, rather than just repeatedly delivering (or consistently ignoring) onboardings?

Investing in Customer Education will improve both your CSMs' and your customers' experiences through:

> Higher customer completion of milestones and project plans for onboarding
>
> Faster time to first value
>
> More efficient CSM resourcing (more time for them to spend on Quarterly Business Reviews, Executive Business Reviews, and other value-add activities)

Kristen Swanson, Chief of Staff for the Customer Experience at Slack, describes Customer Education as "jet fuel for CSMs." By building scalable Customer Education, CSMs can build relationships better and faster, instead of focusing on repeatable, transactional tasks.

Each Customer Education department uses a different mix of formats for onboarding training, based on the need for scale and the stakes of failed onboarding. In this section I'll cover the ones I see most frequently.

ONBOARDING FOR HIGHER SCALE

If you're rolling out your product to large groups of people with a low-touch approach, and especially if most of your users will use the product in a similar way, you'll likely need scalable approaches to onboarding. Here are some that I've found useful.

Getting Started Guides

While not a training, per se, a Getting Started Guide takes the essential actions that the customer must perform, and the common questions they may have, and rolls them up into one short document or video—or, for more complex products, a short series of videos.

When you're putting together Getting Started guides, keep the following principles in mind:

It is a Getting Started guide, not an Everything About Your Product guide. Include only the *most essential* actions that the customer should complete in the first day or two. You can come back to other exciting features when the customer is ready for them.

Give simple examples and use cases. Make it clear what the customer needs to do in order to get to that first moment of value. Try running through a simple example that feels relevant to customers and gives them some quick wins. If you don't know what customers typically do on day one, try shadowing a new user onboarding or a sales call. Pay attention to what customers are trying to do, and what language they use. Mirror that language in your guide.

Make it quick and easy to navigate. Provide clear, easy-to-read headers. Put all extraneous information into other articles. If you use Getting Started videos, place them prominently in your article.

Connect your features to the customers' job. When you introduce a new step or a new feature, quickly remind them *why* they're doing this and how it will make them more effective at doing their job.

Self-paced e-learning

A typical self-paced e-learning program combines text, video, and interactivity—usually hosted on a Customer Learning

Management System. Self-paced e-learning can take more upfront time to create, but it allows you to chunk information into smaller pieces that customers can access on their own time. It provides both scalability for large accounts and engagement for new users as they come on board. On the other hand, if your onboarding needs to be highly customized, and there isn't a core set of subjects or use cases that would apply to large groups of customers customers, self-paced e-learning may not be a great strategy.

Virtual Classroom and Labs

Some people use the term "webinar" instead of virtual classroom or lab, but I think that's misleading. In the true sense of the word, a webinar—literally a "web seminar"—should be like a seminar in a college classroom, where a small group of students engage with each other and with the professor, debate hot topics, and challenge their skills.

But today's "webinar" has turned into a marketing activity where a presenter talks *at* people they can't even see, who are typically checking their email instead of paying attention, perhaps believing that they can successfully multitask their way through training.

Overall, webinars and webcasts have a bad rap with learners. In the 2018 *Voice of the Learner* study by the Digital Learning Consortium, webcasts were rated as having the lowest perceived importance to learners—ranking below audio, video, online courses, and digital reading.

That's why I prefer the term "Virtual Classroom" or "Virtual Lab", to "Webinar." If done right, the virtual classroom is a way to promote interactivity through engaging facilitation, while still allowing participation from those in various geographic locations. The best virtual classrooms promote social learning through Q&A and hands-on projects.

For an example of virtual classrooms done well, check out Box, a file-sharing and collaboration company that delivers multiple online classes each week. These virtual classrooms are open to its entire user base, with many classes taught to hundreds of students at a time. Jesse Evans, as Box's Senior Customer Education Manager, shared the importance of making these sessions engaging and interactive:

"Real education—the kind that has a lasting impact—is about emotional engagement, which means it's about interacting with your attendees, not talking at them. If you remember nothing else, remember this: Never tell your attendees something that they could tell you."

Box's philosophy is to promote some sort of interactivity, such as asking a question to the audience, *once per slide*. Putting this type of guideline in place naturally encourages interactivity, limits the number of slides you can cram in, and prevents bulldozing your way through your content.

There's no better way to learn than by doing, especially when your product is complex or highly technical software. Virtual labs (or "live labs") give you the opportunity to solve problems in a realistic environment. A virtual lab is an environment where you set up an instance of your product for learners to get hands-on practice.

You can use virtual labs for in-class activities or self-study, but you can also use them as sandbox environments for prospects.

Virtual labs do for hands-on activity what virtual classrooms do for instruction. In an ideal world, they provide a simulated environment that mirrors the real-world product environment that the learner will be using.

In-Product User Onboarding

For software companies, what place is better to onboard users than within your product? In-Product user onboarding typically takes the form of guided tours, tooltips, coach marks, and other elements built directly into the product's interface.

Some especially clever onboardings, like in the messaging and collaboration app Slack, use the product to teach you the product.

After you create your username and password in Slack (and perform a few other basic activities that are handled with clickable hotspots and notifications), you get a message from Slackbot. Who's Slackbot, you ask? It's Slack's helpful chatbot.

You know that it's helpful because the first thing it says to you is "To make things easier for your teammates, I can set up a few personal details for you," and then it chats with you to set up your account using understandable, natural language.

The concept of contextual guidance isn't exactly new. Workplace learning professionals have been creating "performance support" tools for years. In the Learning and Development world, performance support includes reference and guidance tools that help people do their jobs—in other words, it's the stuff that happens outside of the classroom, and can range in sophistication from digital walkthroughs to laminate cards that sit by someone's desk. But only in the past few years have companies made more serious investments in their customer-facing product onboarding tools.

Products that rely on free trials to grow their user base often use In-Product Education to onboard those users. Often these are designed by product managers or growth marketers who are eager to show customers all the cool stuff in the product. So what you get are these long real-estate tours that tell you way too much about *what's* there and not nearly enough about *why* you should use anything.

A good in-product onboarding immediately grasps users by showing them the value of what they can do with your product, then gets out of their way until help is needed again. This idea of onboarding tools coming back at strategic times, instead of as one lump transaction, is known as "progressive onboarding."

Later in this book, I devote an entire chapter to In-Product Education.

ONBOARDING FOR HIGHER STAKES

If your customer will incur legal, operational, or even physical risk by not getting educated on your product, that will affect the way you onboard your customers. Namely, you'll need to figure out how to certify that customers won't commit product malpractice, and you may need to use techniques that are less scalable.

Certifications

If I had to make a list of overused education-y terms that get thrown around without a consistent definition, "certification" would appear multiple times. On the same list. In designing your certification strategy, you must understand which type of certification you're building, and why.

The traditional definition of certification is a professional credential—sort of like getting a Certified Public Accountant (CPA) license. You get certified (and maintain that certification) based on knowledge and skills that you've collected throughout a years-long career. These types of certifications are delivered more commonly by professional organizations than by B2B companies, so certification likely means something different in the context of your business.

Designing a certification strategy is kind of like dating—you need to make sure you're on the same page about how serious you are before you start shopping for a ring. Or in this case, you need to be on the same page about how serious and rigorous your certifications are before you start shopping for assessment and proctoring platforms.

Let's walk through the certification seasons of love together.

"We're not really dating; we're just talking"

In the world of SaaS, where most software is becoming very user-friendly, people don't need to be certified, *per se*, because the risk of software malpractice is low. Nothing's going to break if they use the software wrong. Rather, the risk lies in them just not adopting it. So certification becomes a tool for helping organizations prove that they're adopting your software. For these companies, "certification" is more akin to "I took this training class" or "I got a badge."

Often, these certifications are extremely low-stakes, like taking a knowledge check quiz at the end of a course. The customer goes through some sort of learning experience during their onboarding phase, and the CSM just needs a way to verify that the customer learned something. So here, the "certification" can refer to taking the course itself, and maybe having a quick assessment at the end.

This is also typically what people mean when they talk about "certification" in a low-stakes, sales enablement sense, as in, "My team got trained on our new messaging framework last week, and now I'm going to certify them by role-playing a fictional pitch conversation." Translating this to Customer Education, all that "certification" means here is that you have some way of testing the skills that customers learned.

"We're in *like*, not in *love*"

In some cases, you need to go one step further than having the certification just be a course—you want it to be a light credential. Usually, this doesn't mean that the customer has reached a high level of mastery; it means that they're invested. In fact, in its 2018 *Voice of the Learner* report, the Digital Learning Consortium found that 58% of learners are motivated to take training when it leads to the prestige of a credential from a corporation.

HubSpot uses its Inbound Marketing Certification to build foundational skills. Master-level proficiency isn't required; instead, it's a foot in the door. In fact, many of the people who become HubSpot certified aren't customers—they're prospects or even in some cases, students who are learning inbound marketing in a college classroom! People who pass these certifications can share their achievement on LinkedIn or other social networks, but less-advanced certifications aren't likely to carry the same weight as a sophisticated professional credential.

You may also be using your certification program for what's called "assessment-based certificates" (or ABCs, handily enough). Unlike a professional certification, which is meant to represent years of work in a career field, ABCs are certificates that are awarded on a certain topic, usually as part of continuing education, and learners take some sort of assessment to prove that they've mastered the skill.

"Okay, now we're serious"

For many companies, certifications are like a driver's license. You need it to operate the tool. This is especially common for complex, specialized, or technical software, where the risk of software malpractice is high. You want to certify that your customers are competent so they don't break anything.

Often, when you're doing this type of certification, you need to make sure that your customer really knows what they're doing *before* they get their hands on your software in production.

Getting certified as a Salesforce Architect, Developer, or Administrator, for instance, signals to companies that candidates have the right skills to be hired as their CRM administrator, or to build Salesforce apps on their behalf.

To show that you're serious about all of this, you want a higher-stakes assessment. This likely means that the assessment will be timed. You'll need to create question banks that can be randomized by category. You probably want to offer sample tests so that your learners can prepare. You may need to charge for some of your assessments.

You also want to do periodic item analysis, where you look at which questions your test-takers get right or wrong more than the others. Item analysis helps you make sure that the questions aren't phrased confusingly, and that they assess topics that were actually covered in the preparation materials.

"Will you marry me?"

Finally, there's what we would call a "high-stakes" certification. Often these are what you'll find in professional certifications awarded by industry associations—the ones that come with fancy acronyms that you can put after your name and need continuing education credits to renew.

This style of certification is alive and well in the world of partner training and for "architect-level" certifications, where you expect someone to build on top of your product, or to provide a service on your behalf. In these cases, you need to make sure that they're capable of using your product at an advanced level.

Microsoft, for example, invests heavily in these professional certification programs, like the MCITP (Microsoft Certified IT Professional) credential. But before you get too excited about doing high-stakes certifications for your company, know that they require an intense level of effort.

In these types of certifications, you may want the certifying exam to be proctored to ensure its integrity. You may also need parts of the exam to be manually graded, because high-stakes assessments usually need more than just multiple choice questions. In these exams, you often want to provide more robust, scenario-based questions, and you may even require work samples.

When you approach certifications, take the time to understand which type of certification you're building and why. Also, recognize that a certification generally needs both content *and* an assessment, so you can't just build a test without also building a classroom or e-learning course to teach the skills that you're going to certify.

Facilitated courses and classroom training

Most of the scalable onboarding options I just discussed weren't available for customers until recently. Onboarding training used to be conducted during multi-day classroom training sessions, held either on-site at the client's office or at a third-party training center. This placed an obvious constraint on the ability to onboard customers quickly, or reinforce knowledge after the initial onboarding.

Because that's how it was always done, there's an expectation that still lingers around customized, on-site training simply being The Way You Do It. But just as the onset of email spawned the term "snail mail" for what used to simply be known as "mail," on-site classroom trainings as a standard onboarding tool may soon become "snail training."

Classroom training isn't dead, of course. There are several places where it still makes sense:

> For some large enterprise customers, especially those who have centralized teams, on-site training may be used as a way to train up a core team while deepening relationships.
>
> Some companies find success in conducting training and certification roadshows. These tend to work better when they're centered around industry and job skills, not simply software training.
>
> The idea of pre-conference training sessions still seems to be alive and well, because you already have large groups of users in one place. (Whether they're fully engaged for training is a different question.)
>
> In a larger (usually paid) services engagements, especially one where change management or consulting is required, on-site training may be a component of that package.
>
> Maybe most commonly, on-site trainings are still delivered ad hoc by CSMs when they go on-site for quarterly business reviews.

I guess I should correct that last bullet point. Most knowledge-transfer sessions that happen ad hoc aren't really training at all. It's just *telling*.

Your organization must get in the habit of distinguishing "telling" from "training." Otherwise you're funneling time and money into having an expert lecture on a particular subject, only to have the audience forget everything they learned by the next day.

So if you're using ad hoc trainings today and expecting those to help the customer develop skills or change behaviors, ask yourself the following questions:

> Does this session have an outcome that we could measure or observe?
>
> Can participants apply the knowledge that they're learning in the next few days?
>
> Will participants have an opportunity to try out the skills during the session?
>
> Will participants have an opportunity to check their knowledge during the session, to make sure they actually understand the concepts?
>
> Will participants have an opportunity to discuss and debate the concepts, instead of just being lectured at with a periodic "any questions?" thrown in for good measure?

If you can answer "yes" to most of them, you're probably doing a training. If you answer "no," then you're probably just telling the customer things that they're likely to forget.

Be honest with yourself about how you're training customers today: Consider whether your ad-hoc training is simply a "feel-good" activity for you and your customers, or whether it's generating actual results.

ONBOARDING DURING A FREE TRIAL

Before they arrive at the formal onboarding stage, many customers enter a free trial period. This is their chance to find value in the product by using it, instead of just talking to an Account Executive about it. Usually the goal of the free trial is to get customers onboarded quickly, and to have them realize the value in your product so that they'll commit to a paid subscription. This commitment is called "conversion."

So when you're measuring the effectiveness of a free trial, you're primarily looking at:

Acquisition: The number of customers who enter a free trial.

Activation: The percentage of customers who achieve "first value" in a free trial (by using certain features or completing certain actions that are known to lead to conversion).

Conversion: The percentage of customers who convert to paid subscriptions.

Retention & Expansion: The number of customers who continue paying for your product after initial conversion and the number that increase their usage of your product over time.

Because free trials often see a high volume of customers, most companies use scalable education methods at this stage. In-Product Education and "getting started" guides are extremely common, as are self-paced online academies and public virtual classes. Also, don't forget the value of Help Centers during a free trial, as a tool to remove psychological resistance, or friction. When the 30-day clock is ticking, you want to remove any barrier that might cause a customer to stop using your product.

Many companies use their same onboarding trainings and in-product tutorials as free trial education. But if your onboarding training is especially in-depth or complex, you'll probably want to condense it even more for the free trial, so the customer can get moving quickly. If possible, condense your tutorials into small project completions that create quick wins. For example, in project management software, you could give customers a quick sample project to complete. For Optimizely, where the goal was to create an entire roadmap of experiments over time, we started customers with a simple, common hypothesis to test.

In a timed free trial, you also have the option to time your onboarding to go along with the trial. Many companies create 30-day email nurture campaigns to go along with the 30-day free trial. Periodically throughout the trial, you send an email to the customer giving them new ideas, encouragement to keep using your product, and options to get support if they need it.

SINGLE-SOURCING AND REPURPOSING CONTENT

One of the challenges with scalable onboarding content is that it can be slower to update than ad hoc slides. The advantage is that it's more consistent and can serve more customers once it's created. That said, there are a few tips you can use to lower the burden of content updates.

Repurpose content strategically

Atlassian pilots much of its content in conference courses before turning it into self-serve live labs and e-learning. This gives it a way to validate content before turning it into something that's a larger investment. It also means that Atlassian doesn't have to scramble to find content for its e-learning—the content is already there from the pilot.

Sherry Quinn, who leads Atlassian University, says her team was able to repurpose the admin and power-user courses they delivered live at their Atlassian Summit conference (lots of work for a moderately sized audience) to half- and full-day virtual courses (moderate work for a larger audience), and finally after a year of testing the content, into self-paced online courses (moderate work for a *huge* audience). She was able to repurpose the same curriculum, iterating on it each time, to improve the margins and serve more customers at scale.

This repurposing strategy doesn't only work the first time you create your Customer Education department; you can do it for new content as time goes on. If you run live courses or virtual classroom sessions, use them as testing grounds for new content before you turn it into self-paced courseware.

Don't sweat the small stuff

One question I always hear is, "How do you keep content

updated with each release cycle?" And even for sophisticated Customer Education programs, the answer is—you don't. It's not necessary for you to update every screenshot if there's a minor UI (user interface) change in your product. Instead, commit to a regular cadence of review-and-replace, auditing content that hasn't been updated in some time. If you know there are major changes coming up, make sure you incorporate those changes into your courses. But don't worry about updating it for each minor UI tweak.

Furthermore, consider whether you need to feature so much UI in your courses. Taking screenshots of workflows in your product is easy the first time you're putting courses together, since it takes less work than trying to do conceptual diagrams, animations, and so on. But chances are that the core of what you're trying to explain is actually a conceptual process. For example, at Optimizely, we weren't trying to teach what buttons to push in our UI; we were teaching a six-step experiment-building process. Try to remove your in-product UI content in favor of the more conceptual assets that explain process and workflow. Those will endure many more release cycles.

Structure and categorize content in a practical way

As the Internet gets better at organizing content and information, how a user navigates to find pieces of content becomes less important than how machines can discover that same content. As a simple example, it used to be that you would navigate through a link directory like Yahoo! to try to find a piece of information; today you type your search directly into Google and find the information using its algorithm. Instead of browsing through endless categories to find music, you can use iTunes or Spotify to create personalized radio stations based on your tastes.

No matter how clever your information architecture is, it is still useful to tag your content by category, type, and format so that it's easier to find using organic search or your site's internal search. This also makes it easier to maintain and update content over time, especially if you end up implementing a structured content standard such as DITA (the Darwin Information Typing Architecture). These types of structured content hierarchies make content reuse and remixing easier by classifying topics as a task, concept, reference, glossary, and troubleshooting type that can be assembled and combined based on the need. You probably won't start with anything as sophisticated as DITA; the overhead required makes it impractical for many organizations. But most systems do allow you to tag content and place it into categories.

Retention and Growth: Customer Education increases customers' desire to renew and reduces friction

I once got a fortune cookie that read, "Customer service is like taking a bath; you have to keep doing it." After wondering, "Who writes these things?" I taped it to my computer monitor at work.

But just like a few days without showering might leave you smelling a bit ripe, we often neglect our customers' hygiene until the renewal rolls around.

By the end of onboarding, you've put in the work to help your customers gain awareness of your solution. You went through a rigorous evaluation and sales process. And you got them up and running during their onboarding. Now that you've gotten your customers to first value, the job's just getting started.

You've got to love your customers, or you'll lose them. If you don't help your customer get continuous value from your product, they won't renew. If they don't see the value in staying with you vs. your competitors, they won't renew. And if you can't show them the path to increased value, they won't expand.

In many cases, they'll churn. If a customer churns too early, you often haven't recouped your acquisition costs, so you've actually lost money on that relationship. (Your C-level executives may know this as "negative CAC/LTV ratio"—where the Lifetime Value underperforms the Cost to Acquire the Customer).

Why do customers churn before your cost to acquire them pays off? One reason might be because you've been thinking about them in terms of *your* success—how do I keep this customer longer—and not in terms of *their* success? When you don't know what's valuable to the customer, you can't bring that customer value.

While failed onboardings were the number-one source of churn according to the Preact survey discussed in the previous section, your work isn't done once the customer has found first value with your product. You're responsible for bringing ongoing value, which means increasing their desire to use your product and reducing their friction along the way. Remember that ineffective relationship building and poor customer service also accounted for around 30% of churn.

Unfortunately, most companies leave the post-launch phase undefined. That's partially because it's the most customer-driven phase of the lifecycle. Once the product is in their hands, you only have so much control over what they do with it; your customers have to put in the effort to drive their business goals, too. And all of this takes time and effort.

Those who do use Customer Education as part of the post-launch, see the rewards: 12% higher renewals industry-wide, according to the TSIA. Donna Weber, a Customer Education industry consultant and principal at Springboard Solutions, noted that she saw a 10-20% increase in renewals, and a 15% increase in Net Promoter Score, for trained customers.

Customers don't always know how to build momentum after they launch; some companies try to throw CSMs at that problem. The CSMs eventually get to know their customers and become advocates for them (although more often than not, they also get shuffled around every time your customer segmentation changes). High-level points of contact on your customers' side turn over and so do individual team members. Now your CSMs are playing catch-up to rebuild context and train new team members. CSMs are vital for your organization, but their brain power and creativity get misused frequently. Instead of letting your CSMs consult with customers to drive ongoing adoption and value, they're responsible for chasing down renewal contracts or performing the same basic trainings over and over for customers.

Meanwhile, your customer Support team is answering the same questions over and over. Customers get frustrated that they have to call you, and you're not making their lives easier. With the average cost of a North American support ticket estimated at over $15 (based on handling time), and in some cases approaching $50 per ticket, you want to minimize this cost at all... costs.

When it comes to ongoing support and customer retention, Customer Education once again revs up as your scale engine.

SELF-SERVICE DOCUMENTATION IS KEY, EVEN IN THE ENTERPRISE

When we originally created Optiverse at Optimizely, we assumed that it would primarily be used by our smaller, self-serve and mid-market customers. Nearly everyone in the company held the perception that only small customers have an interest in self-serving their content. After all, they don't have CSMs who can hold their hands all the time. We also thought that enterprises, on the other hand, expect their information served on a silver platter by a butler named Jeeves.

We were wrong. It turned out that even our largest enterprise customers preferred to "Ask Jeeves" by using search engines to find information, rather than asking us to solve all their problems. We started to notice that our enterprise customers made up the highest segment of users represented in our Optiverse Knowledge Base and Academy.

What was going on here? One of the reasons we thought that enterprise customers wouldn't respond to self-service content was pure perception—we just thought it "wasn't what enterprises did." The other issue that led to our bias was that we didn't see as many basic support questions from enterprise customers, so we assumed they weren't asking them.

In fact, something different was happening. When you're a small, mom-and-pop company, and you have a problem with a product, you write directly to the company who supplied the product. This is why if you go to any major consumer brand's Facebook page, you see the types of complaint letters that would have previously been sent through angrily scrawled postal mail.

When you're a large enterprise company using software, something different happens. Large enterprise companies usually have centers of excellence, or centralized business units, that manage the overall relationship with the software provider. That center of excellence becomes the first line of defense for questions about the software, so the software company's Support team doesn't end up hearing a lot of these questions.

While you might assume that every customer wants the delightful, personalized experience of speaking to an agent on the phone—do you feel that way when you reach out for support on a product? Would you rather navigate through a phone tree and wait on hold, or get the answer quickly by looking it up online?

The Corporate Executive Board notes in its research that 57% of inbound support calls come from customers who first tried to find information on the company's website. Forrester Research backs this up, finding that 70% of customers prefer to use a company's website to get answers, instead of calling.

Until we talked to these large companies, we didn't realize that the program managers in the centers of excellence were doing exactly what our small and midsized customers were doing: using the Academy to onboard their teams, and Googling for answers to questions.

Given that, the centers of excellence (who largely owned the relationship with Optimizely) were having a positive experience with self-service. They *liked* just being able to Google something and not have to wait for an answer.

The centers of excellence used our resources to train new team members as they come on board, and individual team members are able to get what they need with a simple search.

In order to get to this point, you can use the discoverability and SEO techniques I highlighted in the chapters on Awareness and Evaluation. But your content also has to be solid.

Creating a usable Knowledge Base and documentation set takes upfront effort and maintenance, and it will affect both the volume and quality of tickets that come in, providing your Support team time and focus for more complex challenges.

Having spoken to some other teams who implemented high-volume support documentation programs, or Knowledge-Centered Support (KCS) solutions, we saw that many of those teams ended up with content that was frequently duplicative, untrustworthy, and undiscoverable. Their customers were asking questions like:

> "How do I know that this is the most up-to-date version of this topic?"
>
> "What's the difference between this article and this other, similar article?"

And by asking those questions, I mean that they were giving up on trying to use self service for documentation, and calling the support phone line in abject frustration.

That's why Optimizely decided to take a more curated approach to documentation—an approach that evolved into our "80/20" principle of documentation. We aimed to document the common features, issues, and practices that 80% of our customers would find relevant, and left the edge cases and specifics out. Those edge cases, after all, would generate 80% of the content work while applying to fewer than 20% of our customers.

Training and maturity models: A perfect pair

In the post-launch phases of the customer lifecycle, you're often paying attention to your customers' maturity. In other words, you want to know not just how much they're using your product, but how *well* they're using your product—what advanced features they're making use of, and more importantly what business processes and cultural change they're driving as a result of your product.

Many companies create maturity models to help prospects and customers diagnose how mature their program is. They'll have different criteria, like "program management," "business metrics," and "feature usage" that can all become more mature over time.

Maturity models generally resemble the Capability Maturity Model, which was developed at Carnegie Mellon University and intended for software engineering processes.

Here's an example of a Capability Maturity Model, moving from ad hoc and reactive processes to more mature, well-defined and measured ones:

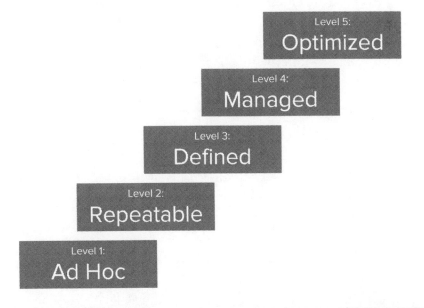

Some have simplified this model to three stages: "crawl - walk - run." No matter which maturity stages you use, though, each dimension gets evaluated on its maturity: whether it's being done ad hoc or systematically, and how much value it's creating for the program at large.

Customers often don't know what stage of maturity they're in, and it's up to you to diagnose them and provide specific recommendations that help them get more value over time.

Chances are, if you have a fairly new Customer Education team, you've only built core content for customer onboarding. You haven't looked into the advanced skills and disciplines a customer needs.

Using a maturity model, you can systematically do a gap analysis to identify where you may be missing content, and how you can create more articles and courseware that would help customers at different maturity levels.

Some great places to start:

> Look at which features your advanced customers use. How do they use them? What are the use cases? Teach your lower-maturity customers how to take advantage of these features.
>
> Benchmark your customer base. What are the best practices vs. typical implementations? The best practices often makes for great advanced content, as they differentiate a power user from a typical user, or a mature organization from a fledgling one.
>
> Determine which skills differentiate a novice and expert practitioner in your field. Creating courseware around those skills helps round out your users' skills, so you're not just teaching them how to use your product; you're teaching them how to be awesome at their jobs.

Are you still stumped on what your advanced customers need? Here's an activity to try:

Make a list of the key skills your customers need to get to first value with your product in the first 90 days. That's skills, by the way, not topics. Just because you covered a topic, doesn't mean you taught the skill. Now go take a look at the topics that you cover in your introductory training that customers receive during onboarding. If those lists are mostly the same, then you're on the right track. But if you're like a lot of companies, you've overstuffed your basic training with concepts and product features that 80% of your customers won't care about as they're first realizing value.

We often complain that it's hard to get customers to absorb all the knowledge from training, as if that's *their* problem. It's not; it's ours. We probably tried to teach them things that they didn't actually need to use at this point in their lifecycle. Get that stuff out of your introductory training, and you'll solve two problems—you'll give yourself more time to teach key skills through interactive activities, *and* you'll have content for that "advanced" training that you haven't gotten around to creating.

CUSTOMER EDUCATION IN THE QBR PROCESS

Quarterly Business Reviews (QBRs) and Executive Business Reviews (EBRs) are staples of Customer Success programs. They provide a structured opportunity to deliver value to your customers' executives. They can also make your customer-side points of contact look like shining stars.

By showing the value that your product creates for your customers, you have a key opportunity to firm up your relationship and learn more about your customers' desired outcomes.

Remember, though, that your users only succeed if they have the skills and motivation to be successful. Customer Education can be a lever during QBRs to show your commitment to the customer's ongoing development. As you develop more robust course catalogs, articles, and other learning materials, you can also recommend specific topics to the customer that will help them grow with you.

Ask yourself: How much does Customer Education come up in these QBR and EBR discussions? Consider whether your CSMs have the tools to be able to report on a customer's consumption of your knowledge resources; whether they're participating in your community; whether they're certified.

Often, if your customers have out-of-date certifications, or haven't taken advantage of your courseware, pointing them toward these resources can be a strong "give" to help them increase their success.

CERTIFICATION PROGRAMS DRIVE VALUE OVER TIME

Many companies use certifications as part of the onboarding phase—maybe even requiring that the customer is certified before they start using the product. Certification takes on a different role in the post-launch phase.

After practitioners pass your foundational-level certifications, they have fundamental skills. Now you can build higher-level certifications to test their advanced, or master-level, skills. Those who really embrace your product and discipline want to be able to show off advanced proficiency and brag about it to the industry.

Certifications (and the courses and learning paths that you build around them) have strong potential to build your customer's LTV, as they can build your customers' competence with your product as well as within their industries.

At this point, your "post-sales" efforts become marketing efforts once again. For example, Salesforce Trailhead and its other certification programs build the careers of future Salesforce admins and delivery partners, making Salesforce customers, as well as the entire field of Sales Operations stronger. At Optimizely, we were creating a category of "experimentation professionals," and our open approach to our Academy and certification programs allowed even our competitors' customers to get certified in product-agnostic experimentation skills. In my opinion, it's short-sighted to worry too much about competitors and their customers accessing your information. The power of expanding your brand to those potential customers creates far more ongoing value.

Over time, practitioners in your field move from company to company. Certification also provides a way for practitioners to show that they're skilled in your product. If those practitioners move to companies who use your product, then your customers know they're getting someone who has the right skills. If they move to new companies, they will hopefully bring your product with them because of the associated trust and value they have in your brand.

Certifications can also be a boon for your Support team. Often, advanced users are helpful because they don't bog down your Support teams with so many basic-level questions. Consider offering support incentives to your certified customers, so more customers will get certified and not ask as many basic questions.

COMMUNITY GROWS OVER TIME

If you have a user community, either online or offline, it can play a meaningful role in your post-launch phases. Why? Customers always want to know what others are doing—and how they're doing it! In your online communities and user groups, have your more advanced users participate and share their experiences.

If you're providing incentives to these advanced user "MVPs" who can share their skills and support others, they will help you not only with your customer support efforts, but also with your company's thought leadership. As they participate in conversations about strategy and best practices, sharing what they know, they'll often find creative ways to use your product or new skills that wasn't even on your company's radar. If you're in an emergent field (as Optimizely was with digital experimentation), these conversations also advance the state of the industry.

What happens when you have an effective community of certified practitioners is that you create a virtuous cycle—as your customers become more mature, they help other customers become more mature, and so on. Everybody benefits.

BRING IT ALL BACK TO ATTRIBUTION

Let's say that you didn't invest in Customer Education and instead had CSMs and Support agents individually drive your certification programs, community efforts, and post-sales trainings. You'd quickly find your team without focus, and you'd have to hire more expensive people than is practical. Yet I see several companies who expect their individual CSMs or other related roles to drive these types of programs as initiatives on the side.

But there's danger in relying on individual CSMs to do everything themselves. They should be trusted advisors and domain experts, but that doesn't also mean they can scale your post-launch experience. An investment in a few Customer Education professionals now can save you an army of new, expensive CSMs down the line.

That means, as Customer Education professionals, we have to be able to measure Customer Education's impact and tell the story of its efficacy on an ongoing basis.

Christine Souza, who led Knowledge Management, Education, and Community at AppDynamics through its acquisition by Cisco, compares the way we talk about Customer Education to the way marketers used to talk about what they did:

"Marketing went from 'spray and pray' to highly targeted metrics. We can do the same. To do that, we need to be able to tell the story of our business."

And that doesn't mean "learning business-speak," in a vague sense. We won't magically be invited to sit at the executive table just because we know how to "speak business." But what does telling the story of our business look like? Often, we do it in the wrong way.

Christine says, "Customer Education leaders tell their boss that we just trained 400 people, but software executives think on a different order of magnitude. They want to hear about 40,000 people—but we don't have 40,000 people using our product. Those numbers work for Marketing teams who attract tens of thousands of leads, but our story is different."

The same is often true of training revenue. We might find our revenue numbers impressive, but on average, training revenue is a rounding error compared to a company's overall revenue.

Instead of talking about raw numbers who consume our training, Christine recommends tying Customer Education to the customer's journey. Is your product harder to implement than it is to sell? Does your customer base have skill gaps that need to be filled so that they can use your product? Is there a need to improve customers' time to realize value? Those are stories we can use to frame the work we do.

Here's are some ways I recommend looking for stories about the impact of Customer Education:

> Show how your Customer Education programs influence NPS. What is the NPS for your trained customers, or your active community MVPs, vs. those who aren't trained?
>
> Do this same analysis with ticket deflection and product adoption. You'll almost certainly see a lift for customers who are actively engaged with your Customer Education programs vs. those who aren't.
>
> Talk to your Support team about their experience with trained vs. untrained customers. One of my favorite stories comes from Avis Beiden, a Customer Education leader who discovered that her company's Support team was stunningly able to predict whether a customer was trained based on the quality of the questions they asked. For each ticket, the agent responded to the question, "Do I think this customer received training?" and their accuracy was startling.
>
> What percentage of your churned, renewed, and expanded customers use your Customer Education resources? Conduct

this analysis to (a) find out whether there's a strong correlation between renewal and education consumption, and (b) look at your penetration rates in general. You'll quickly see which parts of your Customer Education ecosystem are underutilized.

These stories help to show the *results* of Customer Education on the broader business, not just the *activity* you're doing.

One final tip from Christine on presenting to executives: know your audience.

"If you wouldn't cognitively overload your learners, why would you do it to your execs? Focus on ways to tell the story that are simple and visual. Some execs prefer detail, and you can always keep that in the appendix of your presentation. That way, you'll be able to answer those detailed questions on a moment's notice."

If Customer Education is doing its job, you'll see customers who have fewer barriers to success as they continue using your product and become more mature over time. This is the recipe for higher customer lifetime value, and if you do it using scalable customer education, it's also the recipe for higher CLTV with lower operating costs.

Where does Customer Education sit in an organization?

Asking where Customer Education fits in an organization is a bit like asking where the spleen is located in the human body. We have a general idea, but most of us aren't completely sure, and we get uncomfortable when asked. Let's walk through some of the common organizational approaches, with pros and cons.

CUSTOMER SUCCESS

It's most common in modern SaaS companies to see Customer

Education within Customer Success: the Customer Education Manager role aligns with the Customer Success Manager (CSM) and Customer Support representative (CSR) roles. Because this configuration is pretty widely accepted and relatively uncontroversial, let's keep this one short.

Pros: Customer Education aligns cleanly with other Customer Success roles, by capturing and scaling knowledge and training that's commonly delivered by CSMs and CSRs in the early stages of a business. With this alignment, it's easier to set shared goals around number of customers trained, number of issues documented, customer contact rate, CSAT (customer satisfaction) score, and product adoption rate.

Cons: If your organization doesn't place CSMs and Support representatives in the same part of organization, you may find yourself torn between whether Customer Education primarily works with Support (on ticket deflection) or CSMs (on customer training). I'd recommend keeping Customer Education neutral, and having it report to the same level that your CSM or Support functions would.

PROFESSIONAL SERVICES

Another option for housing your Customer Education function is as a professional service. Some earlier-stage companies don't offer professional services, and instead have services reporting into Customer Success. If that's the case, see the "Customer Success" section above. More mature organizations tend to have separate professional services arms, where they may house training services. This is especially common for more technical or complex products.

Pros: By placing Customer Education here, you can align the training services that you provide with other professional services. This makes it easier for you to share resources like Engagement Managers, who scope custom engagements with customers. Until recently, this was the one of the most common places you would find Customer Education (or "Education Services") in a software business.

Cons: Most modern Customer Education programs don't operate on a pure services model, especially in younger companies. There are two reasons I can think of for this: First, Customer Education teams now own more than just training activities. Their responsibilities include things that aren't services, like customer communities and documentation. Second, education is becoming more consumerized. Customers increasingly demand educational resources as part of their package (not an add-on) in order to enable their team. So while you can certainly offer paid (or discounted) services for custom trainings and certifications, be aware that many Customer Education services shouldn't be monetized.

MARKETING

In the age of inbound marketing and demand generation, helpful customer-facing content can drive leads, and ultimately buying decisions. For that reason, you may decide that having polished Customer Education materials can create demand by addressing helpful topics *and* supporting existing customers as they approach renewal. I see this structure less frequently, but when I do see it, it's most commonly in support of industry-oriented education. For example, Gainsight's Customer Success University teaches more general Customer Success management skills—not just how to use the Gainsight software.

Pros: If done right, Customer Education will both support and benefit from marketing efforts. Customer Education will help your company position itself as a thought leader in its category, especially if your programs offer industry-focused best practices, not just tool training. It also serves as a differentiator for your brand, in the same way that publishing a variety of ebooks and webinars is. If you have a Customer Marketing team; and especially if you run user groups, customer advocacy programs, and communities; then it may make sense to house Customer Education here as well. This organizational structure also offers you tight alignment to communication design (which will add polish and professionalism to your materials) and marketing automation (which will drive up pageviews and enrollments in your courses).

Cons: Placing Customer Education within a Marketing team creates risk that the team's resources will be diverted away from Customer Education after you create one or two versions of your materials. Customer Education can be treated as a "campaign" that you can be pulled off of, then refocused on other campaigns. Be prepared to re-invest in updating your materials as they go out of date. Customer Education is not a campaign that can be sunsetted; it's an ongoing investment.

PRODUCT

Especially in more technical organizations, Customer Education sits in the Product team alongside Technical Publications and Documentation. This is particularly relevant if your primary goal in Customer Education is to drive ongoing product adoption— and especially if you're pursuing In-Product Education efforts.

Pros: Customer Education programs are similar to software features—they must be built, maintained, and eventually retired. In fact, many content-focused teams use Agile development processes to build educational content and programs. This placement also gives Customer Education strong alignment with your Product Managers and Product Designers, who are typically the subject matter experts for product-oriented content. If In-Product Education is a core component of your strategy, this can be a smart placement.

Cons: For more technical Product teams, you may experience a disconnect between the level of technical skills required to be a Product Manager compared to a Customer Education Manager. Product teams also aren't often well-equipped to handle training services or similar customer activities.

HUMAN RESOURCES OR SALES ENABLEMENT

I'm going to group these two together, not because they're entirely similar, but because the rationale for putting Customer Education in these areas of the organization is incredibly similar.

Pros: As your organization grows, you will likely have functions and roles focused on Learning and Development (L&D) and Sales Enablement. Given that you're already building these competencies elsewhere in your organization, it might be tempting to share your Instructional Designers, Trainers, Administrators, and so on between Customer Education and internal enablement activities. Typically in this structure, both internal L&D and Customer Education report into the Head of Learning.

Cons: This may be the structure that sounds most tempting in theory, but it's the one that's hardest to pull off in execution. It's true that a customer-facing Trainer and an internal L&D Trainer have similar skill sets. But, if you think about it, so do Sales-humans and Recruiters (they just "close" different types of business for different audiences). L&D-oriented Trainers and Instructional Designers are typically more oriented toward human performance issues, because they receive direct or indirect feedback from the end-users of their content, and they can directly measure the users' performance in their organization. Customer Education, however, requires more focus on creating content that is easily discoverable and digestible to learners outside the organization, where they do not see the impact ultimate performance impact on the end-users. If you're a large organization with enough training and documentation people to effectively allocate and channel them into the right parts of your organization, this structure might work for you; but for most smaller companies, I don't think this is a strong setup.

THE CUSTOMER EDUCATION TECHNOLOGY STACK

THE CUSTOMER EDUCATION
TECHNOLOGY STACK

In the world of software, a "technology stack" is a set of technologies that work together. In the world of Customer Education, it refers to all the different tools and systems you use to run your education programs.

When new Customer Education leaders start building their programs, they must decide which technologies to use in their stack. After all, they have to figure out the best way to publish documentation, host and track courses, manage certifications, stand up online communities, and more.

In this section, I'll go through the components of a typical Customer Education stack and discuss some considerations as you evaluate the various types of stacks. But before we dive in, I'll share three caveats.

Everyone's stack is a beautiful, unique snowflake: No two Customer Education stacks look exactly the same. Most Customer Education portfolios don't include every system I've listed in these chapters and many choose other technologies I haven't discussed. Also, there's a wide range of suppliers in several of these categories. You should start with, and evolve to, the set of tools that best support *your* department's needs, not replicate someone else's stack that happens to make sense for *their* business.

It's easy to get distracted: When shopping for each of these systems, be on guard for flashy features that sound innovative. Some of these shiny features turn out to be marketing inventions, not actual innovative products. Don't buy a system because it has something fancy-looking; keep asking how the system will solve your core problems.

Kick the tires, don't check the boxes: Most companies walk into their buying process with a RFP (Request for Proposal) or at least a list of requirements for their evaluation. The system that allows you to check the most boxes is rarely the best system, so prioritize the features that you consider most essential to the success of your strategy. Asking for a sandbox environment will help you see how the system *actually* operates. On the flip side, a supplier may check all the boxes on your RFP, but throughout the process they provide you with mediocre service, don't share knowledge between members of their team, and only half-listen to your questions. What's going to happen once you sign, and they're no longer on their best behavior? Undo, undo!

According to learning research starting in the 1980s, one of the most commonly held beliefs about learning is that people learn 70% on the job, 20% through "social learning" where they interact with others, and only 10% through formal instruction. This tends to surprise people who believe that customers come in knowing nothing and then walk out of a one-hour webinar suddenly imbued with all the product knowledge they could ever hope for.

While the 70/20/10 model has been debated over the years— especially the actual percentages—it's still a useful guideline to think through the different technologies you need to support customer learning.

When you're considering how you'll invest in different components of your technology stack, keep in mind that each platform can support different types of learning. For example:

Knowledge Base and In-Product Education platforms are effective at serving "on-the-job" (70%) learning, because they serve as references as customers go about their work.

Community platforms map most easily to the social learning (20%) component, but if you use virtual training tools effectively, they can provide social learning as well.

Even though a Learning Management System (LMS) is most commonly used to deliver and track formal training (10%), modern systems are built to support more social and on-the-job learning as well.

Your "On-the-Job" Stack

Because most learning occurs on the job, the tools you provide for informal learning will often be the most widely used of any educational system you have. Knowledge Bases and Help Centers let customers quickly find reference materials and answers to their questions. Digital Adoption platforms expose education and help directly within an app or site.

The point of these systems often is not for customers to "learn" something. If you can contextually deliver a support article that helps a customer solve a problem in the moment, it doesn't matter if they "learned" how to solve it. What matters is that you helped them do their job.

Enable your customers to find these informal learning tools and use them in the context of their jobs. To make these systems effective, you need them to be easily discoverable—otherwise what could be an "on-the-job" learning moment will turn into a "frustrated-with-the-job" moment, and all of a sudden your product is getting a bad review from an angry user. Whoops! We'll pay extra attention to ease of use and discoverability as we go through this section.

KNOWLEDGE BASES AND HELP CENTERS

The Help Center is a core pillar of many Customer Education functions. In fact, it's often the first tool that Customer Education teams have access to, because so many Help Centers are included with support ticketing systems.

What is a Knowledge Base or Help Center?

"Knowledge Base" and "Help Center" have slightly different connotations (a Knowledge Base is where you house knowledge, and a Help Center is where you send people to get help). Some companies use "Knowledge Base" to refer to the thing that houses the Help Center, User Guides, and other docs. For the purposes of this section, I will use "Knowledge Base" and

"Help Center" interchangeably.

Your company probably has Knowledge Bases both for your company and for customers. For example, HR teams publish Knowledge Bases and wikis explaining benefits and policies.

Knowledge Bases also help Support teams. To illustrate, imagine that you're managing a large call center in the 1990s. The agents in the call center have some questions that they answer for customers over and over again, so those answers should be scripted out and easily referenceable. You could accomplish this by giving them a binder or a laminate with the answers on them, but the papers would start stacking up quickly. And what about the less-common, but still repeated, questions? What binder do you put those in? To make the answers more discoverable, you put the answers in some sort of *base* where *knowledge* can go, housed on the company intranet or on a wiki.

As businesses migrated to the cloud, so did their Knowledge Bases. Online Knowledge Bases became more prevalent thanks to wiki tools and support ticketing systems bundled with Help Center products.

Today, nearly all Knowledge Bases for Customer Education purposes are housed online. According to Atlassian, a company you may know better as the creator of Jira and Confluence:

> A Knowledge Base is a self-serve online library of information about a product, service, department, or topic.
>
> The data in your Knowledge Base can be from anywhere, but usually comes from several contributors who are well versed on the subject - enough to give you all the details. Subjects range from the ins and outs of your HR or Legal department to how a new product, hardware, or software works. The Knowledge Base can include FAQs, trouble-shooting guides, and any other nitty gritty details you may want or need to know."

Atlassian even defines it as *self-serve* and *online*. While some companies still keep their Knowledge Bases locked behind a vault of login gates that remind you of the opening credits of *Get Smart*, most of the platforms you see these days tout features that make information more easily discoverable for customers.

What to look for in Knowledge Base software

For many tech companies, Knowledge Base software was mandatory but perfunctory. It was a tool your Support team used to find knowledge topics to resolve issues, and in many cases, it was barely usable (sometimes even by the Support team).

But in the age of self-service, you miss opportunities when you don't optimize your Knowledge Base strategy. Knowledge Bases, at their best, can be both an effective self-service resource that lowers support costs *and* a competitive differentiator for your business.

When you evaluate Knowledge Base software, consider both how it makes information discoverable and how it makes collaborative authoring easier. Next I'll present some features to consider in your evaluation.

Search-first *and* browse-first navigation

At Optimizely, we did quite a bit of research into whether our users searched for information from our Knowledge Base homepage, or browsed through the categories to find information. We found that there wasn't a significant difference between those two behaviors, so we built an experience in Optiverse that served both "search-first" and "browse-first" users.

What does a search-first user need? A prominent search bar helps. Even better if that search bar can auto-suggest content as the user types. If you let users filter search results page, it will narrow down the possibilities to find just the right article.

How about a browse-first user? A good category structure is key—most Knowledge Base platforms offer categories. But equally important is the ability to lift certain articles out of their categories and onto the homepage. For instance, some platforms let you expose "featured" articles on the homepage, outside of their natural categories. Others show a feed of recently published or updated articles.

Front-end customization

With a Knowledge Base, you have plenty of opportunity for customization to make your articles more readable and content more discoverable. A system that gives you greater control over front-end customization (HTML, CSS, and JavaScript) will allow you to build custom elements over time.

For example, if your system doesn't include these elements by default, you may want to add:

Callout boxes (like "Note" or "Tip") that help break up the flow of information and highlight key points

An in-article table of contents or left-hand navigation, which is helpful for longer-form articles and especially useful for single-page developer documentation

Tools to magnify images, especially screenshots

Tabbed information (for example, if the same process works slightly different based on browser or operating system, a user could tab to the correct one)

Categories and tools for reuse

Content reuse is a hot topic in the world of knowledge management. The logic goes: If you've written the content once, you should be able to simply reuse that content in other places. Once it's been updated in a central repository, have it automatically update in all locations.

Sounds simple, but content reuse takes a significant amount of upfront work, requiring you to set up information typing models that may also change over time. For many growth-stage companies, it's not feasible to set up the correct infrastructure for content reuse until they have matured. The amount of work and rework it would take in a growing company wouldn't allow you to generate a positive ROI.

In the early stages of growth, you may want your Knowledge Base system simply to let you "reuse" articles across different categories. This allows you to edit one "source" article that publishes to multiple categories. For example, if you've published an FAQ about billing, and you have both "FAQ" and "Billing" categories, you can publish the article to both sections.

As your organization grows and matures, being able to categorize and reuse content systematically becomes a more attractive proposition. Once you have enough content and enough places for it to be published, you want a system that will be able to help you reuse content effectively. Look for systems that support knowledge management (KM) and knowledge-centered support (KCS) practices.

User feedback tools

Most Knowledge Base systems let users upvote or downvote articles, depending on whether they were useful. When you're evaluating Knowledge Base systems, don't just look for whether this feature exists—dig into *how* it works.

For example, can you change the feedback structure? If the default voting system is positive-neutral-negative, can you remove the neutral option? Can you branch the feedback and ask a follow-up survey question if the article is downvoted? Is there any place to collect free-text responses from users?

Additionally, who gets to give feedback? Some systems don't let users provide feedback unless they're logged in—which, for open Knowledge Bases, is only a minority of your visitors.

Authoring and editing workflows

If you have only one or two people writing and editing articles, as most companies do at first, then you don't need much in the way of authoring or editing workflows. As you start to grow and include more people in the authoring process, you need better insight into articles as they move from draft, to review, to publication, to revisions.

Some systems provide the ability to categorize articles by these statuses, and they also provide authoring or editing permissions based on the status of the article. For example, someone with "author" status would be able to write a draft article, but once it's moved into review, they wouldn't be able to publish it.

While many organizations use Google Docs or similar tools at first to handle collaboration during the authoring and editing processes, some systems also provide native collaboration tools so that your authors and editors can interact without leaving the system.

Look out for how your system handles revisions. When an article has already been published, and you need to revise it, does your system let you create a new draft version? Some systems will pull the *original* article back into draft mode so that it's inaccessible, but other systems let you branch off and create new draft versions, which you can work on while the original remains published and intact.

Versioning, history, and audit logs

As more hands touch your documents, it's more important for you to know who wrote what, and when. For example, let's say you accidentally publish articles containing errors, or someone writes about a feature inaccurately. You'd probably want to give that person feedback! You'd also probably want a way to roll back the article to a previous version.

Especially in knowledge-centered support (KCS) processes, where you have many Support agents writing articles at once, you want to have the ability as an editor or a program manager to see an audit log of article versions, and perhaps roll back to previous versions. Some systems can provide you these version histories as "diffs" where you can see what text was added or removed, line by line.

Another helpful tool for auditing is the ability to organize and sort articles by factors like the last update, creation date, upvote/downvote count, and status. As a Knowledge Base manager, you want the ability to do both systematic audits (putting your oldest or most-downvoted articles up for audit every quarter), as well as random quality audits.

Search Engine Optimization

No matter how clever your article categorization scheme is, many customers would prefer to use Google as the front door to your docs. Ultimately, your best SEO tool is writing and updating content on relevant keywords, and your Knowledge Base platform can help in a few ways:

> **Human-readable URLs:** Have you ever noticed a URL that went something like *http://www.example.com/blog/5-simple-tips-for-washing-your-great-dane*? That text isn't there for show; it's there to help make the URL more readable to humans and to search engine crawler bots. Ideally, your Knowledge Base system automatically appends the article title or "slug" to the URL, while still providing an article ID that never changes (even if you change the article title).

> **Alt-text:** Try hovering over an image on a website, and you may see a little bit of text pop up. This is known as "alt-text" and it's helpful for visually impaired visitors to your site. It helps them understand what's in your images. But do you know who else it's helpful for? Search engine crawler bots! Alt-tags are one of the ways that a search engine's image search knows how to find the right images. You can always add alt-tags manually in the HTML of your site, but your Knowledge Base system may have a solution that lets you insert alt-text without digging into the guts of the HTML.

Widgets and performance support

Information in a Knowledge Base must be easy to find. Search engines are one way; in-product guidance is another. Over the last few years, an abundance of performance support, In-Product Education, and Digital Adoption platforms have popped up, offering users a way to get support directly within a site or app. I'll come back to these in the next section, but be aware that some Knowledge Base systems have widgets that let you embed article links or search for relevant help articles directly in your product.

Integration with support ticketing systems

Because much of the content for your Knowledge Base comes from Support teams, the source content often originates in support tickets. On the other end of the cycle, Support agents want to be able to reference help articles frequently and easily. That makes support ticketing systems vital for two-way integration. For some Knowledge Base platforms, it's really easy to integrate with support ticketing systems because they are sold together, as a bundle.

That said, most third-party Knowledge Bases also offer some sort of integration. Look for the ability to turn support ticket text into article drafts. Also look for features that make it easy for Support agents to discover relevant articles as they're answering tickets.

Analytics

As you publish more articles, those articles are viewed, and then upvoted or downvoted. Different people come in and edit them over time. Agents use them in support tickets.

How much of that information does your system provide access to?

Because you don't want to be flying blind on your program's health or operations, look for reporting and analytics that help you answer questions like:

How many articles were updated each month?

How many articles were published each month?

Which people wrote or updated the most articles?

Which articles got the most, or least, views?

What was your overall upvote count, downvote count, and upvote-to-downvote ratio?

Which articles generate the highest or lowest upvote-to-downvote ratio? Which *categories*?

What search terms are used most frequently in your Knowledge Base search? Which articles do people click when they enter those terms?

Which agents link the most articles from their tickets? Which articles are linked most often?

Most systems won't answer all of these questions in their native analytics tools, but they may provide data pipelines for you to export the raw data into your data warehouse, where you can do deeper analysis.

Additionally, check whether your system of choice can give unique IDs to users. Gordon Mak, a learning technologist who has worked at LinkedIn and Box, recommends using these unique IDs to attribute Knowledge Base usage to other downstream activity to find out, for example if Knowledge Base visitors end up using your product more.

IN-PRODUCT EDUCATION

Whether you call it "digital adoption," "in-product guidance," "performance support," or some other term yet to be coined as of the writing of this book, In-Product Education is one of the quickest-growing categories within Customer Education.

Many early-stage companies assume that they don't need In-Product Education. They think the product should be so intuitive that onboarding isn't necessary.

Let's dispel a myth: Needing In-Product Education doesn't mean that your product is designed poorly. To quote Casey Winters, former entrepreneur-in-residence at Greylock Capital, "There's a quote popular in Silicon Valley that says if your design requires education, it's a bad design. It sounds smart, but it's actually dangerous. Product education frequently helps users understand how to get value out of a product and create long term engagement."

In-Product Education doesn't mean you have bad design, nor should it compensate for bad design. Good In-Product Education complements good design.

What is an In-Product Education system?

Software companies are quickly realizing that when it comes to user onboarding, feature activation, and contextual support, there is now better place to get product help than within the product itself.

When it comes to In-Product Education platforms, there are a few major "flavors":

Product Analytics and Guidance: These systems provide rich analytics on user paths and let you analyze how people use your product. You can use those insights to create walkthroughs, tooltips, and other cues that help customers get what they need.

Guidance Only: These systems focus exclusively on letting you build and offer in-app walkthroughs, surveys, tooltips, announcements, and the like. The analytics components of these products are minimal or nonexistent.

Contextual Support Only: These systems usually take the form of an in-product widget that sits at the bottom of the screen and presents contextual information based on where the customer is in the product. Based on where they are and what problem they may be having, they can see recommended solutions and search for related information.

Once you've decided which "flavor" works best for your product, you can start investigating the actual features. In this section, I won't discuss the product analytics components—entire books have been written on analytics. Instead, I'll stick to the In-Product Education components.

What to look for in In-Product Education software

In-Product Education is a little different from other types of software in your Customer Education stack, because it lives directly in your product. This creates some considerations that you wouldn't have to deal with in a system that sits somewhere else and operates relatively independently. It also means that, in most cases, it's going to have to blend in seamlessly with the rest of your product.

Front-end customization and templating

At the risk of sounding like a broken record, it's more important than in any other system to have In-Product Education that you can customize. In most cases, you want the content you build to look and feel like your product—if not identical, then at least intentionally similar. If your users are cruising along, enjoying your product, and then a weird, unformatted window pops up, they're going to think someone hacked into your product and is trying to steal their credit card information.

Front-end customization is pretty standard for these systems, but it's still worth evaluating how seamlessly they blend into your product. Some systems can get pretty close, but they still don't look *quite* the same.

Some systems also give you the ability, once you've made certain front-end customizations, to save those as templates that can be reused.

Make sure you can embed different types of content in your In-Product Education. A common use case is to embed relevant videos within in-product guides and walkthroughs.

Personalization and data objects

This is going to get a little technical, so if you feel like your eyes are starting to glaze over, just skip to the next section. In-Product Education becomes far more powerful when you can personalize it. After all, if the customer is logged into your product (or if you use an Account-Based Marketing tool to capture customer information), then you can use that information to deliver more targeted content.

Here are some ways you can use different attributes to customize In-Product Education:

Names: In *How to Win Friends and Influence People*, Dale Carnegie wrote that "A person's name is to him or her the sweetest and most important sound in any language." If you know your customer's name, why not greet them by it?

Accounts: If you know which account the user comes from, or which company they work at, you may be able to display content specifically recommended for that account. This doesn't typically work at scale for all customers, but for strategic customers it can help to solidify your relationship.

Industry Verticals: Most companies have at least a few target verticals that they serve. Each of these industries may use the product in different ways. If you know the industry your user works in, you can supply sample use cases, stories, and other tips to help them find value in your product. This works not only during onboarding to inspire your users, but also as they continue to grow and mature along with your product.

User Role: Most B2B software products have different user roles or permission levels. Often these roles also imply that they will use the product in a certain way. For example, in the Knowledge Base platform example I used earlier, authors and editors had different user types.

Time and Frequency: A customer in the first few weeks of onboarding probably wants to know something different than a long-time power user. So does a user who has lapsed for months and hasn't used your product since the onboarding stage. If you're capturing time and usage information, you can use that as context to recommend certain features or re-inspire lapsed users.

Feature Usage: You may want to display some content to users who have already used (or not used) certain features. For example, if a user has already used Basic Feature, you can recommend Advanced Feature. But you wouldn't want to recommend Advanced Feature to a user who hasn't even used Basic Feature.

Here comes the more technical portion: It does matter *how* you get that data. Depending on how the In-Product Education (or Digital Adoption) platform operates, the data might come from tracking cookies, from information stored in the browser's local storage, or from two-way integrations with another system of record that stores the relevant information. In each case, you need a way for the information to be passed to your Digital Adoption platform so it can be displayed or personalized. Often this has to happen at page load—and this is what creates a conundrum. If the information used to customize the experience is being collected from the page itself, but the page hasn't loaded, then you'll have a loading delay at best and an error at worst.

All this is to say: Sit on the demo call with someone technical enough to understand the nuances of how data will be collected and populated, and make sure that it's the right fit for both your product and for the type of information you want to use to personalize the experience.

Launchers and reactivation

Think about the last time you started using a new product. Did you rigorously review the entire manual or dutifully walk through the guider screens step by step? Maybe if you were building an IKEA bookshelf you did, but if you were like most new users, you probably skipped the "Getting Started" stuff and didn't come back to it until you had questions.

In general, users prefer to jump into a product and play around before they're ready to learn about it. According to research from the Nielsen Norman Group, a user experience (UX) research firm, "People do not launch an app to spend time learning how to use the interface, but rather to complete a task in as short an amount of time as possible, using the least amount of effort possible." If you're not ready for a product tour, you rush through it or dismiss it.

But unlike having a manual that you can open up, many software products are more like the notes from *Mission Impossible*: "This tape will self-destruct."

The rationale for this makes sense at first: It's a "New User Experience" (NUX) or "First Time User Experience" (FTUX), so it should only be shown to new users. Most of the information from the tour shouldn't be necessary after that, so why devote any precious real estate to reactivating it?

But what if the user just dismissed the NUX tour the first time, or didn't pay close attention? All those little guides that show up during the initial onboarding just go away. Like the time and effort you invested in collecting Beanie Babies in the mid-90s, there's no way to get that back.

These days, many In-Product Education systems handle the disappearing information issue by providing "launchers" or other little widgets that allow users to pull up relevant guides, contextual help articles, or checklists. Investigate whether your platform of choice has this, and if so, how much customization it will require to host the content that you want.

Branching

Do you remember those old *Choose Your Own Adventure* books? As the reader, you'd be exploring the ancient Hall of the Sphinx, and then all of a sudden the book would tell you that you hear a noise behind a loose brick. If you want to remove the brick to see what's behind it, turn to page 67. If you want to ignore it and keep moving on, turn to page 72. So you turn to page 67, and wouldn't you know it—you've just been mauled by a mummy!

In-Product Education should be like this—not the mummy part (although I think that would be fun), but the *Choose Your Own Adventure* style of guidance. For example, let's say that an in-product guide has popped up to troubleshoot an issue. The guide recommends that you try a solution. You try it, and it doesn't work. Does the guide now let you navigate to a different solution based on the outcome? Or does it just stop, so you can get angry and call support?

Or let's imagine a happier case. Using contextual information, a guide may suggest three different case studies to you based on your industry. By choosing one of them, you can branch to another path in the guides.

Many e-learning tools can accomplish this using simple branching logic, but they usually don't let you publish directly within your product. If you're interested in creating these types of experiences within your product, investigate whether your In-Product Education tool supports branching, and if so, how much customization is necessary.

A/B Testing

When we first started using In-Product Education at Optimizely, we naturally wanted to run some tests to understand whether the new guides were effective—and ideally which guides worked better than others. That's where A/B testing came in: to compare two versions of our product experience and see which was more effective.

We decided to run an experiment where a control group was exposed to the product without any in-product guides, and a variation group did see guides as they onboarded in the product. For the variation group, we looked at how many of the users engaged with the guides. We then compared the control and variation groups to understand whether the guides influenced their later product usage—specifically whether they implemented a set of key features in Optimizely.

Without disclosing actual numbers, here's what we observed:

> Within the variation group, a relatively small number of users went through all of the new guides the first time. But a larger percentage came back to them later after dismissing them.
>
> Compared to the control group, the variation group ended up using the key features two to three times more!

We concluded, based on this experiment, that in-product guides had strong potential to increase feature adoption during onboarding. After all, the group who saw the guides likely had a better sense of why these key features were important, how the features would help, and how to set them up.

Without A/B testing, you won't truly know how your In-Product Education influences user behavior. So whether you get a system that integrates well with an A/B testing tool, or one that has its own A/B testing features, I'd recommend this as an area to investigate.

Bear in mind that, as always with A/B testing, you need a high enough sample size to support your conclusions. Otherwise the results you're looking at aren't meaningful and could be attributed to random chance. So unless you have a large user base, you may not be able to test your features quite as much as you'd like.

Reporting

If you recall from the beginning of this section in In-Product Education, many tools provide robust product analytics. I won't go deep into the requirements for product analytics, but your In-Product Education system should at least offer basic reporting to help you answer basic questions such as:

Which flows or tooltips are used most often?

Which ones are dismissed most often before they're done?

Where do people commonly drop off in a given flow?

How often do people reactivate a flow that they've previously dismissed?

If there is a Call to Action (like a button to click), how often do users complete it?

An In-Product Education system that also moonlights as a product analytics tool will likely be able to give you these types of insights and more (like user pathing reports), but I'd recommend that you dig into the reporting that any potential In-Product Education tool provides.

Your "Social Learning" Stack

While social learning presumably accounts for 20% of learning, there actually aren't many systems dedicated to social learning. Knowledge Bases and Learning Management Systems often include commenting and collaboration features, but for many companies, the customer Community platform is the hub of social learning.

Although I discuss only one type of social learning platform in this section, social learning should occur in other systems and venues—for example, during interactions in a virtual training or in self-study cohorts of a Massive Open Online Course (MOOC). And because social learning is... well... *social*, much of the inter-action also occurs person-to-person outside of a forum that you control. However, a community will give you an opportunity to harness those types of interactions so they can benefit a wider group of people.

There are quite a few community forum platforms for B2C companies, where they serve as an extension of the company's Support team. Think about how often you've tried to search for a troubleshooting solution, only to find the answer on a commu-nity forum instead of the company's help site.

I see only a handful of "big names" in community software for B2B companies. B2B companies use Community platforms for support, too, but they also use communities to build "communi-ties of practice," where experts can share their success strategies.

Your online community strategy will dictate which features are most important. For starters, it's worth asking whether you are even ready for an online community. Unlike the ballpark in *Field of Dreams*, if you build it, they will not necessarily come. Community platforms require continuous effort to answer questions, moderate responses, clear out the spam, and archive outdated information. What some companies are actually looking for is a customer advocacy platform, which lets a smaller group of customers engage directly with your brand and is generally not discoverable through organic search. Customer advocacy platforms let you create contests and missions for your customers, and reward them in return. In this section on community, I won't be discussing customer advocacy platforms—just online community forums.

Front-end customization and SEO

In the previous chapter on Knowledge Bases, I discussed the importance of having flexible options to customize the user experience. I also stressed the importance of making sure that content is easily discoverable for search engines. For communities, both of these factors are true as well. Most community software is built to be discoverable and customizable.

Investigate how easy the system is for your end users: you won't get traction on your community if it's hard to find content, or to post or reply.

Try browsing through the platform from the homepage, looking for new or updated content. Then try searching for information from a search engine and landing in the platform that way. In each case, is it easy to find what you're looking for and jump into a conversation quickly, or is the experience filled with confusion and friction? If it's hard for you, it'll be harder for your users.

User feedback and analytics

Similar to how articles are upvoted or downvoted in a Knowledge Base, most community forums let users upvote or downvote content. Investigate your potential platform's approach to this: does it allow both up- and down-voting, or just upvoting? Do user ratings influence how content is displayed or ranked in a search? Can massively downvoted information be systematically audited or flagged for removal?

Most forums have a concept of "best response," where a certain answer can be flagged by moderators as the best answer to a question. Determine who in your community can choose a "best response," and how a best response may display more prominently or visibly in the discussion thread.

Some platforms also routinely survey users to measure engagement, satisfaction, NPS, or intent. In doing this, they can give you insight into what users are attempting to do in your community: Were they looking for support? Making a purchase decision? Trying to answer other people's questions? Sending an idea to your product team? These insights let you analyze the impact of your community on the rest of your business.

Community platforms should also offer analytics on your user activity, response time, and other key behaviors. Even if you have a high-level goal metric, like your number of Monthly Active Users, you can use your analytics to dive deeper into your community health and figure out how to make it healthier over time.

Moderation, permissions, and perks

Because communities are a team sport, you'll likely have multiple moderators in your system. Look into what permissions your users, moderators, and administrators have, and how they can be modified.

You may also want a system that can draw a distinction between internal and external moderators. In essence, you may trust internal representatives from your company to perform certain actions that you wouldn't assign to volunteer moderators.

It's also worth looking into what perks you can provide to your "MVP" users. Many community programs provide incentives for certain super-users—the ones who answer tons of questions and actively consult with customers on the forums. These incentives can take many forms, but a helpful framework to use is "SAPS"—status, access, power, or stuff. This may be handled by your customer advocacy platform instead of your Community platform, but it's still worth investigating whether your Community platform can provide:

Status: Badges, ranks, or titles—and the ability to share these achievements on their social networks

Access: Private forums or other areas of the community

Power: Additional moderator privileges

Stuff: Swag or other goodies—for example, the ability to send stickers or little prizes to users who reach certain levels

Idea boards

In addition to support forums and strategic discussion boards, many online Community platforms also provide a space for users to upvote different feature requests. These often become a key component in "voice of the customer" initiatives. By looking at the most-requested features, and what users have to say about them, your Product Managers gain additional insight into potential new features and user stories.

Social and Single Sign-On

Many Community platforms are now trying to integrate more broadly and deeply with other social networks. After all, if you can use social media widgets to help customers access the community from other networks, you've increased the power of that community.

For example, users may prefer to access your community through your company's brand page on Facebook, or your company's Twitter account.

And if they can log into the community using credentials from another social network (using single sign-on technology), they won't need to spend as much time and effort creating a new username or trying to remember a password that they forgot.

Your "Formal Learning" Stack

Even though it theoretically represents only 10% of total learning, formal learning usually marks a critical moment for customers. When your customers are first onboarding, you have the opportunity to use formal training programs to arm them with the skills and motivation they need to be successful. Additionally, the 10% represented here also includes moments like certification, where your customers can prove that they've reached a certain level of expertise—even if they learned much of what they know from the other 90% of their time.

LMS

The Learning Management System (LMS) is a core pillar of most Customer Education functions. Many Customer LMS platforms are rebranding themselves as "Customer Enablement/Learning/Training Platforms." If you see this type of language, you're probably looking in the right place; I will call them LMS platforms here.

While you can run your team without an LMS in the early days, you will be manually delivering and tracking all of your training without one.

What is an LMS?

An LMS handles course enrollment and delivers self-paced online courses, tracking activity along the way.

Your company may have an internal LMS for its own employees—this is where you go to take compliance courses and IT security trainings. It tells you how much of the required training you've completed, and you complain to your HR department that they shouldn't force you to spend time in a system that looks like it's made from the desecrated bones of Windows 95.

If you took online courses in college, you may have used an LMS, like Blackboard or Moodle, which housed your course content and let you have discussions with other students.

And what about direct-to-the-learner online course providers like Coursera, EdX, Udacity, Udemy, and Khan Academy? Those are essentially MOOCs (Massive Open Online Courses) sitting on top of an LMS.

Talented Learning CEO John Leh, an LMS industry expert, notes that there were over 700 LMS systems as of 2016, and that number has only continued to rise as technology becomes more accessible.

And 97% of those systems are not going to work for you.

In fact, in the 2016 TSIA Technology Spending report for Education Services, the LMS was among the most-used technologies—at nearly 80% penetration—and the least satisfactory, according to their satisfaction ratings of each technology.

Why? Many don't have a clean user interface that's required for customer engagement. Others don't provide robust analytics. Hundreds are primarily designed for purposes like compliance training, academia, professional associations, or other things that are enough unlike Customer Education that you won't be able to provide your learners with a great experience.

Because there are so many LMS platforms, your LMS search can be a minefield. To choose an LMS for your Customer Education function, you'll want to focus on a "Customer LMS"—sometimes also called an "Extended Enterprise LMS," "Customer Learning Platform," "Customer Training Platform," "Customer Enablement Platform," or similar. Regardless of what it's called, a good Customer LMS is built with customers in mind.

What to look for in LMS platforms

A good Customer LMS is centered around customers, which means it has to work like the other systems you would put in front of your customers.

Remember these two key differences between internal learners at your company, and external (customer and partner) learners:

You can't usually fire customers if they don't do what you want.

Customers pay you money, and may be paying you even more money to take your training.

Your LMS must keep customers engaged, because ultimately

you have less control over what they do. This is doubly true if the customer is paying for the experience (and therefore will naturally complain about it more). I'll highlight some key attributes for your consideration in selecting an LMS.

User Experience

Why do companies invest in their user experience (UX)? It's not simply to "delight" the customer. Delight is abstract. Good products have good UX because if they don't, customers will get frustrated and stop using the product. Yet most LMS platforms look and feel like someone stopped updating them around Y2K.

Why don't LMS platforms look and feel like they want to be used? Conventional internal-learning, HR-driven LMS platforms don't have to worry about user adoption, because they cater to learners who *have to take the training.* They're serving mandatory compliance training and similar types of courses. Even if other types of content get added to the platform over time, the typical business case for an internal LMS is to track learner activity for performance evaluations or compliance reasons. If they don't take the training, your company can be in deep trouble, or the learners can get fired.

The threat of firing doesn't work so well on your customers. Instead you have to engage them with attractive, relevant content and an interface that makes them want to spend time learning.

Most people know intuitively whether a product "feels" modern. I recommend that you take several steps beyond that and ask each supplier to give you a sandbox environment where you can load in your content. That way, you (and anyone else helping you pilot the system) can navigate through your content from a learner's perspective.

If you don't have a wealth of content to load in, you may also be able to get access to other companies' Customer Education sites that use the same systems you're evaluating. Seeing these systems "in the wild" should give you a good sense of their UX.

When you see the system through your learner's eyes, you'll start to notice interesting quirks in the experience that you may not have noticed during the product demo. Maybe the "next" button isn't appearing when you expect it to be. Maybe it's surprisingly hard to navigate between courses in a learning path. Maybe the gamification features that you saw in the demo aren't so appealing through your "learner" lens.

Customization

For every three Customer LMS platforms you look at, at least one will pitch you with, "We can make it look just like your corporate site!"

What they're trying to say here is that the more an LMS can reflect your brand, the more likely it is that learners recognize what it is and engage with it. It's not a bad pitch; you don't want your LMS instance to look like it's completely disconnected from your brand standards. You also don't want it to look like every other instance of that LMS out there. That's the customer experience equivalent of showing up to a party and you see someone else wearing the same outfit. *Awkward.*

When you evaluate a Customer LMS, I recommend evaluating not just whether they *can* customize the look and feel, but find out *to what extent* they can customize it, and *how much effort* it takes to customize. Let's break down these three criteria:

> *Can they customize the look and feel?* Some LMS platforms simply can't customize their look and feel, aside from allowing you to upload your logo in a pre-designated location. That's like me putting on a cape and telling you I'm Batman. Probably won't be fooling people any time soon.
>
> *To what extent can they customize?* Each system offers a different level of control over customization. Some lay out a panoply of options and toggles for you to tweak. Others provide you full control of the front-end—usually through CSS, and in many cases JavaScript. If you have control over JavaScript, you essentially have full control over customization (but also often full responsibility when you break the

site). For the platforms that offer you endless toggles, ask yourself critically which ones you're actually likely to use. It's easy to get saddled with a system that has so many options that it's nearly impossible to administer.

How much effort does it take to customize? Let's say your potential LMS platform shows you a bunch of fancy, customized portals that look just like their companies' corporate sites. The first question to ask here is how long and how many resources it took to customize. As the old saying goes: "Do you want it fast, cheap, or good? You can choose two." In many cases, the "good" examples you're seeing were not done fast or cheap. So it's up to you to figure out how much effort was involved in the final product. It's also important to ask about what kinds of customization will actually break the system. For example, one of the LMS platforms I used in the passed allowed my team essentially to hack the interface to customize it, but we couldn't upgrade to the next version of the system because it wasn't compatible with any of the customizations we had made.

Content Discoverability

One big advantage of modern LMS platforms is that they offer learners more control over their experience. That's a boon because it gives learners more control. The feeling of control is especially important for adult learners whose idea of fun isn't an afternoon spent browsing a training catalog. On the other hand, it means you're trusting learners to find the content they're looking for.

A good Customer LMS will provide tools to help learners discover content more easily, and may even be able to curate or recommend courses using tags or machine learning.

Keep an eye out for features such as:

Search: Almost every LMS includes a search bar to find different courses or pieces of content. But keep in mind that in many cases, learners don't know what they're searching for. Unlike a help site where the user has come in with a problem, an online academy often helps learners discover what they *don't know they don't know*. Dive deep into how intelligent the search functionality is: Does the platform do a simple keyword-based search, or does it handle synonyms and spelling variations? Does it make any sort of algorithmic course recommendations?

Learning path hierarchies: Many Customer LMS platforms are structured around the "course" as the core unit. Each course contains lessons. And in many systems, courses can be organized into paths or series. The advantage of being able to curate courses into paths is that it makes them more discoverable. Instead of browsing one large catalog for a specific topic, learners can enter into paths organized by role, skill level, and more. Some questions to ask here, depending on the experience you want to create for learners, are:

> Can the same course be shared between paths or does it need to be re-created?

> Does the platform offer analytics into a learner's journey through paths, or just through individual courses?

> Is the UI for paths clear, including how to navigate from one course in a path to the next?

> Can users skip between courses in a path, or are courses locked until you complete previous courses?

> Has the system designed course series simply as collections of courses, or as true linear paths?

Curated catalogs: Most LMS platforms have a concept of "learner groups," where you can organize learners based on characteristics like what account or company they belong to, what role they have, and what level of subscription they have. You might choose to curate certain pieces of content based on these characteristics to create a more personalized experience. After all, if you provide fewer starting points, but make stronger recommendations, you'll help learners avoid the paradox of choice, where more choices can lead to fewer decisions.

Recommended content: Because an LMS often caters to learners who *don't know what they don't know*, it's helpful if the system can automatically recommend related courses and content. Some LMS platforms use tags to recommend related content, and I expect more will use machine learning algorithms to do this in the future.

Ungated Content

In an internal LMS, everything in the system is typically housed behind a login wall. Authentication is handled by your HR Information System or another internal identity provider. And why shouldn't it be? All your learners work at the company and have company credentials, so they can log in as they would for any internal system.

For a Customer LMS, it's a different situation. Because your learners are customers, partners, and sometimes prospects or the general public, it's unwise to place everything behind a login wall. Imagine how frustrating that would be for your potential learners: They're not logged in—maybe they Googled some information about your product—and now they find a link to your online academy. *This looks interesting*, they think, and they click the link to see what's inside, only to be smacked in the face by a plain-looking login prompt: "Please log in using your account information," and now your customers are asking, "What account credentials?" "What's my password, again?" "How do I just find out what courses are in here!?"

Most customers aren't even that generous with their time and patience. They might ask *one* of those questions before leaving your site to go watch YouTube videos of cat jumping fails.

When evaluating a Customer LMS, pay attention to how much you're able to place outside of the login gate. Many systems now allow you to put your homepage and course catalog outside of the login gate if you want, so users can browse your courses and learn what's in them before they need to log in. Some allow you to create logged-in and logged-out versions of your course description pages.

Many, however, are actually internal LMS platforms masquerading as Customer LMS platforms, and they haven't really thought about their logged-out experience. And it's your customers that will pay the price.

E-Commerce

Even if you're not putting a price tag on any of your courses at first, you'll probably consider it down the road. In addition to making your CFO happy, assigning a price tag to your training content also subconsciously makes it more valuable to learners.

Spend some time evaluating how your Customer LMS handles e-commerce. What payment gateway do they use? Can it generate invoices? How is billing reported back to your finance team? Can courses be bundled into packages and sold? Can you create subscription pricing for your content? Can you generate different types of discount codes for your courses, and can those codes be unique or reusable? If you sell training in other countries, does your system correctly handle foreign currencies and taxes?

Unless you've already been selling training, you probably won't know all the details of your pricing and packaging strategy from day one. Look to your Customer LMS to provide a level of flexibility to support your evolving pricing strategy.

Consumption-based pricing

Most internal LMS platforms are built around the idea that you have a certain number of seats in the system. Those seats represent employees at your company who will consume a certain amount of training each year. The number of seats you'll need is fairly predictable, since it's based on the number of employees you train each year.

Customer Education is not so predictable, and the way a Customer LMS is priced should reflect that. Sure, you could make an assumption about the number of seats based on the number of users being onboarded each month, but that number is surprisingly hard to calculate once you consider that each account being onboarded has a different number of users, existing accounts also onboard new users, and even your own company employees may use the content you create.

If you use seat-based pricing, you'll likely find yourself in a position where you're constantly having to add and remove active users from the available seats. This means you'll almost instantly need to hire a training administrator to keep up with the extra work this creates.

I vastly prefer consumption-based models, where you're charged based on the volume of enrollments or active users (who consumed content in that month). Make sure to review the pricing model with your LMS provider—you'll need pricing that reflects the way your content actually gets used.

What's all this I've been hearing about "LRS" and "xAPI"?

There's been a lot of talk about "the future of the LMS." Since LMS software first appeared in 1990, it's gained adoption as a way to track and administrate learners' activity in courses—and, as time goes on, to create and publish those courses as e-learning.

Most LMS platforms report on learners' activity using a set of standards called SCORM (Sharable Content Object Reference Model—don't worry, this won't be on the test). SCORM has been the most common way to report on e-learning progress and completion since it was first released in the year 2000. Much like the USB standard allows all sorts of peripherals to communicate with your computer, SCORM allows learning experiences to report back to your LMS.

This pairing of LMS and SCORM works decently if all of your learning happens in the LMS, and all you care about measuring are course enrollments, course completions, student hours, and quiz scores.

But increasingly, education teams recognize the fact that learning (maybe even *most* learning) happens outside of the LMS. People watch videos on YouTube, read books, go to conferences, and attend informal trainings that don't get tracked in an LMS. To account for this, a new standard was released in 2013, called

Experience API (or xAPI for short).

xAPI allows you to report on learning activity from many different systems and pass "statements" about what happened into a centralized system called a Learning Record Store (LRS). These "statements" may be something like:

Rich took a course on project management (in the LMS)

Tina scheduled six meetings with her stakeholders (in the calendar)

Ethan completed a certification on intermediate project management (in the LMS or at an event)

Vecepia received positive feedback from ten stakeholders (in a survey tool)

As you may have noticed in the example above, an LRS may track information from an LMS—but it doesn't necessarily replace it. Unlike an LMS, an LRS doesn't handle training schedules and registrations, host e-learning courses, or allow you to create content. It's simply a data repository.

For Customer Education, the role of the LRS often gets replaced by a CRM, where all client data is stored. By creating "training records" in a CRM, training data flows into the same system where other customer records are stored.

For internal learning, xAPI provides a way to track organizational activity and informal learning that previously wasn't trackable. It gives Learning and Development teams insight into different types of training people take, how they apply what they learned, and what results they got.

For Customer Education, the jury is still out on xAPI.

Organizations store customer data in systems such as CRMs, Marketing Automation and Account-Based Marketing platforms, Customer Success systems, and so on. Each of these systems is designed to report into a data warehouse, where the data can be joined and analyzed.

Because customer data reports into a central data warehouse, you may be able to use xAPI statements to pass information from system to system, but you may also be able to use other types of integrations and data connectors to report on and analyze data coming from your LMS, CRM, and others systems, all within your data warehouse. You or your business intelligence team would then build reports using a data visualization tool.

VIRTUAL CLASSROOM & LIVE LABS

For many companies getting started with Customer Education, the webinar is their first choice for delivery. They're relatively cheap and easy, and you don't have to plan that much for them. That said, if you remember the earlier section of this book on customer onboarding, you may remember that webinars have two pitfalls:

> Most training webinars aren't interactive, so it's hard to stay engaged or retain any of the information.
>
> You need to continually promote webinars and virtual classes to get attendance.

A good virtual classroom system will help you work through these issues. The problem, often, is finding a good one.

Your first option is to use traditional online meeting platforms. Some of them include webinar versions that are adapted from their original meeting software. They include different ways to dial-in, screenshare, and video chat, which makes them seem like they can be repurposed easily for training.

The biggest problem with many of these solutions is that meetings and webinars aren't exactly trainings. As a consequence, online meeting platforms don't provide a good way for you to interact with participants. There may be a Q&A window and a way for participants to "hand-raise." Some may offer the ability to quiz or poll your participants. But your options to truly engage participants are limited. Also, these platforms often don't provide many customization options, don't give you usable analytics, and don't integrate with other systems that you may use (like an LMS or Marketing Automation platform).

Aside from online meeting platforms, your second option is "webinar" or "virtual event" platforms that are primarily designed for Marketing teams. These are designed to host large webinars, often with Q&A functionality and other types of interactivity. Many of these also offer group chat where you can interact more freely with participants—and better yet, they can interact with each other.

These systems tend to offer more opportunities for interactivity, and because they're designed for Marketing teams, they more consistently offer integrations with common marketing automation systems. They may not have all of the "virtual classroom" options you're looking for, but many come close. The biggest drawback to many of these systems is the cost. Marketing teams tend to have more budget to throw around than incipient Customer Education teams.

As a third option, there are some systems that are explicitly designed as "virtual classroom" or "live online class" tools. These usually include more tools for interactivity, like collaborative whiteboarding and enhanced quizzing and testing.

These systems can provide a great experience for learners, but many of these systems don't integrate with other systems of record, like your CRM or Marketing Automation software, so while the classroom experience is more robust, you might not be able to create as seamless of an enrollment experience or do much tracking on the back end.

That said, you can also think outside the box. Dave Derington, who leads User Education at Azuqua, has started to explore running virtual classes using Twitch, a webcasting company better known for live-streaming video games. In his words, "Twitch is the most amazing Instructor-Led Training Platform that you're probably not using."

On one hand, it lacks many of the features that we're used to when it comes to running virtual courses. "Unlike most platforms," Dave says, "Twitch was built for scale. The customer experiences a buttery-smooth stream nearly all the time regardless of the number of participants."

Regardless of which option you pick, consider whether it's worth using instead of the meeting or webinar software that your company just happens to use already. In addition to interactivity and integrations, consider:

Video and audio quality: These are not created equally across platforms. There's nothing worse than lagging out while you're trying to interact with participants, or getting disconnected.

Web-only or download: Some platforms require software to be downloaded and updated, while others are hosted in the cloud. Not all learners work at companies that allow third-party software to be downloaded.

Simulive option: Some platforms allow you to record a session once, then play it while you interact with participants in the chat. If you're planning to conduct the same training week over week and don't mind it feeling a little "canned," this option may be right for you.

There's also a related category of software I didn't discuss earlier: live labs. For more technical products, especially ones who host longer virtual classes (for example, some companies do full-day or multi-day online courses), live lab software may be a better solution—or at least a complementary one—compared to webinar platforms.

Live labs are simulated software environments that provide opportunities for learners to experiment in a safe space. For complex software products, where mastery involves working hands-on in the product, live labs are an effective way to conduct hands-on training because the learners are actually working in the software, albeit with simulated data.

E-LEARNING AUTHORING TOOLS

Self-paced e-learning provides a way to learn without a live instructor. That bad IT security course you took where you had to click through endless screens of monotonous content? That's e-learning. But so are games, simulations, videos, and interactive e-learning modules that let you explore content in creative ways and test your skills.

In the past, in order to author e-learning, you'd hire a custom e-learning development company like the company where I first worked out of college, Enspire Learning. Working together on project teams comprising a Project Manager, Instructional Designer, Multimedia Designer, and Front-end Developer, we would develop custom courses published in Flash and deploy them to our customers' LMS platforms.

Some of these courses were traditional click-through e-learning; others were more creative, offering experiences like branching conversation simulations or even engaging learning games.

In the years since I worked at Enspire Learning, a new category of e-learning software, called "rapid development" tools, took the industry by storm. Now a single content developer could create and publish courses without using a four-person team. Coinciding with 2008's Great Recession, which slashed training budgets, rapid-dev tools quickly took over the world of Learning and Development.

Rapid development e-learning tools are a little bit like Power-Point, but with branching and interactivity. At worst, the output from these tools resembles a PowerPoint deck, or that bad sexual harassment training you had to take that one time. At best, they let you design complex activities involving interactive function-ality like drag-and-drop, ranking, click-to-reveal hotspots, and even light games and simulations.

Along with the rise of rapid-dev tools came, perhaps not surpris-ingly, more quickly produced, lower quality e-learning. Because the interface of many of these tools resembles PowerPoint, training professionals who were pressed for time and budget largely uploaded slide decks into these tools, with perhaps some cursory interactivity, and more bad click-through e-learning was born. I empathize with these training professionals. It's difficult and costly to put together good training, not to mention creating good e-learning with "rapid-dev" tools is... not quite rapid.

That said, forward-thinking content developers were also testing the limits of these tools, producing more creative works using their design prowess. Using interactivities like hotspots, drag-and-drop, and quizzes, some interactivity was possible.

Rapid-dev e-learning tools also started to evolve over time, adding concepts like variables, states, and triggers, which let content developers create more complex and meaningful interactivity.

Today, given enough time and skill, it's possible to produce high-quality e-learning using rapid-dev tools that would have taken an entire team to develop in the past. But there's still also a lot of click-through, PowerPoint-y stuff out there.

Most recently, "form-based" authoring tools have started to supplant rapid-dev tools. Form-based authoring allows people to create templated activities by entering their content into forms. The templates are often visually appealing, unlike their predecessors, but the content must adhere to the limits of the template.

Finally, some authoring tools center more around video, letting you quickly produce screen capture video and annotate it with callouts, highlights, animations, and other similar features.

All this is to say that the quality of work done in rapid-dev or form-based tools is only as good as the skills of the person producing it, and the amount of time that person has to complete it. So when you're evaluating authoring tools, consider not only the features they offer but the skill level required to use those features meaningfully.

Consider how your authoring tool will publish content. Most systems now offer the ability to publish as HTML5 or Flash. Now that Flash is nearly extinct, it's important to have some options for how content is displayed.

As far as reporting, most authoring systems also allow you to report using SCORM, and an increasing number support xAPI. Some even let you add your own JavaScript to send other types of data as needed.

CERTIFICATIONS & ASSESSMENT PLATFORMS

As I discussed in an earlier section, when people use the term "certification," they can mean many different things. It's crucial to nail down your certification strategy before you find the right assessment software: your strategy and your software are inextricably linked.

Let's return to the certification seasons of love to see what might be required in an assessment platform (or if you even need one).

The low-stakes approach: "We're not really dating; we're just talking"

If your company says "certification" and means "going to a class and maybe taking a test at the end," then you can swipe left on buying a full certification platform. Instead, most LMS platforms do this without the need for an additional system.

Light credentialing: "We're in *like*, not in *love*"

If you're using certification as a light credential, or offering assessment-based certificates, you *may* want a dedicated assessment platform depending on the rigor of the assessments—but don't start calling the caterers and photographers just yet: many LMS platforms have this type of functionality as well. Even if there are a few pieces missing, you may be able to supplement them through an integration with your CRM, where you can store information like the date of credentialing.

The operator's license: "Now we're serious"

When there's more risk involved in a certification, or you're testing on more advanced skills, you'll need a more robust platform to support it. Remember that at this stage, you'll likely need timed assessments, randomizable question banks, cheating prevention, and sample exams.

If you're looking for this level of rigor, it might be time to start looking for an assessment platform. You may not need full proctoring at this point, but many assessment platforms allow you to do unproctored online testing.

The high-stakes approach: "Will you marry me?"

When the stakes are high and you're certifying architect-level positions, or advanced service partners, you likely want the certifying exam to be proctored. You can either have your test-takers go into a room where a proctor watches them, or use remote proctoring solutions that use face and noise detection to make sure that your test-takers aren't looking things up on another laptop or having answers whispered to them.

Not all assessment platforms offer the right level of proctoring and cheating detection, so if you need to conduct true high-stakes certification, be sure to discuss these options in depth with your potential certification platform. Many certification platform providers also have psychometricians on staff and offer supplementary services for high-stakes exams, like doing the item analysis for you, helping you inventory questions, grade results, and figure out what the right passing scores should be. (Also a perk: getting to tell customers you worked with a psychometrician!)

Digital Badging

One emerging trend in certification and credentialing is the idea of digital badging—a credential that can be carried across different platforms. So, for example, if a person passes a course on your software and gets a badge for completing that course, a prospective employer can then see that badge when reviewing applications.

Increasingly, formal, four-year college degrees are supplemented with shorter credentialing programs, bootcamps, and assessment-based certificates. For customers and lifelong learners, there is value in being able to show different credentials and certificates in the places where prospective employers are searching for candidates.

Digital badging is still in its early stages, but it is maturing thanks to standards such as Mozilla's Open Badges standard, which according to its website offers "connected, verifiable credentials represented in portable image files" to educational institutions, non-profits, and large employers like IBM.

Unlike many trends in the world of L&D, this one I predict won't just be a fad. As time goes on, I expect to see more LMS and assessment platforms support digital badging standards as a way to communicate competencies and achievements, rather than treating badges simply as "digital stickers."

Supplementing Your Stack

In the previous sections, we looked at the different components of a Customer Education technology stack. That said, it's often not enough just to choose the tools. In many cases, you'll also need to customize the look and feel of your platforms, connect the data to other systems, and decide whether to buy the systems or build them yourself.

CUSTOMIZATION & DESIGN

In many of the earlier sections, I stressed the importance of front-end customization. Essentially, what that means is that you should have as much control as possible over your HTML, CSS, and JavaScript. Even if you don't write front-end code, you can conceptually understand what these front-end languages do.

Let's walk through them:

HTML: This is the basic skeleton of your content. HTML essentially gives you control over *what* is on the page—letting you divide content into headers, paragraphs, images, and so on.

CSS: While HTML gives you some control over the look and feel of your content, you can't rely solely on it unless you want your site to look like it was built in 1998. CSS gives you control over *styling*. It lets you customize the fonts, images, colors, and even device compatibility on your site. Have you ever resized a page from desktop-size to mobile-size and it looked terrible? That's life without CSS.

JavaScript: While CSS gives you control over look and feel, JavaScript gives you control over *interaction*. Most of the things you actually do on a site are powered by JavaScript, like submitting forms, creating and dismissing popups, upvoting or downvoting an article, and so on.

Any product that lets you publish to the web will give you a different level of control over these languages. Some give you essentially full control over each of these languages, so you can build any sort of design or interactive elements you desire, as long as you have the budget for custom development. Other products lock down their systems, giving you a few customization options but not allowing you to insert any of your own CSS or JavaScript.

If it's not important to you that the system you're evaluating looks, feels, or works any different than what you see in the demo (except maybe for inserting your company's logo or changing the color scheme a bit), then front-end customization is probably a "nice-to-have," not a "must-have," for you. But if you're looking to have your Customer Education systems mirror the look and feel of your product, or have their own unified brand, you'll likely need to do extensive front-end work—meaning, lots of CSS and JavaScript coding. People tend to underestimate how much front-end work is needed, and how expensive that work is in time or hours. Don't make that mistake.

For example, when we created the first version of Optiverse at Optimizely, one of the main features we included was a unified navigation system between our Community, Academy, and Knowledge Base. This made it easy to move between the three systems and search for content in all three. It also created the illusion that all three sites were one platform, not three different systems linked together.

To do this, we needed to do a significant amount of customization—in some cases, pushing the boundaries of what our systems allowed. To understand how your prospective Customer Education systems handle front-end customization, I recommend asking the supplier to show you several versions of their site "in the wild." Ask to see some that have low or no customization, some with moderate front-end customization, and some that are highly customized. Additionally, ask about the risks of high customization. Depending on what you want to do, and especially when you start to execute complex CSS or JavaScript, you can end up breaking the system's functionality, which means you may not be able to take advantage of updates to the system without doing more front-end customization work.

Finally, be realistic about the costs (in dollars and hours) of customization. Consult with a design and development agency about the cost of designing and implementing a customized experience. There are many independent, third-party front-end contractors available for this type of work. You can also do this work in-house, of course, if you have access to your design and development teams, but again, you need to be realistic about the hours it will take to complete a project like this.

DESIGNING FOR DATA & INTEGRATIONS

Data, data everywhere, and not a drop to measure. When you're selecting Customer Education systems, you'll want to measure the impact they have. I cover *what* to measure in a later chapter, but for now, you must consider how the tools in your stack are going to even *let you measure*.

There are typically two types of data that you're looking for in a Customer Education system:

Activity data: What are people doing on your site? What pages are customers visiting, what courses are they completing, and what are they upvoting or downvoting? What articles or courses are your authors writing, and when do they get updated?

Effectiveness data: This is more about your program's performance—how do your Customer Education programs drive product adoption, renewals, expansion, support reduction, and so on?

When looking for those types of data, there are a few places to look:

The system's native reporting: Some systems have their own, built-in analytics and reporting capabilities. But with most of these systems, they're not built to be analytics tools. (The main exceptions here are In-Product Education tools that actually *are* built to be analytics tools.)

Your CRM system: Many Customer Education systems integrate with common CRMs, where other key customer information is stored. For example, many LMS platforms can create training records in a CRM, so that you can track which customers were trained and when.

Your business's data warehouse: Even for systems that give you good reporting out of the box, you will still want a way to get data out of those systems and into your organization's data warehouse, where your other key data is stored, so you can compare data from that Customer Education system to your other Customer Education systems, and other business data. That's how you get your effectiveness metrics.

Each Customer Education system will have its own way of handling its own native reporting, and its own method for getting data into your other systems of record.

When you investigate different systems, spend time walking

through the reports that you have access to, right there in the system. Do these give you all the information you need? In most cases, probably not.

Perhaps more importantly, investigate their solution for exporting data. I've seen these solutions come in a few flavors:

CSV exports or other data dumps: Some systems export data into a CSV file on a periodic basis (such as every night), which can then be uploaded into another database or system of record.

APIs and data connectors: Some systems provide an API (which, if you're not familiar, is essentially a connector between two systems) so that you can export data in real-time into another system of record. APIs typically require some work to set up.

Integrations: Some systems build integrations with other systems of record, like a CRM or Marketing Automation platform. Each integration can be different, so make sure you actually investigate how the integration works, how you set it up, and what data is passed.

You probably aren't your organization's expert on data architecture, so I recommend getting someone from your Sales Operations, Business Intelligence, Data Science, or Data Engineering team to help you during the evaluation—you're looking for the person or team in your organization who connects various systems into your data warehouse.

Data Engineers don't always get consulted before systems get implemented, and they have to deal with the pain of integrating them later. In many cases you're actually making their lives easier if you bring them in early and ask them to help you evaluate potential systems. If you don't bring them in, you risk having a potential supplier say to you, "Sure, that can just be built using an API," which sounds simple until you realize it's months of custom engineering work.

Want to make your Sales Ops and Data Engineering teams' lives even easier? Typically, they'll want to see each company's API documentation, as well as any other documentation on integrations or data connectors, so ask the supplier to provide you with these beforehand.

BUILD VS. BUY

To build or to buy—that is the question. For each system in your Customer Education stack, you have the option to buy it from a supplier who specializes in that tool (for example, an LMS provider or Community platform). You also have the option to buy a mega-suite that offers multiple tools in one platform. Finally, you can build these systems yourself. Each has trade offs, so let's walk through the pros and cons of each approach.

Buying specialized tools

Most teams who are new to Customer Education don't start by buying a mega-suite of education tools. They start by buying specialized tools for each Customer Education platform (or using the tools that the company already has): an LMS, a Knowledge Base, a Community platform, and so on as they add new programs.

> **Pros:** Specialized tools are more likely to be good at what they specialize in. For example, a company devoted just to selling Customer LMS platforms has more likely thought about what features are necessary to serve this purpose. Specialized companies also tend to have more domain expertise and can advise you on your setup.
>
> **Cons:** Specialized tools typically don't connect to each other easily. Your LMS probably won't seamlessly integrate with your Knowledge Base. Even if they integrate through an API, not all APIs are created equal. You'll also be working with multiple suppliers, and the costs can add up.

Buying mega-suites

Some teams choose to use one larger supplier or suite for all their Customer Education needs. As of this writing, it's not the most common approach, but these all-in-one solutions are growing in the market.

Pros: A mega-suite's tools are more likely to integrate with one another (though it's not guaranteed in the case that the mega-suite simply acquired different technologies and didn't connect them to one another). You don't need to sign multiple contracts or work with multiple vendors.

Cons: Mega-suites are less likely to have thought through the solution for each individual Customer Education system. Instead, they're more likely to use the same type of solution to solve multiple problems. You may find that they don't have the features you need.

Building custom systems

Some teams build their Customer Education systems from scratch—for example, on top of a Content Management System. This seems to happen either for departments that are completely new (so there's less at risk if they start from scratch) or departments that are relatively mature (and have outgrown the limitations of their previous systems).

Pros: You have nearly complete control over the experience and functionality.

Cons: Custom systems take time and money to build—and front-end development is not cheap. If you've never had another LMS, Community, or Knowledge Base platform, then you may not know what features you actually need to build. You may end up doing more re-work on a custom system if you don't get it right the first time.

There's no one correct approach, but if you're new to Customer Education, specialized tools are more likely to help you figure out what you want (or don't want) in a given system.

BETTER CONTENT BOOTCAMP

If you could only make one initial investment in Customer Education, what would it be?

A fancy LMS to track all your learners' data? An ace Trainer and a polished marketing deck for them to read to customers? An admin to manage all your sessions and enrollments? A machine that magically implants product knowledge in people's heads?

I'd pick the last one if I had the R&D budget for it, but short of that, I'd invest in powerful content.

In Customer Education, you live or die by your content. It's what separates your world-class, differentiated program from that terrible sexual harassment course that you had to take in 2002. Because a Customer Education department will push content to so many "surfaces"—live classroom, e-learning, Help Centers, communities, in-product, and more—content fuels your Customer Education engine.

But not all content is created equal. Most education content is *bad*—it's dull, overwhelming, or both. It's "death by Power-Point" or long-winded lectures. People go through entire Master's programs to become skilled in Instructional Design, and to figure out what makes content *actually* stick and translate into job performance.

Although most Customer Education professionals don't have time for a Master's program, picking up a core set of Instructional Design and content development skills will go a long way.

In this section, I'll dismantle the received wisdom about education that leads to bad content, then I'll share a set of "Instructional Design 101" theories that you'll actually be able to use on the job to make better content.

Where content goes wrong

Training is one of those things that most people think they understand, because they spent several years in school and usually have gone to a bunch of (bad) trainings in their lives. So when they start building training, or asking their team members to put together trainings, they subconsciously model them after the trainings they've seen.

One of the reasons that Customer Education doesn't get prioritized in organizations is that education is one of those things that most people (including your executive stakeholders and subject matter experts) don't think is that hard. "How hard can it be to train customers? You just have to sit them down and explain the product to them!"

Whether they say it aloud or not, they're making a few dangerous assumptions about Customer Education.

First, "If I put an expert in front of my customer and have them share what they know, then the customer will know it too." Let's call this assumption **Sage on the Stage**.

Next, "If the customer needs help with something or wants to learn about it, they'll find it. We just need to include all the content that the customer should know." Let's call this one **Spray and Pray**.

Why are these assumptions dangerous?

As it turns out, they make for some really dull trainings. An *expert* dumping *knowledge* onto a customer is usually boring, overwhelming, or both. You end up creating educational experiences where an expert talks at the customer at length. Or boring, click-through e-learning. Or long, detailed docs that no one reads. Or a massive content catalog that goes unused.

It's not just that these experiences are boring—the greater danger is that they're ineffective and a waste of everyone's time. They don't generate outcomes or behavior change. If you put an expert in front of customers to deliver knowledge, and the customers don't do anything with that knowledge, then you've wasted the expert's time *and* the customer's.

But the greatest danger is that even if your education is boring and ineffective, you often aren't measuring it enough to see how ineffective it was. Customers come back after training with really basic support questions, or they simply don't adopt your product. And you're scratching your head wondering why this is happening. After all, you trained them, didn't you?

I'm pretty sure the reason that a lot of organizations don't invest more in Customer Education is because of something I call the "But I Trained Everyone" effect. (Let's call it the BITE effect—because bad education really bites.) Symptoms of BITE include putting a lot of effort into live classroom trainings that you don't measure, customers nodding their heads in training sessions but not absorbing anything, and writing documentation that doesn't actually deflect support tickets.

But we trained everyone! Why didn't they learn? The core of the problem lies in our mental model of how customer education works. It goes like this:

Step one. Simply lift the knowledge wholesale from the expert's brain

Step two. Cram it into the customer's brain

Step three. Voila—learning has occurred!

In reality, we learn in more complex ways, through a variety of learning styles, and usually only when we're ready and motivated to learn. But when we falsely assume that the goal of education is to yank as much knowledge out of one person's brain and cram it into someone else's, we end up with education whose goal is to cram in as much content as possible. Your education programs look like this:

You have outlines that progress feature by feature, and are

designed around making sure that a certain percentage of your features are covered in the content.

You're more focused on features than what the customer's going to do with them.

You don't answer the question of *why* a customer would want to use the feature.

You don't address how your product fits into your learner's everyday job.

You don't give your learners opportunities to reflect on how your features will help them, or to practice their skills.

Effectively, you have a list of content, but no strategy to engage the learner.

Instead of taking a *content-first* approach, you must take a *learner-first* approach. Make it about them. From day one of your Customer Education team, when you still have blue skies and green fields ahead, you have an opportunity to prioritize what actually matters to the learner—to help them do the things that make them successful. Here's what learner-first design looks like:

Your outlines are designed around making sure that customers understand how to get value from your product, and what use cases would best motivate them. You're willing to leave out features if they're not essential to this stage of the customer's journey.

You're more focused on use cases and workflows than describing features in the abstract.

You prioritize *why* a customer would want to use the feature, not just what the feature is or how to use it.

Your content helps or solves problems in your customer's everyday job. You address other things they might be responsible for besides using your product.

You include opportunities for learners to reflect, interact, and test their skills.

But before we can create education that overcomes the BITE effect and actually helps people learn, we have to dismantle the pervasive "Sage on the Stage" and "Spray and Pray" myths in our organizations.

DISMANTLING "SAGE ON THE STAGE"

In school, you had a teacher or professor who would spend most of their time at the front of the class delivering information to you. We treat trainings the same way: there's usually an instructor at the front of the room, or leading the webinar. Even e-learning implicitly has an "instructor," usually the expert who put all the bullet points in there.

The instructor lectures, the students take notes, and knowledge has transferred from one head to another, right? Wrong. Here's the irony: even the expert who's up there lecturing probably didn't learn this stuff by hearing it in a lecture.

So how do we help our "sage on the stage" make sure that the knowledge actually gets out of their head? The problem is that experts can no longer remember what it was like to use the product as a novice.

When we do something enough, we forget what it was like to learn it, so it becomes harder for us to teach it. Think about something as simple as driving to your own house. You rarely need to think about every step of it because you do it so often. But if a friend is driving to your house for the first time, they need a GPS to assist them. They're paying more attention to each turn and each exit sign on the highway.

In 1990 a Stanford graduate student named Elizabeth Newton asked her subjects to choose well-known songs that they would try to have listeners guess. The twist? They could only communicate what the song was by tapping out the melody with their fingers.

This study, also notably cited in *Made to Stick* by Dan and Chip

Heath, illustrates a principle known as the Curse of Knowledge. When the tappers were asked to guess how many times the listener would recognize the song, they were confident that the listener would guess what the song was 50% of the time. After all, the song sounded so clear in their heads! In fact, though, the listeners wouldn't guess the song nearly as often as the tappers estimated—the reality was 2.5%. The tappers were suffering from a cognitive bias: because they could "hear" the song clearly in their heads, they assumed that stripped of its proper context, the listeners could "hear" the song too.

We suffer from the curse of knowledge, too. Talk to the average subject matter expert and they take the position of, "How hard can learning this be? It's all pretty simple when it boils down to it." They're hearing a song in their heads, but the people who are supposed to be learning can only hear tapping.

I like to informally and unscientifically recreate this experiment when I'm explaining Customer Education to a more general audience. I have someone clap out a song and see if the audience can guess what's being clapped. They rarely do. Once you realize that it's a lot harder to hear the song than you think, you realize what the true purpose of Customer Education is: you have to take all the tapping and clapping, all the distractions and noise and interference, and build enough context that the customer can hear not the tapping, but the song.

How do we do this? We must stop designing for *content* and start designing for our *learners* first. Designing for the learner first means asking yourself what will motivate your learners to use your product. Ask questions like:

> How does your product help customers do their jobs better?
>
> What other challenges are they having in their jobs that would conflict with your product?
>
> What will they be able to accomplish by using it?
>
> What types of use cases are they trying to achieve?
>
> Who are the different personas who use your product, and how do they use it differently?

What "basic" skills do you need from day one, vs. "advanced" skills down the line? Are you introducing these all at once, or pacing them out?

How, if at all, would your product help its users get promoted in their organizations?

By answering these questions, and working what you learn into your content, you're less likely to come out with a jumbled series of product features and more likely to intentionally create a coherent story that helps your customer find value.

One of the best ways to start making learner-centric content is to put yourself in the learner's shoes. Sit in on your customer onboarding calls, but envision yourself as a customer. Ask yourself, from the customer's perspective: *Will I learn how to use the product by listening to someone talk over slides for an hour? How many chances did I get to ask questions? Did I even know what questions to ask? Did I get a chance to practice any of these skills? Exactly how excited am I about these stock photos?*

Basically, this is the Golden Rule of Customer Education: do unto your customers as you would have them do unto you. As you create Customer Education, keep asking: *If I were a customer, would I want to take this course?*

DISMANTLING "SPRAY AND PRAY"

When many Customer Education professionals first start their teams, they start scrambling to create content: Help Centers, docs, classroom training, webinar training, online academies, communities, certifications, in-product tutorials, live labs, and the list goes on.

That's gotta be overwhelming if you're starting from scratch. But there's no use in frantically creating content if the content doesn't actually drive results.

The big mistake that Customer Education teams make is building all these *things* without thinking about how *effective* those things are. If you ask them what the point of educating customers is, they might say, "So they know how to adopt our product." Or maybe aspirationally, "So that they become experts."

And so they end up building training programs that are essentially large collections of knowledge and expertise. These get delivered in unreadable and undiscoverable docs, long and boring classroom trainings, webinars where participants dutifully check their email the entire time, online academies with staggeringly high drop off rates, tumbleweed communities, certification programs that don't mean anything to a user, and so on.

Was "knowledge" or "expertise" really the goal? That's what your business may think customers want, but is it really? It's not true that customers just need information dumped into them so that they become experts. More often, they'll forget all that great knowledge you dumped on them if they aren't going to use it in their jobs. It simply cycles out of their short-term memory.

You've probably heard the statistic that you forget 50% of what you learned within *one hour*, 70% within *24 hours*, and 90% within *one week*.

Scientists have been studying the "forgetting curve" since it was first hypothesized in 1885 by Hermann Ebbinghaus. Using a series of nonsense syllables, he tested his ability to remember the words and found that his ability to retain memories followed, essentially, an exponential curve where he forgot the most in the first day, then gradually less over time.

Today's cognitive science around this isn't quite so rigid in the 50%-70%-90% numbers that I quoted earlier, but the basic idea of the Ebbinghaus Forgetting Curve still holds: without anything to strengthen our memory, we'll forget the information quickly.

Complicating all of this is the fact that memory doesn't work the way we think it does. Cognitive science has led to an interesting discovery. While we think that memory is like a video camera that captures information and plays it back at varying levels of fidelity, it's actually a little more like video editing software: every time we access a memory, we also alter it a little bit, infusing it with a bit of the present.

TAKE A BITE OUT OF BITE

At this point, I hope you're able to spot symptoms of BITE when you see them. Pay attention to the way other people in your business talk about documentation, training, and education. Can you spot it now?

Now that you can see "Sage on the Stage" and "Spray and Pray" approaches at work, you'll need better models to replace them.

Writing Learning Objectives that don't suck

The problem with "Sage on the Stage" is the Curse of Knowledge, so you need a way to make sure that customers understand *why* the content is relevant to them, and that they're actually able to turn knowledge into action. In other words, let's leave "knowledge" behind and start thinking about outcomes.

The best way to do this is by writing solid *learning objectives* for each piece of content you create—whether it's a course, article, or video. Similar to how a business objective clearly defines the outcome of an initiative, a learning objective shines a bright light on what the person will be able to *do* after going through the content.

If this sounds like a hassle, it's not—I promise. Once you know what the person will actually be able to *do*, you can measure whether they do it afterwards. All of a sudden, instead of asking vague questions like, "How do you know they learned? Were they nodding and smiling?" you're having a conversation about behavior change and performance outcomes.

That sounds good— maybe you're nodding and smiling right now—but most people skip over the work of writing good objectives because they haven't really thought about what behavior they're trying to change.

David Ogilvy, known as the father of advertising, once said, "People who think well, write well." This couldn't apply more to learning objectives. If you treat them as a hassle, and don't really think about the outcome, the learning objectives are going to be perfunctory and so will your training. You won't be thinking critically about the gap between what you (the expert) know and what the learner knows.

The problem with learning objectives, however, is that most of them suck.

How many times does this happen to you: you enter a training, and you just see a list of topics that will be covered on the agenda. Maybe the slide says "In this training, you will be able to:" and then there's a list of bullets written in Trainer-ese.

The instructor walks through the list, and tells you when the bathroom breaks will be, and then you're off to the races. But do you care about those agenda topics? Probably not! You care about what you're going to be able to *do better* as a result of the training. So when setting the learner's expectations about what will come in the course, tell them (concisely) what they're going to be able to do.

Learning objectives tell the learner what they'll be able to *do* if they're successful in the training.

Most sucky learning objectives read something like: "Understand the four stages of the Capability Maturity Model."

Gross. "Understand the four stages?" Is that an outcome? Can you take a video of me *understanding* the four stages? What would that look like if you took a picture of me doing it—rubbing my temples vigorously? Maybe you can open up my brain and see if understanding has taken place.

So let's try fixing the verb first. Maybe you change it to "Describe the four stages of the Capability Maturity Model."

Is that a good learning objective? It's *better*. I can take a video of you describing the four stages of the model, and I can give you feedback on whether you said the stages in the right order. What I don't know is whether this will matter on your job.

Better to skip to the stuff learners actually care about. What's the stuff they're actually going to be able to do better in this training? Or what's the problem they're going to be able to solve if they read the help article?

So maybe we'll tie this objective to a job-related skill: "Create a two-year plan for your department based on the Capability Maturity Model."

I'm going to be able to *create* something? For my *department*? Now we're getting a specific, measurable outcome. At the end of this training, I could take a video of you creating your plan. I could evaluate how well the plan hews to the Capability Maturity Model. I could even give you some qualitative feedback on how to use other components of the model.

At this point, you might be thinking, "That sounds like a good objective for a longer training, but you couldn't teach me how to do that after, say, reading an article."

That's probably true. In Customer Education, you typically have an audience with broad skill levels—your novices won't be able to do complex objectives after reading an article. So your learning objective and your format must match.

How do objectives and formats mismatch? It happens all the time.

On one hand, you may simply be providing reference material or an answer to a common support question. Creating an entire course or branching simulation around a simple topic like this is the equivalent of bringing a wolf to a dog show: it's impressive that you did that, but you overdid it and it's scary.

On the other hand, many companies do the opposite and underinvest in learning. For example, they might put together a

30-minute "demo" webinar and expect users to be completely proficient in using the product afterward. (This is the BITE effect at work again.)

We need to create training that actually drives the outcomes we want to see. Often we create something called "product knowledge" training where knowledge itself isn't the outcome; the desired outcome is actually application. We teach "product knowledge" because we want people to *use the product*. If we want to see our customers apply product skills, then we need to create room during the training for them to test those skills out, and ideally we should be able to measure by the end of the training whether they actually applied the skills!

To summarize the whole line of thinking we just went through, I like to ask a few questions about learning objectives before I start creating content:

> What is the *verb* I want to see people do after they read this article, watch this video, or take this training? Could I see them perform that action?
>
> Will the objective help the person be *better* at their actual job?
>
> Is it *realistic* that the person would be able to do the objective after this learning experience, or is more training required?

Check your verb first. If the sentence you've written is about what the learner will be able to "know," "understand," "comprehend," "learn," etc. then that's probably not a good learning objective. Instead, find the actual skill that the learner will take out of the course. That's your verb.

The learning objective should be something that applies to the learner's job—after all, most adult learners don't care about gaining knowledge or skills unless they can use it somehow.

Regardless of whether you're building a course or writing an article, ask yourself what you expect the learner to do after they've completed it.

Know something: Do they *really* just need to know or understand something? It's possible, but most of the time you'll want to push on this and ask what they're going to do with this knowledge. Your learning objective might be "Remember what each status type means so that you can tell which stage of the process a report is in."

Do something routine: Articles and simple trainings can teach procedures—for example, you might create an article on how to export a file. That doesn't require judgment; the customer either did it or they didn't. If they practice doing it a few times, they'll probably be able to do it just fine in the future. These typically can be handled with an article or a quick video. Your learning objective might be "Export a file to CSV."

Do something complex: For skills that require judgment and practice, you'll usually need more than a simple reference doc or video. This is where more extensive training is necessary—often with practice and reflection opportunities built in (but we'll get to that in a few steps). Your learning objective might be "De-escalate a sensitive customer call."

One more note about learning objectives: It's important that you (and your stakeholders) know what they are, so you can design learning around them, but it's not always important for learners to see them in the same way.

You don't need to include the boring learning objectives bullet-point slide at the beginning of your training. You can make it fun—for example, I know a few Trainers who use the *Mission: Impossible* method ("Your objective, should you choose to accept it, is to..."). Others discuss them in terms of customer needs ("You've told me you need to be able to add users, configure your widgets, and set up your *boîte diabolique* in the admin control panel. By the end of the training, you'll do all three of those things").

Learning objectives also help set expectations in written content, like help articles. I recommend starting each article with an objective, as in "This article will help you:"

With articles, you can be a bit more forgiving on your verbs, because some knowledge articles really are just there to help people understand a concept. They're just references. In these cases, a "This article will help you" section makes the article more scannable and signals to the customer that they're in the right (or wrong) place.

But if the article helps customers use a feature or solve a problem, then use "This article will help you" to describe the actual skills and situations the customer may encounter.

EVERYTHING IS 80/20

So much for "Sage on the Stage," and onto our next myth: "Spray and Pray." The problem with "Spray and Pray" is cognitive overload: the more you present at once, the less likely any of it is to get absorbed. You need a way to make sure that you're not presenting too much information at once, and that what you do present is actually vital to achieving the learning objective.

When it comes to learning objectives, more isn't better. And yet we still treat our training agendas or catalogs like they're the buffet at Caesar's Palace. During the design process, many people inventory every single thing they want a customer to learn about a given topic, and make sure it's jammed into whatever timeframe they have for the course.

Think about the last software product you learned how to use. Did you master every feature on day one? Probably not. You probably started with some basic use cases. You played around a little bit, tried and failed to do some fancier stuff, and then eventually you got more skilled if you needed to.

When you're designing onboarding training, you may be tempted to walk through every feature because this is the primary opportunity you have to train your users. You might also think that the content is helpful "just in case." Paradoxically, the more information we're exposed to before we're ready for it, the less likely we are to act.

When we're pummelled with irrelevant content that we're not ready for, we experience cognitive overload. In his research on cognitive load theory, educational psychologist John Sweller found that our working memory (the part of our memory that processes information in the moment and lets us take action based on the information) can overload if it receives too much information at once.

I know—the idea of missing a key piece of content is the stuff of cold-sweat nightmares. But remember: You'll have opportunities to fill more content gaps later. On the other hand, you don't necessarily have another opportunity to engage your learner and get them to care. Customers don't learn on your timetable, so cramming in as much content as possible isn't going to help them succeed.

In other words, you need to move from a "content-centric" mindset to a "learner-centric" one.

Think critically about what you want to expose customers to on day one, and what information can or should come later. Which activities will actually lead your customer to first value with your product? What are the common areas that will trip them up before they can achieve value? Those are the areas to focus on.

Instead of cramming in all the content you can, your goal should be to identify the 20% of content that creates 80% of the outcomes for learners.

This "80/20" ratio has a rich history. In 1896, an economist named Vilfredo Pareto observed that around 20% of Milan's population owned roughly 80% of the wealth. As it turns out, this pattern—sometimes referred to as "the vital few vs. the trivial many"—holds in other areas as well. Joseph Juran, a management consultant, took the "Pareto principle" and applied it to business—for example, in quality assurance, 80% of the problems come from 20% of the root causes.

The exact percentage here is less useful than the principle: instead of spending time documenting *everything* and creating courses for *every* topic we can think of, how can we focus on the 20% of learning that will generate 80% of the benefit for customers?

Unless you're in a regulated industry and some lawmaker says you need to, you don't have to document or train on everything. The thought of having training or documentation that isn't 100% complete sends chills down completists' spines. But ask yourself a philosophical question: If you document an edge case, and no one's there to read it, does it matter? (This also applies to release notes, which commonly require the most time invested for the fewest readers.)

If you look across your support and Customer Success teams, chances are that there's something at least resembling a Pareto distribution: 20% of topics generate 80% of tickets, or drive 80% of ad hoc training requests. Obviously, you should start with those. But let me suggest something bolder: what would happen if you didn't publicly document the other 80%... until it becomes part of the 20%?

If you recall from the chapter on customer onboarding, you can use a Pareto distribution to determine what should go in your onboarding courses as well. Instead of stuffing your onboarding training with every topic a customer could need, you can forsake the false god of thoroughness and instead focus on the 20% of skills that will actually drive a customer to first value with your product.

What do you do with the stuff that isn't your "20%" core documentation or training? You can still find ways to make those topics accessible to customers, while setting expectations about where to find what information. For instance, many companies encourage customers and Support teams to discuss edge cases and other "non-canonical" topics in their Community. The results are still searchable, but there's not as much expectation that the solutions are "blessed" by the company.

This was one of the main reasons that Optimizely chose to consolidate the Knowledge Base, Academy, and Community sites into one platform called Optiverse. The Community content is still searchable from the same place as the Knowledge Base, but when a customer searches for a certain topic, they have different expectations about the information based on where they find it:

> In the Academy, they're looking for content that's linear and interactive—organized into an engaging path for them.

> In the Knowledge Base, they're looking at a smaller set of canonical documentation, where they can expect a certain level of editing and polish.

> In the Community, many solutions are user-contributed and timestamped (so an out-of-date solution is easily identifiable). If a certain solution on the Community becomes widely discussed or searched for, then you always reserve the right to make it canonical and move it into the Knowledge Base.

Taking a less-but-better approach to education increases discoverability, ease of maintenance, and your likeliness to improve your company's ticket deflection and customer satisfaction goals.

Yes, you'll still have customer complaints. There will inherently be topics that you "missed." But steer into that skid for a moment—don't you have customer complaints right now? The point is to see if your trend improves overall.

BOOSTING YOUR SIGNAL

Now you've moved away from "how much content can I fit in this course?" and towards "how do I help the learner get from their current state to the desired outcome?" You've defined learning objectives and defined the "20%" content that's necessary to guide the customer toward their goal. So how do you actually guide them there?

Learning new skills and managing change is like hiking a winding mountain trail. You're trying to get from point A to point B, but the path isn't straightforward, and there are boulders poised to fall on you if you take a wrong turn into the wilderness.

If your job is to get someone from A to B along this path, how do you do it? Do you just list out the directions for them and hope they'll be able to do it? That's not going to be helpful to someone who's never traveled that route before.

Instead of a "sage on the stage," your role in training is to be the "guide on the side," helping learners along the path. You can point out some of the obstacles that they'll encounter on the way, and show them some shortcuts, but you can't walk the path for them.

But Customer Education poses an additional challenge in this metaphor: often, you're not right there by the customer's side. At some point you have to leave your on-site training or hang up the phone, and then they're still responsible for getting from point A to point B.

As the customer hikes the trail, you're less like a sherpa walking by their side, and more like a ranger communicating via walkie-talkie. You try to communicate with the customer and help them along their path, but you can't always see what they see. Instead, you can do everything possible to boost the signal strength of your walkie-talkie.

In this section, I'll share some ways to boost the signal strength of your communication, so your message comes through clearer—even when you're not right there by the customer's side.

Build a schema

John Bransford and Marcia Johnson had a hypothesis about the value of setting the right context when they conducted psychological experiments in 1972. We can do the experiment together. Read the following paragraph (the same one they showed to participants in the study) and see if you can re-explain it after you're finished reading:

"The procedure is actually quite simple. First you arrange things into different groups. Of course, one pile may be sufficient depending on how much there is to do. If you have to go somewhere else due to lack of facilities that is the next step, otherwise you are pretty well set. It is important not to overdo things. That is, it is better to do too few things at once than too many. In the short run this may not seem important but complications can easily arise. A mistake can be expensive as well. At first the whole procedure will seem complicated. Soon, however, it will become just another facet of life. It is difficult to foresee any end to the necessity for this task in the immediate future, but then one never can tell. After the procedure is completed one arranges the materials into different groups again. Then they can be put into their appropriate places. Eventually they will be used once more and the whole cycle will then have to be repeated. "

Okay, what?

If you don't know what that paragraph is referring to—if you lack the context—then I may as well have just read to you from the untranslated Voynich manuscript. (What's the Voynich manuscript? If you don't have prior knowledge about that, then I bet that analogy made you feel alienated. Educate, don't alienate!)

But what if I told you that the process being described above is... doing laundry? Try re-reading it now; makes a little more sense, doesn't it?

Bransford and Johnson's experiment played out roughly the same way. The participants who were told that the paragraph was about laundry *before* reading it had substantially higher recall when they were asked to restate it.

This experiment was getting at the idea of *schema*. A schema is just your mental model for something. So in this case, you have a schema for laundry—you can imagine sorting clothes into whites and colors, or separating out delicates. You can imagine the washing machine and the dryer. You can imagine going to a laundromat or doing laundry at home. Maybe you've had a visit from the repair company and can relate well to the "expensive mistake" bit.

Because you already have a schema for laundry, you don't need to close-read the text to understand what's going on. When you come across a phrase like "you arrange things into different groups," your schema fills in instantly that "things" are items of clothing and "groups" are loads.

Now you have the curse of knowledge—you'd struggle to go back to a time when you didn't know what those words meant. But if you had to describe this process again to someone who lacked a schema, wouldn't you try to give them more context than what was given to you?

For some reason, we forget this concept when we try to educate customers. We use language that makes complete sense to us— probably the same jargon and buzzwords we freely throw around in our internal meetings—but makes learning more difficult to customers.

On the other hand, draw upon your learners' prior knowledge in areas that they *are* familiar. Your customer isn't a blank slate; they're probably coming into your training with previous experience. Today isn't the first time they've logged into a computer, learned about software, or even (for some) had experience using your product. Start by getting a sense of the learner's prior knowledge, perhaps through a challenging pre-test or scenario for them to solve—we learn best when we're challenged—or at least through some sort of activity that asks them to reflect on their previous experience.

Jesse Evans had a golden rule for his training programs at Box University: "Never tell your attendees something that they could tell you."

In other words, if you think your learners may already be able to answer a question using prior knowledge, ask them instead of saying it yourself.

How do you know what a learner's prior knowledge is? Ask! If your product helps customer service professionals improve the service they provide, try asking about previous good and bad customer service experiences they've had (or were responsible for). If you're teaching a certification course on project management at your user conference, try asking about a previous project gone off the rails; you can probably use that example later when you're exploring how your software can enhance project management. And of course, if you're working with customers who have used your product before, have them share their experiences of using your product.

Instead of using buzzwords or treating customers like a blank slate, use the power of the schema to your advantage. For example, you can take complex ideas and boil them down into memorable mental models (MMMs).

Mnemonics are good examples of mental models that stick. If you learned the order of colors in a rainbow as "ROY G. BIV" (Red, Orange, Yellow, Green, Blue, Indigo, Violet), the order of operations in mathematics as "Please Excuse My Dear Aunt Sally" (Parentheses, Exponents, Multiplication and Division, Addition and Subtraction), or the scientific classification system as "Kings Play Chess On Fuzzy Green Stools" (Kingdom, Phylum, Class, Order, Family, Genus, Species) then you're more likely to have that information seared into your memory and easier to recall over time.

In my previous role at BancVue, which created software products and marketing for community financial institutions, my team frequently traveled to train front-line representatives. At some point, the Trainers started asking the representatives to remember the features of a checking account with the acronym "FRAN" (Free, Rewards, Ask to Qualify, No Fees). That got a few eye-rolls back at the home office but rave reviews from the participants. This worked better than any job aid we could have provided.

Analogies and similes are also good examples of mental models. In *Made to Stick*, Dan and Chip Heath attempt to describe a pomelo—once without a schema, and once with it.

Without using a schema, they describe it as "the largest citrus fruit. The rind is very thick but soft and easy to peel away. The resulting fruit has a light yellow to coral pink flesh and can vary from juicy to slightly dry and from seductively spicy-sweet to tangy and tart." That's a lot of words, and "the resulting fruit" is one of the most awkward phrases I've ever seen committed to the printed page.

But by using an analogy, they describe it as "basically a super-sized grapefruit with a very thick and soft rind." That doesn't have quite as much detail, does it? But it's a lot simpler and gets the point across.

What's In It For Me?

How do we move from content-centric knowledge dumps to learner-centric outcomes? Just like you should justify your Customer Education function with a rationale for how it will help your business, you should also start your trainings and docs with a solid "why."

In training, this is often referred to as the "WIIFM" (you might heard it said out loud as "Whiff 'em")—What's In It For Me?

Note that this is different from an agenda. An agenda tells you what will be covered and when you're getting breaks. That's important for expectation-setting but pretty lousy as a "why." Just seeing a list of topics isn't going to motivate anyone.

Often, when we begin designing documentation and training, we think about all the topics and features we want to include, but we miss the WIIFM. When you focus on teaching your product, feature by feature, you're engaging in content-first, not learner-first, design.

The WIIFM has to be job-relevant and get to "why" a customer would want to use your product. It also has to be something that matters to the customer, not something *you* think they should care about.

One of the big mistakes I see is that companies spend their training time essentially re-selling the product to a room of users who didn't buy it. That's an understandable impulse—the sales pitch worked well enough to get someone to sign a check. But re-selling the product to a bunch of people who are responsible for using it every day won't be an effective motivator.

You're going to have to find a different angle—instead of "how this product improves your business," the WIIFM for your audience here will probably look more like "how this will save you time," "how this will make you better at your job," "how this will help you make better recommendations to your customers," and so on.

Let's use customer onboarding training as an example. A good onboarding training will address how your product works and what to click, but that's not the point of the training. All of those "what to click" sections should be framed in a broader process or workflow—and that process should help your trainees do their jobs better. Product adoption is a two-way street: if you're not helping make their jobs easier, then they won't really care about using your product well.

At Optimizely, one of the high-level value propositions was that a culture of experimentation could reduce costly investments that later failed. That didn't matter as much to an individual user. Our actual users cared more about the fact that they could now quickly deploy a change to their website without waiting for Engineering support. Some of them cared more about being creative and becoming pioneers in the field of experimentation. In addition to the "culture of experimentation," we appealed to those other, more personal values in our trainings.

When I worked at BancVue, the bank's or credit union's officers cared that the products would help them increase deposits. The front-line representatives and tellers we were training didn't care about that, but they did usually care about increasing their customers' satisfaction.

Now, at Checkr, we're helping employers in a regulated industry make decisions that affect real people's ability to work. By training them, we're not just helping them use a product; we're also helping them balance their organization's trust and safety needs with candidate fairness. We're helping them make more consistent and compliant decisions to protect their organizations from risk.

So before you ever talk about how your product works and what buttons to click, make sure that you've gotten your learners' attention and that they feel like by learning how to use your product, they'll be better at their jobs.

Building motivation

How much time do you set aside in your day for learning?

Despite the fact that Bill Gates, Jack Ma, and Elon Musk deliberately set aside an hour a day for reading and learning, most of us don't feel like we have the time. And we especially don't want to spend that time learning how to use a new product.

We'll only put in the time if it helps us achieve a result—and even those results are pretty narrow. In fact, most adult learners care about very few things when it comes to learning: *Will this solve a problem I'm having or avoid it in the future? Will this afford me some new opportunity or increase in status? Will this help me grow professionally or personally?*

When it comes to learning a given skill or subject, people can be *intrinsically* or *extrinsically* motivated.

Intrinsic motivation means that you're motivated from within yourself to do something. Maybe you think it will be fun, or you understand why it's important, or you just want to. We can learn for intrinsic reasons: For example, if you really love the idea of data analysis, you may take it upon yourself to learn SQL. Or if you want to move to Paris at some point, you'll probably be more motivated to take that French class.

On the other hand, we're extrinsically motivated when we do something out of obligation, pressure, compliance, or external incentives. We're there because it's required, because we feel like we must, or because someone's paying us to do it. We go to sexual harassment training because we'll get in trouble if we don't. We go to professional development events to maintain accreditation status. We go to workplace trainings so they don't fire us and keep paying us money.

Edward Deci, author of *Why We Do What We Do: Understanding Self-Motivation*, and Richard Ryan conducted several studies to explore how different rewards motivated people. In these studies, he had participants complete a puzzle, then watched to see whether they would continue solving puzzles afterwards. In other words, were they self-motivated to continue challenging themselves?

Deci found that people tend to be more intrinsically motivated when they feel like they're making decisions autonomously. The more control and choice they feel like they have, the more likely they are to stay motivated. You can accomplish this in your courses by giving learners multiple paths through content, or more control of the agenda.

The research also revealed that people also tend to become more intrinsically motivated as they become more competent at something. Provided that we feel autonomy and self control over what we're learning, the feeling of becoming more competent makes us want to continue to challenge ourselves.

On the other hand, it turns out that a lot of common extrinsic "motivators" actually caused participants to lose interest in performing the task afterwards. Those who were offered money, who were threatened or evaluated, or who competed against peers, ended up *less* intrinsically motivated to keep solving puzzles than the group who was just asked to solve the puzzle for its own sake.

By adding extrinsic motivation to a task, it *decreased* the likelihood of that same task being intrinsically motivating in the future. So be careful with the way you use rewards, incentives, and even competition. The goal of most training is to get people to do something well *after* the training, so you don't want to do something that will increase motivation during training but decrease motivation later.

In any course, you'll probably have a combination of intrinsically and extrinsically motivated learners. From course to course, people may even switch between categories. Just because you're intrinsically motivated to learn one thing, that doesn't mean you're intrinsically motivated to learn everything. A given person can be intrinsically motivated to learn one skill, but not see the value in learning a different one.

Here are a few considerations for managing motivation in your courses:

Respect people's time. Extrinsically motivated people would rather get up to speed quickly than learn *everything* now. Even intrinsically motivated learners are still pressed for time. They're juggling your educational experience with other tasks and duties.

Remember that competence is motivating. Provide opportunities for learners to see how they're improving their skills, and be sensitive to learners who are frustrated that they're not yet competent at something.

Find attention-getters. If someone isn't intrinsically motivated to learn, you may be able to find interesting stories, statistics, or use cases that will at least get their attention and make them more motivated to continue. Sometimes starting with a surprise will create that "lightbulb" moment that you're looking for, since you've caught the learner off guard and prepared them to think about a topic in a different way.

Use suspense and mystery. Mysteries are such a successful genre because they tap into something fundamental in the human brain. It's why the podcast *Serial* was on everyone's phones in 2014. It's why two of the top ten Nielsen-rated shows are, at the time of this writing, franchises of *NCIS*. The majority of *Harry Potter* books are centered around mysteries that the characters have to solve. So if you can set up interesting mysteries for your learners centered around the content, you may be able to increase their motivation.

Beware of gaming the system. When someone is extrinsically motivated by money, prizes, or even certification credentials, they'll do exactly what's needed to get the reward. So, for example, if you set a requirement that users must enroll in a certain number of courses to win a prize, but not that they complete them or prove that they learned anything, you may have a bunch of extrinsically motivated learners racking up course enrollments but not learning a thing.

What about gamification? Gamification has been hotly debated in both Marketing and Education: is it motivating or not?

If we take Deci's research into account, it would seem there are parts of gamification that are actually intrinsically motivating: for example, if our games are actually fun. But there are also many styles of "gamification" that rely on extrinsic motivation, like points, badges, and leaderboards.

I see people try to solve the problem of boring content by making it more "fun" with *Jeopardy!* games or by "gamifying" it using badges and leaderboards. But not everyone is motivated by competition, so leaderboards don't work for everyone. Badges only work if the person cares about having a badge. And *Jeopardy!* is not necessarily fun—it's a memorization game that's better for memorizing facts than for changing behavior.

That said, game mechanics *can* help you present objectives and scenarios in a more immersive way—so, for instance, a course on Discovery and Root Cause Analysis could use mechanics from a mystery game like *Where in the World is Carmen Sandiego?*

The Customer Education team at Optimizely had a tradition of hosting "gamification nights." We used them as an excuse for the whole team to get together, kick back, and play some board games together. Even once we became a global team, we continued to host these nights when our international team members came to town.

Beyond just having some fun together, we also used gamification night as an opportunity to learn more about how games motivate us, and apply those lessons to our own learning experiences in Optiverse.

How do you know if you've motivated your learners? You need to investigate whether customers are doing what you trained them to do, after the training is over. If they're not, is it because they need more training? Or is it because they're not motivated?

Some skills require training and practice to master—maybe it takes multiple sessions to master. Most people aren't born knowing how to play hockey, how to handle a customer service call, how to open a checking account for a customer, or how to conduct a statistically significant experiment. These are all skills that require some training, instruction, and practice to get right.

Look at your product analytics, or reach out to your customers to find out whether they're doing what you trained them to do. If you expect them to master complex skills after only a little training, your expectation might be unrealistic—the Curse of Knowledge strikes again.

On the other hand, there are things that customers need to do that aren't really skills, but just knowledge. For example, you generally don't need training to log into a product. If your product is simple enough, you probably also don't need to train someone on common tasks like creating a new user or entering billing information. If you're spending valuable training time on those topics—get them out of your training! Those belong in reference docs or other support materials, which you can provide as part of training.

Simple tasks usually don't require retraining. If customers aren't doing this really basic stuff, it's not because you didn't train them. So what's happening? It might be a basic awareness issue, as in they didn't know that a feature exists—so you can tell them (or use something like In-Product Education to alert them). It might also be motivation, as in they know what to do but they don't care. No amount of training gets someone to care if there's a different, underlying issue. This is where CSMs should be spending their time getting to the root cause, instead of just training *at* customers.

REMOVING NOISE

Let's go back to our walkie-talkie analogy. Maybe you've boosted your signal, given your customer better maps and tools to get the lay of the land, and distributed some field rations so they don't go hungry. You've equipped them with a better schema, a compelling WIIFM, and some motivation.

But remember that any signal can be impeded by noise. If a blizzard hits, there will be interference in the signal. This "noise" can make the signal a lot fuzzier, and it can take your customer off course. So what types of "noise" exist and how can you remove them?

Words matter

Every customer is unique in some way—and they'll be quick to tell you so. There's some customization they need from your product, or some reason why their industry is different from your other customers'. This means that, even though a lot of your content may be similar from customer to customer, you can learn how to speak to customers in their own language.

Find the terms they relate to (and avoid the ones that make them angry)

When I worked at BancVue, our primary training audience was the front-line staff of community banks and credit unions. Not having worked in the industry before, I went on-site with a credit union to do some shadowing. At one point, I asked one of the employees a question about their customers. I may as well have just stepped on their foot and ground it for three minutes.

What was going on? It turns out that credit unions don't have "customers"; they have "members." Because credit unions are member-owned, they don't think of their account holders as customers. When they hear "customers," they think of banks: their competition.

I learned an important lesson here. In the live trainings we delivered, I knew we'd have to adapt the scripts and materials to refer to "customers" for banks and "members" for credit unions. For e-learning, where it was impractical to maintain two separate versions, I tried to use more neutral terms like "clients" or "account holders," which at least didn't give anyone a pulmonary embolism.

Avoid buzzword bingo

We often write like the worst versions of ourselves. Instead of clear and concise prose, we offer drawn-out, jargon-filled technobabble. We end up with content that is dull, dry, and confusing.

How many times have you gone to look up a help article, only to find it dense and impenetrable, filled with jargon you don't understand?

Or you go to a training, and the Trainer is lecturing in tech-talk or marketing-babble? You're probably thinking, "Just talk to me like a person! I came here to learn how to do something, not to hear you pretend to sound smart."

The first time a customer is exposed to a topic—if they lack prior knowledge—everything sprawls out before them like the western Kansas prairie. It's flat. *Really* flat. There are no hills, no contours, and no landmarks.

If we don't set the right context for customers, and help them understand what to pay attention to (and why it's important), they're going to hear a bunch of words before they have any sense of what those words mean. Good education is like a topographic map, helping learners see where some of the peaks and valleys are—what's worth paying most attention to, and how to use some information as landmarks to put others in perspective.

Instead, a lot of docs are written by people who understand the technology very well, and the customer very poorly. And trainings are conducted by people who are paid to sound smart, not to help people learn. If we're going to help people learn, we have to put things in their terms. We have to set the right context before we introduce new information.

Try auditing your articles and scripts for common buzzwords and jargon, and replace them with plain language, clear analogies, or more engaging examples and stories.

CREATING COURSES THAT BOOST SIGNAL AND REDUCE NOISE

If you can create strong learning objectives, find your "80/20" balance, build a strong WIIFM, and eliminate other noise, you'll already be ahead of most knowledge-dump training.

What can you do to take your courses to the next level? Here, I'll share some of my favorite techniques to boost signal and reduce noise.

Start with a bang

When you deliver Customer Education, you're at war—and the enemy is in disguise.

We tend to think that, by training customers, we're fighting the great evil known as ignorance. If we can just open up our learners' brains and stuff enough expertise in there, we'll be praised as heroes and our images will be graven into the walls for generations to come.

That's what the enemy *wants* us to think. Because the enemy isn't ignorance; it's distraction. If we're not compelling from moment one of our virtual classes, we've lost to Operation Inbox. If our e-learning doesn't grab attention, we find ourselves on the receiving end of the Course Abandonment Maneuver. If our live courses are dull, then our participants pull the famous defensive tactic known as I-Have-A-Meeting-To-Go-To-And-Yes-It's-Totally-A-Real-Meeting-Nope-Not-An-Excuse-At-All.

That's why TV shows, movies, and other media put so much effort into their first moments—to hook you in. Think of the plane crash in *LOST*, the desert chase in *Breaking Bad*, the dawn of mankind in *2001: A Space Odyssey*, or the heart-rending story of Carl and Ellie in *Up*.

You don't need a movie studio's budget to create a memorable opening. One of my favorite opening moments is in the 2017 podcast *S-Town*, where narrator Brian Reed starts with this:

> "When an antique clock breaks, a clock that's been telling time for 200 or 300 years, fixing it can be a real puzzle. An old clock like that was handmade by someone. It might tick away the time with a pendulum, with a spring, with a pulley system. It might have bells that are supposed to strike the hour, or a bird that's meant to pop out and cuckoo at you. There can be hundreds of tiny, individual pieces, each of which needs to interact with the others precisely."

He poetically walks through what seems like a pretty mundane description of clock repair, describing the difficulty of fixing an old clock. He talks about "witness marks," which he describes as "clues to what was in the clockmaker's mind when he first created the thing."

Now, two minutes in, he's still talking about clocks:

> "I'm told fixing an old clock can be maddening. You're constantly wondering if you've just spent hours going down a path that will likely take you nowhere, and all you've got are these vague witness marks, which might not even mean what you think they mean. So at every moment along the way, you have to decide if you're wasting your time or not.
>
> Anyway, I only learned about all this because years ago an antique clock restorer contacted me, John B. McLemore, and asked me to help him solve a murder."

Boom. All of a sudden, in one sentence, our expectations are yanked away. This isn't going to be a boring, if well-intentioned, profile of the clock-making process. We're going to learn about a murder. The earlier language—*puzzle, witness marks, clues, hours going down a path that will likely take you nowhere*—now snaps into focus.

The whole introduction takes around three minutes, but it sets the tone for the entire series. It shows you, without exactly telling you, what's going to be important for the next few hours.

The first moments are among the most important. Yet many courses don't start with anything memorable or attention-grabbing. They start with an agenda (Save it for after you got their attention). Or a long-winded introduction to who the facilitators are (No one cares unless you're a celebrity). Or those canned slides talking about the history of your company (No! No! Kill it with fire!). These types of intros are supposed to bolster our credibility, but they actually destroy it by boring our learners.

What can you do to make intros more memorable? You can do some of the work through interesting content. Try adding an attention-grabbing story, a mystery to be solved, or a controversial fact that will open some eyes and get brains running.

You can also grab attention using media. If you have extra development time to spare, spend it on creating an engaging introduction using video or infographics.

In classroom environments, you can actually hand over the intro to the learners. Go around the room and ask them what they want to get out of the course, or about problems they're having in their jobs that you might be able to solve in this training session.

Jesse Evans recommends using the crucial 60-second window at the beginning of online classes to facilitate interactivity. In the classes he developed and led for Box University, he would always ask learners to:

> Type something in the chat box to everyone else ("Say hello in your favorite language") to get people talking and demonstrate that learners can interact with each other.

Type something in the chat box to presenters or private chat ("How many of you have taken a class with us before?") to show that there's also a safe space to ask private questions.

Type one final thing into the chat pod to everyone as a transition into the actual course materials.

Break it up

Have you ever thought about why phone numbers have punctuation in them? If you want to order contact lenses over the phone, why do you call 1 (800) 266-8228 instead of 18002668228? It's the same number.

In 1956, a Princeton cognitive psychologist named George Miller published a paper titled "The Magical Number Seven, Plus or Minus Two: Some Limits on Our Capacity for Processing Information." (That's an amazing title, by the way.) In his research, he found that the number of objects that an average human holds in their working memory is—you guessed it—seven, plus or minus two.

Unlike long term memory, the working memory is more immediate and more susceptible to forgetting. So when you first provide information for the first time, it enters the working memory. Thus it needs to be digestible.

One of the best cures for the common working memory is chunking. Chunking refers to dividing large pieces of information into smaller, more digestible pieces. That's why 18002668228 is much easier to remember as 1 (800) 266-8228. The punctuation helps group the 11-digit number into four chunks in a familiar pattern.

How do you incorporate chunking into your learning experiences?

The structure of your courses matters. I'll cover this more deeply in a moment when I discuss microlearning, but making each course and lesson more digestible makes them easier to remember and places less in the working memory.

Bullets and lists can help. If you have three main points to make, consider putting them in bullets. Or if you have a six-step process, reinforce what those six steps are.

But don't bullet-point your learners to death. If you put a slide up with "the 24 top techniques to improve customer service," then you have a great recipe for at least 23 forgotten techniques.

Highlight objectives at the beginning, and key takeaways at the end. This primes the working memory to pay attention to what it's going to absorb, and reinforces that absorption at the end of the course.

One form of chunking that has taken the education world by storm is "microlearning." Broadly, microlearning means breaking up learning into smaller chunks to make it more discoverable and consumable. But how small should the chunks be? And is "microlearning" real or just a fad?

Surely you've heard the statistics about Millennials with their shortening attention spans. And let's not even dare to think of the generation *after* Millennials who, as of the writing of this book, are officially entering the workforce. The way that journalists and pop-science writers stereotype these generations, you would think that they're neck-and-neck with goldfish in a race to the bottom of the attention aquarium.

If you're nodding along with this knowingly, you might be surprised to know two things; first, goldfish aren't proven to have particularly short attention spans; and second, most of that human attention span research is bunk.

Yes, there's a trend toward information becoming shorter and more digestible—but there's no proof that it's generational; it's more likely a factor of information becoming more accessible via technology. In the past we held days-long training sessions for customers not because they had longer attention spans, but because the technology available to us mostly involved airplanes, slide projectors, and handouts. It wasn't feasible to implement microlearning in that environment, except perhaps through Train the Trainer programs where we could empower someone at the customer's site to continually train their own employees.

While there are certainly still benefits to face-to-face instruction, length is not chief among them. Technology has given us many ways to break up learning experiences into smaller chunks that are more relevant and timely, so we can hold our learners' attention and present information when learners need it most.

Microlearning doesn't just make customers happy when you tell them that your courses are "bite-sized"—it also can be better for learning retention.

Cognitive and psychological research has shown that spaced practice is better for long-term retention than massed practice (a.k.a "cramming"). The more opportunities we have to practice something, the more likely we are to remember it and apply it. And the more spaced out the practice is—in other words, the more we have to retrieve the information—the more likely we are to remember it.

Put this into practice by including periodic activities and knowledge checks in your courses, instead of a single final test or certification. Learners will actually remember more if they learn in bite-sized chunks over a longer period of time and try practicing what they learned, instead of taking everything in a day or two and then hoping for the best.

To embrace microlearning, use the following techniques:

> **Break your courses into smaller chunks.** We frequently make the mistake of trying to cram many topics into a session; instead, use the learning objective as your unit of measurement. Each small chunk of a course should teach one skill in a matter of minutes, then it's time to move on to the next chunk. Learners don't like scanning through an hour-long recorded webinar for the one piece of information they want.
>
> **Repackage your chunklets.** Now that you have smaller courses centered around learning objectives, you can repackage them. Alessandra Marinetti, who led Customer Education for LinkedIn and now for Box, recommends packaging shorter courses into paths for your different customer personas to make them quick but relevant.

Deliver it in context. If you create short modules or videos for microlearning, see if you can weave them into your product experience. Many In-Product Education platforms allow you to embed video directly into tooltips. What better time is there to see a video introduction to a feature than while you're learning to use that feature?

Tell the learner what they'll learn and why it matters. Since learners can drop in and out of microlearning sessions easily, you only have a few seconds to engage them. I usually like to start with a quick value statement in a friendly, inviting tone (like "In this video, we'll set up alerts so that all your team members know when you make updates."). This statement should quickly explain the learning objective and the value of learning it—while still sounding like a human.

Show, don't tell. Often we learn better through stories, analogies, and statistics than long-winded explanations. If you can start your microlearning sessions with quick (30-second) attention-getters, you can often convey a point more efficiently than had you not taken that time.

Keep videos and content pieces short. Like, under-five-minutes short. If you use a video analytics platform, you can see exactly when viewers drop off in your videos, but the rule of thumb is to limit your videos to five minutes or less. This means that you'll need to script them out beforehand, and edit them down to remove needless clicks and pauses. Most modern video-editing software makes this relatively easy.

Keep your entire course short, too. In their *Voice of the Learner* report, the Digital Learning Consortium showed a significant preference toward learning in "doses" of 20 to 45 minutes, even if those doses are smaller units in a larger curriculum.

Use a "show it, try it" structure. Even a 20-minute course may provide time for 10 minutes of explaining and demonstrating the concept, then 10 minutes of having the learner try it out themselves. This provides a quick feedback loop to let the learner know whether they've mastered the skill.

Flip it over

For years, most companies trained their customers using a traditional classroom model. Like a college course, there would be an in-classroom lecture delivered by a "sage on the stage," and followed by some homework. If learners were lucky, that "sage on the stage" also knew how to be a "guide on the side" and open the classroom up to interactivity, debate, and reflection.

While this is the accepted model, and few customers are going to yell at you for proposing a traditional classroom training, it presents some challenges:

You're putting a lot of pressure on the Trainer to act both as the "sage" and the "guide."

The traditional classroom model lends itself to the lecture format because the information is new to most of the learners. They don't yet know what questions to ask.

People walk into the classroom with different levels of expertise, so you have to decide whether to cater to the least knowledgeable person asking all the basic questions, or the seasoned veteran who's folding their arms in the back.

More and more, both academic and corporate classrooms are starting to "flip" from this traditional model. Technology is making it easier to disseminate information outside of a classroom, which presents opportunities to change the way that people learn. Most Customer Education teams aren't completely eliminating the in-person classroom time, but they are thinking critically about how to make the classroom time more valuable.

So what is a "flipped classroom"? It's not a situation where all the desks are upside down when the learners walk in (although I guess you could use that as an icebreaker before training). Instead, it's about flipping the sequence of classroom and homework.

In the traditional classroom, you went to a lecture and then got homework. In a flipped classroom, you essentially do the homework first. For most Customer Education programs, the homework is something like an e-learning module or article that explains the basics of the concept. That way, when the learners are together in the class, they don't have to sit there and listen to someone lecture at them. They actually get to drive the agenda, ask meaningful questions, and try more hands-on situations.

Customer Education leaders are sometimes afraid to flip their classrooms because it requires more improvisation (which means you need a Trainer who can adapt on the fly), because they're worried that customers won't do the pre-work (which means you need CSMs who can hold customers accountable), and because it's just not the way things used to be done (which means you need to help your team get with the times).

Yes, it does take more work to build a habit around flipped classrooms—but they end up being more valuable in the end. When trying to implement flipped classrooms, which involves selling the idea to your internal teams and customers, you could start by being transparent about the goals and the options. For instance, here's a script your CSMs could use with the customer:

"We know it's hard to get your team together for four hours of training, and we want to make that time as valuable as possible. That's why we've spent time developing this self-paced e-learning that will help get your team on the same page and able to ask more meaningful questions when we're together in the training class. Can your team devote one hour to this pre-work?"

And if the customer pushes back: "If they're not able to take an hour, we can use the e-learning as homework, but we've found that the classroom time isn't as valuable when we do that. Which do you think would be more effective for your team?"

Another tactic is just to treat this as matter-of-fact. It's not up for debate; it's the way things are done!

"As your team gets up to speed, we want to do everything we can to help you get value as quickly as possible. Our most successful customers follow our recommended training plan, which begins with one hour of product knowledge e-learning. This helps your team be on the same page, and they'll be able to ask more meaningful and targeted questions in the classroom training. Can you let me know when your team will be able to complete the e-learning, so we can then get your classroom training scheduled?"

Either way, it's becoming increasingly common to withhold one-on-one time or classroom trainings until customers have completed some pre-work. The key, I've found, is for CSMs to be comfortable positioning the value of flipping the classroom. If they're confident in your self-paced learning and how it benefits the customer, then customers are more likely to accept the plan of action.

As the idea of pre-work becomes more common, you can offer flipped classroom options with confidence. If you also have social learning programs like a customer community, you can even extend your flipped classroom by having the cohorts who went through your courses join a private forum afterwards for continued discussion.

Make it interactive

If you're able to cut down your learning into bite-sized chunks and flip your classroom, it means that you'll be able to focus on making each individual experience more meaningful and interactive. Most trainings don't do this—we typically talk at learners instead of training them.

Why don't more trainings have interactivity? Why do we still allow an hour of talking at customers to be considered "training"? If your "trainings" are actually lectures and your "e-learning" is just a click-through "page turner," without any opportunity for learners to reflect or test their skills, then you're offering a passive experience.

It's harder to create meaningful interactivity than it is to put a subject matter expert in front of customers and lecture. Now we're back to the fundamentally flawed idea most of us have about training—that if we put an expert in the room and have them open up their head, remove their brain, and stuff it into the learners' heads, then knowledge is effectively transferred. Sorry, but it still doesn't work that way!

In most trainings, the facilitator does 80% of the talking. Imagine what your training would be like if your facilitator only did 20% of the talking.

Does everything need to be interactive? Help Center articles certainly don't, but I would argue that training does. If you expect behavior to change or skills to build, then you need to give learners an opportunity to practice the behavior and build the skill. You actually do your learner a service by putting less content in each course, and focusing instead on reinforcing the content in different ways, like text, video, simulations, and inter-activities.

Have you ever heard that people remember 10 percent of what they read, 20 percent of what they hear, 30 percent of what they see, and 90 percent of what they do? As we saw earlier with the Ebbinghaus Forgetting Curve, this isn't precisely true—the research on the percentages is pretty murky—but what is true is that getting hands-on practice makes training more relevant than if we just hear a lecture (or see a video) about a given topic.

Jesse Evans used a "I do, We do, You do" structure for courses at Box University:

> **I do:** The instructor briefly walks the learners through the skill that's being trained—still making sure to pause for inter-activity and questions *at least* once per slide.
>
> **We do:** The instructor has the class walk through the skill in a guided fashion, using a simplified scenario. The instructor asks, "Okay based on the scenario, what's the answer to the first question of the method? The second? The third?"
>
> **You do:** Now, the instructor gives another scenario, which learners work through on their own. They provide their answer, followed by why their chose their answer. This gives the instructor an opportunity to add more commentary or correction as needed.

Many Trainers and Instructional Designers use an approach called "Tell me, Show me, Let me try":

Tell Me: The instructor briefly introduces the skill, with emphasis on *why* it's important.

Show Me: The instructor walks through the skill in context, showing how it's done. This provides a model for students and allows them to ask questions.

Let Me Try: Now it's the learner's turn to try it out. This typically takes the form of guided practice, where the instructor gives feedback as the learner tries out the skill.

Note that you can use these models both for in-person training *and* self-paced content. For example, if you're building a self-paced online course, you could "tell" with a quick text snippet, "show" with a quick demo video, and "try" with a simulation activity created using a sandbox environment or an e-learning authoring tool.

Through interactivity, we learn by doing, and we learn more from our failures than from passively absorbing the "right" information.

Learning by Doing

When we include opportunities for practice, our learners can make mistakes and learn from them. Practice activities also give learners a chance to restate what they learned in their own words, and to put learners in the active teaching role instead of the passive student role.

Have you ever wondered why the best way to learn something is by teaching it yourself? We're going to need to talk about the brain for a moment—I promise it won't be too painful.

Research shows that your memory encodes information when you have to get it out of your head, not when you try to cram it in. When you first learn something new, it gets stored in your short-term memory. You probably try to get it to "sink in" by repeating it over and over, or re-reading the information.

If you do nothing else, the information will gradually fade away. But if you actively challenge yourself to recall the information—by quizzing yourself, by putting it in your own words, or by teaching the information to someone else—over time, that memory will encode into long term memory through the hippocampus. The more we try to recall information—and the more we space that recall over time—the more likely it is to encode.

In *Make it Stick* by Peter Brown, Henry Roediger III, and Mark McDaniel, one of my favorite books on the cognitive science behind learning, the authors describe the unique style of Mary Pat Wenderoth, a biology lecturer at the University of Washington.

She interrupts her lectures with periodic questions. When her students start to open their notes, she tells them not to look at their notes, but instead to try remembering the information themselves, in their own words. She asks them to imagine they're in the woods, looking for the information. The clearer the path her students can carve to find that information, the stronger the pathways in their brain become.

Learning by Failing

Oscar Wilde once said, "Success is a science; if you have the conditions, you get the result." But you don't get to success until you've learned from failure. For every quote about success, there's a more interesting one about failure.

Take Ray Dalio, for instance. He's the CEO of the hedge fund Bridgewater, and he famously said that "Pain + Reflection = Progress." Other CEOs, especially those in Silicon Valley, tend to embrace the mantra of "Fail Fast and Learn" or "Fail Forward."

And here, what's true for CEOs is true for Customer Education. If we're never given a chance to try something, and potentially fail at it, it's harder to learn from the experience. Many people are afraid to fail because it will hurt their ego, but if you take a learning approach to failure, considering it acceptable and even desirable as a learning experience, you'll often remember more from what you got wrong, instead of when you breezed through easy content and got it right.

So when you create learning experiences, consider starting with challenging scenarios that will force learners outside their comfort zone. And when you're writing assessments and quizzes, avoid easy "gimme" questions that you know the customer will get right. You know the ones I'm talking about—where the right answer is glaringly obvious and one of the distractor options is a joke answer.

Failure Leads to Feedback

We don't learn or move forward unless we experience some pain and reflect on it. As learners, we need the chance to try and fail in a safe space, and then reflect. And we can't reflect without getting meaningful feedback on what we tried. This can be done automatically if you've created your training using learning software that offers feedback, or can be done through peer grading in a user community, but we need feedback to keep learning and growing.

Quizzes and knowledge checks aren't just a way to keep track of learner's scores—they are great opportunities to give feedback. In fact, more and more cognitive science research shows the benefit of learning from testing. First of all, testing provides feedback on what we did well and where we can do better: we learn from failure more than we learn from success, so a test can potentially do more for a learner than a lecture where there's no chance to fail.

The authors of *Make it Stick* present a series of studies on "the Testing Effect," where periodic testing is shown to increase long term retention of knowledge and skills. In effect, needing to periodically retrieve and use what you learned helps you retrieve it more easily in the future.

Remember that spaced practice is more helpful in the long term than cramming. So before you decide that your one final certification exam is how you want to do all your assessment, consider placing more knowledge and skill checks throughout your courses.

Feedback doesn't necessarily need to be a box that pops up saying, "You got this question right!" or "Sorry, please try again." In fact, I'd argue that those are pretty basic, poor forms of feedback (even though they're the easiest types of feedback to build).

If you're able to, go beyond this simple "green checkmark/red X" feedback. After all, just telling someone that they got something wrong doesn't help them understand *why* they got it wrong, or what material they should return to if they want to better understand the concept. Try telling your learners what they should go back and study, or point them in the direction of the right answer so they can learn from their mistake.

Another reason why this simple style of feedback isn't always useful is that it only really helps for multiple choice or true/false questions. To get to deeper levels of learning, we often have to do more than just answer multiple choice questions. Often we need to walk through scenarios, complete projects, or try to demonstrate the skills we learned.

Feedback can manifest in different ways. The traditional place for feedback is the end of the scenario or assignment, where you give detailed feedback on how well they did. That said, you can also pause and give feedback throughout to help guide the learner on where they go next.

But sometimes the best feedback is experiential—for example, in a *Choose Your Own Adventure* book, when you make a choice, you experience *feedback* on that choice based on which page you turn to. The mummy that mauled you on page 67 is a form of feedback teaching you not to go around pulling bricks out of the Hall of the Sphinx. The same is true in games, where your actions often have immediate feedback. If you can *show*, not *tell*, the learner what effects come from their actions, you can often facilitate deeper learning.

And for everything else, job aids

If you've flipped your classroom and focused training on interactive skill-building, what happens to the rest of the content you were supposed to train customers on? Instead of trying to address it all during a course, let customers access that information afterwards using support resources and job aids.

What's a job aid? It's a tool that your customers can use on the job. This could be a flipchart, a laminate, an interactive spreadsheet, or an online Knowledge Base. These tools account for the fact that learners won't remember everything from training. With job aids and other post-training references, you equip them with the right resources to retrieve that information later.

Often in training, your time is better spent on interactivity, working through scenarios together, and practicing skills that will stimulate better recall later. Meanwhile, all that other reference information should be easily available to learners so they can simply look it up later. This is where Knowledge Bases, In-Product Education, and communities become effective tools in a Customer Education program. They make it easy to find the information on-the-job, long after the Forgetting Curve has taken its toll.

Building better content

Now that you learned all those theories, it's time to start improving all your content!

Hey, where'd you go? If I may coax you out of the trembling fetal position that you've entered, let's focus on this mantra:

You can't do everything well, but do *something* really well.

That's right, perfectionists—you can't do everything well. Not at first, and realistically not ever. If you try to do everything well, you'll most likely do nothing well. The old saying here is, "Don't let perfect be the enemy of done."

But my strong opinion is that you should find at least one way to differentiate yourself, measure it, and invest in it as a differentiator for your Customer Education function.

Sort of like your product should have a Unique Selling Proposition (USP), your education programs shouldn't just be fully airlifted from other industry "best practices" (which are often just mediocre practices), received wisdom, or necessarily even any of the techniques I provide in this book. Find something unique and special that you can invest in early—something that will stand out to your business and your customers. Even doing *one* thing in this chapter well will take you a long way.

Okay, let's get going. Time to improve our content.

GETTING IT WRITE

Clear, concise, and zippy text lessons can engage learners more than boring "interactive" e-learning pieces. Well-written Knowledge Base articles and guides serve as your first line of defense against unnecessary support tickets. If you don't gate your written content, it can also help you claim SEO value for your company.

With that in mind, craft clear, concise, and helpful writing.

Style guides

If you visit http://voiceandtone.com, you'll notice that the email marketing company MailChimp brilliantly reserved this URL for their written style guide. That's right: they take enough pride in their writing that they went through the trouble of reserving voiceandtone.com to build a style guide micro-site.

When you first arrive on the site, you see the following message:

"Before you write for MailChimp, it's important to think about our readers. Though our voice doesn't change much, our tone adapts to our users' feelings. This guide will show you how that works."

Then you can click through different examples of copy you'd find across MailChimp's blog, social media, Knowledge Base, legal copy, and more—each categorized with an imagined user's feelings and some tips for writing with the user in mind.

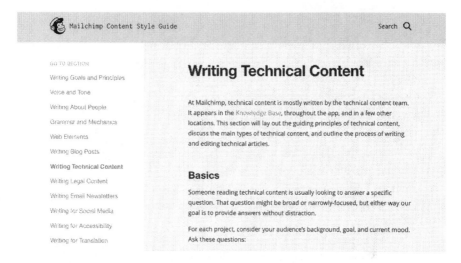

MailChimp's online style guide. https://styleguide.mailchimp.com/

MailChimp's Knowledge Base articles are meant to appeal to users' interest and curiosity. And though the example they give is more verbose than, say, their in-app copy, it holds true to the tips they provide:

Be straightforward. Your priority is to answer questions and inform readers. Unlike their public site, which can be clever (but not silly), or their in-app success messages, which can be funny and casual, the point of the Knowledge Base is to be helpful above all.

Avoid marketing speak. This resonates with me; when I work with some Support agents who are writing articles for the first time, they may write to customers with a friendly and helpful tone, but they start writing articles as if they were selling a timeshare in the Florida Keys. Be helpful, not flowery!

Keep your language and style consistent across articles. You likely have several ways to describe key concepts in your product. For example, at Optimizely we would always debate whether the thing you ran was a "test" or an "experiment," and whether the person who went to the site was a "visitor" or a "user." At Checkr, we debate whether the person getting background checked is a "candidate" or "applicant."

A style guide helps you capture the right voice and tone, and helps your writers stay as consistent as possible.

For example, at Optimizely, we started our Style Guide with this statement of purpose:

> Our customers are here to learn or get help. This context helps determine the approach we take. A friendly, helpful voice meets them where they are; a little humor and personality can make the process delightful.
>
> Customers who read a KB article should think, "Great, I can do this. I'm going to get started!" They shouldn't react with: "Yikes, this looks complicated. I'll figure it out later."

When you're setting your own voice and tone standards for articles, consider which voice and tone values you'll use. For example:

Human: Write in a friendly, relatable voice. When you're done, read it out loud. Trim down extra words and long sentences. Aim for a natural rhythm.

Helpful: Anticipate the customer's perspective; meet them where they are. Make it easy for customers to find the information they're looking for. What is the person thinking about when they first start reading? What do we want that person to be able to do by the end of the article?

Clear and concise: As the Economist Style Guide notes, "Clarity of writing usually follows clarity of thought. So think what you want to say, then say it as simply as possible."

Concrete: Be specific. Use examples (one, maybe two). Don't write in marketing-speak; say what you mean.

Actionable. Don't just tell customers what to do; show them how to do it. Provide helpful resources when you can. You may even want to define a "Call to Action" in some articles.

You can even provide resources like Hemingway (hemingwayapp.com), which lets you enter text, then see opportunities to make it more clear and concise.

Your style guide will also help set conventions for ambiguous areas of writing and style, and frequently missed points. For example:

> **You vs. I:** Do you write articles in the voice of the user—for example, "How do I use Widget X?" Or do you always use second person, as in "How do you use Widget X?"
>
> **Pronouns:** Do you use "they" as the singular pronoun (as in "When a user enters the product, they first click Button X"), "he," "she," "he or she," or something else?
>
> **Link text:** Do you link to <u>this article on using Widget X</u> or do you only link the portion that specifically talks about <u>Widget X</u>?
>
> **Contractions:** Are they OK? Or are not they?
>
> **Prescription:** Is it OK to write "You can use Widget X to solve this problem" (which makes it sound like an option), or just write "Use Widget X to solve this problem"?
>
> **Common product language:** Do you "click," "press," "hit," or "click on" a button? (Hopefully not "hit on.") Do you "log in" (as a verb) or "login"? "Set up" or "setup"? Do you "enter" or "fill in" a form field?

Finally, your style guide can even cover visual guidelines, such as what dimensions to use for screenshots and how to annotate or highlight images.

When you're first putting together a style guide, it doesn't need to be comprehensive—in fact, that may be overwhelming as you go from *no* style guide to *mega* style guide. Instead, start with the essentials: what are the most common inconsistencies your writers make? What are the biggest questions they have about writing? What are the essential tips that would help them get over the hurdle of writer's block?

Images

Novice writers are often told to "show, don't tell." While that advice usually refers to writing descriptively and artfully, in Knowledge Base articles you can literally show instead of telling.

Instead of writing long descriptions about how to go through a certain product workflow, use screenshots and even animated GIFs to show the process in action—especially if this is an action you want the reader to take. Seeing the process modeled visually reduces the effort it will take to recreate it.

After all, if you're reading a description like, "Click the settings button in the upper-right in order to activate the admin interface," that might raise more questions than it answers:

> What's the settings button? Does it say "settings" or is it a little gear icon?
>
> The upper-right of what? The entire window? The small section of the product that I'm in right now?
>
> What's the admin interface? Have I seen that before?

You could have saved the sixteen words it took to write the description, and all those mental questions the user had, if you had just taken a screenshot and annotated it. It's true what they say: a picture is worth at least sixteen words.

Longform and shortform content

Whether you're using your documentation for training, marketing, or customer support, consider search-friendliness. You want your documentation to be easily found through organic search as well as any search/knowledge management tools you're using on your site.

Conventional wisdom in the world of Knowledge-Centered Support tells you to write a lot of short, single-serve articles on specific topics so you can easily monitor which ones get used and which ones don't, and so the customer immediately understands whether they're looking at the relevant article. Then you can use "related article" functionality to suggest similar topics.

For a lot of companies, this works well. For others, this conventional wisdom leads them to a sprawling, unmaintainable tangle of single-serve articles, where it's really hard for a customer to tell which one is the most up-to-date, or which of these several related articles they should even be looking at.

The bigger your library of content gets, the more difficult it also becomes for Support reps and others in the organization to maintain the content, because there's more risk of duplicative or out-of-date content.

Instead, experiment with grouping shorter articles (especially those that aren't your most frequently viewed) into longer-form articles. In many cases, you may get more upvotes on those articles because, even though the customer had to scroll more to find information, they didn't have to click around between many different articles.

VIM, VIGOR, AND VIDEO

Written content is great, but video works better in many cases—especially for visual workflows that users can replicate.

If you happen to have a videographer on staff who can help with higher-production videos, all the better. But for smaller companies who don't, screen-capture video tools often allow you to produce videos relatively quickly with screen recording, callouts, and light animation.

Although video content has a higher production cost than written articles, articles with video tend to receive better feedback and are perceived as easier to understand than written instructions. This makes video worthwhile for the most common issues, topics, and workflows.

Video topics come with an inherent tradeoff: videos that take longer to make last longer, but videos that can be produced quickly usually need to be redone frequently.

Product Videos: Quick but disposable

Videos showing workflows in your product can be produced more quickly, but they have a shorter shelf life. You'll need to re-record them as your product changes. These are typically better served as quickly made, low-production videos.

Even for quick-and-dirty workflow videos, a little professionalism goes a long way. Learners are willing to forgive quite a few things, but audio quality isn't one of them. Invest in a professional-quality microphone (Many of my colleagues in the Customer Education world use the Blue Yeti USB microphone, which as of this writing is approximately $110 on Amazon).

One common question I hear is around video maintenance: While videos can be engaging, visual ways to communicate ideas and workflows, they also take work to maintain. For instance, when your product interface changes, you'll likely need to update videos to reflect it. I recommend having a strategy or philosophy around how often you'll do this? For instance, do you update the videos every time *any* change is made? Do you only update it when *major* changes are made? What qualifies as major? Do you audit videos on a regular basis to update them, with the most current product UI? How often?

I recommend auditing videos periodically and setting a threshold for what constitutes a "major" change, or enough "minor" changes to constitute a re-do. Learners are generally forgiving if the UI in the video looks slightly different, but sometimes if you make enough slight changes, the product will look significantly different. Any major change in functionality should also be a cue to re-do the video.

Another way to make video maintenance less burdensome is to make fewer product videos. Do you need a video for every feature of the product, or could you better spend that time doing your *top* features and *top* support issues? Avoid abstract feature tours for their own sake, and keep videos focused on workflows and practices that aren't intuitive in the product UI.

You can validate where to spend time on videos by spending some time with your customers. Watch them try to use your product, and look for the places where they just can't do what they want to do easily. If something is intuitive and easy to do, you probably don't need to spend time training on it. The trouble spots are the most fertile grounds for videos.

Conceptual videos: Slower but evergreen

The other area where videos may be helpful are "evergreen" topics, which don't go out of date as fast as your product UI. For instance, you may want videos discussing the strategy behind using your product, or industry topics that are related to your product.

These types of videos take longer to make because you have to figure out what will be on the screen at all times. Whether you use animations, stock photos, text, or recorded slides, you'll need to storyboard these out in advance. They'll also take longer to edit together.

On the low-production end, some people create slide decks and take video of those. On the higher-production end, some people use "talking heads" of experts discussing topics, live-action video, and motion graphics or animations. Unless you already have a videographer on staff and ready to help you, you probably don't want to start on the high-production end. One minute of high-production video can take weeks to produce.

IMPROVED IN-PRODUCT EDUCATION

Do you remember Clippy? The vaguely predatory anthropomorphic paperclip in late '90s-era Microsoft Office? The one who interfered in your progress more often than he helped you accomplish a task?

Twenty years later, we're still squandering In-Product Education opportunities on unhelpful copywriting, intrusive pop-ups, and information overload.

In-Product Education and Digital Adoption platforms have strong potential to increase user engagement and product adoption, free trial conversion, and ultimately account renewal. But, like most tools, you get out what you put in.

In-Product Education is a newer "surface" for many Customer Education professionals, but it's rapidly gaining adoption. If you're just getting started with user engagement or In-Product Education platforms, the following techniques will help you get started in the right direction.

Determine your strategy

In-Product Education tools are versatile, so you may be tempted to use them for anything that catches your fancy. But remember that once you build content, it has to be maintained and QA'd like any other product feature. It's best to start with a clear idea of what you want to build first. Here are some common options:

Drive adoption in the New User Experience (NUX) or First-Time User Experience (FTUX). The FTUX is the very first time you see a new product, and the NUX is a little more general, referring to the phase where you're still a new user. Typically In-Product Education in this experience helps to give the user some initial confidence and inspiration in using the product. Some Digital Adoption platforms even provide onboarding checklist features.

Drive conversion in a free trial. Similar to the function of a NUX, products that have free trial periods need to make sure that customers are up and running as quickly as possible, so that they'll see value in the product before the trial is over.

Reduce support burden. What's better than putting trouble-shooting tips in your Help Center? Putting them directly in the product! In-Product Education helped Optimizely reduce its most frequent support issues by making it easier for customers to get help.

Product and Growth Marketing. In-Product Education platforms can be used to target customers who haven't yet used certain features, exposing them to the value of those new features. Similarly, when your engineering team releases new features, you can cue users as to what's new.

New Products, Versions, or Redesigns. When you add new products to your portfolio, or redesign existing ones, there's a risk that customers become disoriented and disengaged. Here, providing them with a new path to adoption can help increase their desire to switch to the new version of the product and reduce friction along the way.

Use the right tool for the right interaction

Many In-Product Education platforms come equipped with several interaction types and templates. But when do you use which one?

Walkthroughs: These are the traditional step-by-step guides, which progress using a "Next" button. Different steps can either exist as free-standing modals (also known as "pop-ups") or they can be anchored to elements of your UI. Use these sparingly for key workflows in the product. Generally you should give your user the opportunity to stop these and resume them later. Users are less likely to drop off if they *chose* to enter step-by-step walkthroughs.

One-step modals: Unlike walkthroughs, these appear once and are then complete. Usually you would use this for a quick alert or update to the user. Again, because they're disruptive to the overall experience, try to keep these to a minimum unless the user clicked something to activate them.

Tooltips and badges: These are the little question mark icons that you click to learn more about something. Although users opt in to these by clicking them, they're usually quite small, so they're used to house a quick definition or explanation of a UI element. I recommend putting a "Learn more" link at the end of these, leading to your Help Center.

Banners (or "butter bars"): These are non-intrusive elements that still allow users to interact with the product. Generally, you would display these for issues or updates that are pervasive in nature, like a reminder to upgrade to a new version of the product or an announcement of an upcoming event.

Error states: These are essentially special modals that only appear when there's some sort of error. Now the user probably wants help, so it's a good time to offer them the option to go through a troubleshooting education flow in the product, or at least to link out to a relevant troubleshooting article.

Each of these cues presents a different way to convey information or prompt action.

Keep your flows short: The drop off struggle is real

When In-Product Education tools first became widely available to Customer Education teams, many of us had a tendency to use them as a basic product training. We'd send users through multi-step product onboarding tours, jamming as many steps as possible into the flow. In old-school Performance Support systems, you could do this because you generally had a captive audience of internal users.

But through analysis, we found that users generally won't stick around for more than three or four steps. Past that, you're probably telling them how to use the product instead of showing them through their attempts to interact with it.

For your walkthrough-style flows, ask yourself: what is the least amount of information you need to convey so that your user understands why they're supposed to be using this feature and what to do with it? Be ruthless with trimming out unnecessary steps—and even words.

Pendo, an In-Product Engagement platform, ran an analysis in 2016 to measure the average drop off in multi-step flows. As you may imagine, the results were dire. Even in two- or three-step flows, the average completion rate was around 30%. By four steps, completion neared 20%. By 15 steps, completion rate hovered just above 10%.

Here's what I take from these statistics:

> If 20% of your users finish an eight-step flow, and you have 100,000 users, then that's still 20,000 users who finished the entire flow (and presumably more who made it almost to the end). That may not be a bad thing.
>
> But I still suspect that the low completion rate is a product of us forcing multi-step flows upon users who aren't ready for it, so we should aim to keep our walkthroughs as concise as possible and as opt-in as possible.

One way to account for opt-ins to your walkthroughs is to try to reclaim the users who dismissed your onboarding earlier. **Make your flows progressive—avoid the "one-and-done" onboarding style**

How many times have you been given a product tour before you're ready for it? User research shows that most users are not ready for an extensive product tour the first time they use a product. More likely, they'll try to play around with the product (and maybe fail), and only then will they want to know how to do certain things.

So why do so many product tours show up the very first time you enter a site or app, waste your time before you have any context, and then disappear forever?

The mistake I see often is placing the product tour in a first-time user experience —the very first time a user enters a product. Instead, product tours and other key walkthroughs should be incorporated more broadly and progressively throughout new user experience. During your user onboarding phase, the goal of your In-Product Education isn't to do a complete product tour, but to gradually expose new features and use cases.

Try to use a progressive style with checklists, progress bars, or steps if it's an onboarding use case. The LinkedIn progress bar is a famous example of this, where you'd be asked to complete different profile steps on the road to 100% completion.

If your tour displays only once, the first time the user enters your product, and can never be reactivated—no one's going to look at your tour.

Experiment with style and multimedia

Typically, in-product help has taken three forms:

A step-by-step walkthrough done with popups or modals

"Coach marks" or instructional overlays that appear as an overlay on top of the interface (where the screen fades and there are arrows pointing at everything with labels)

A "contextual support" drawer that could be opened to give (usually verbose) information about the product

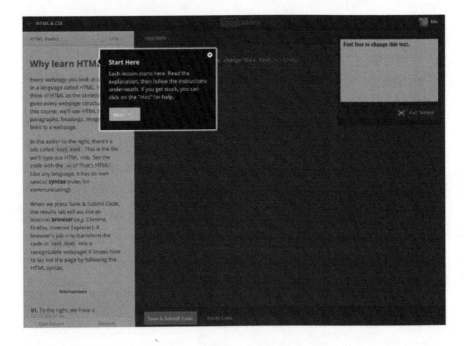

CodeAcademy uses walkthrough modals to introduce you to its UI.

Headspace provides coach marks in its UI.

Those work in some, but not all, cases. Be willing to experiment with different formats. Think about how much you want your in-app engagement flows to be fully integrated into the interface (so that it just looks like part of the product) vs. how much you'd like it to be more of a standalone experience.

For example, one of the most innovative user onboardings can be found in the communication app Slack, which embeds its onboarding and its help within its own chat interface. To onboard in Slack, you're not clicking into every feature. You're talking to a chatbot who progressively shows you things you can do.

Dropbox also takes an inventive approach, building assistance into its own UI. The first time you onboard in Dropbox, you get to see some sample files that help you learn how to use Dropbox's features.

Not everyone has the resources to do this, nor does everyone have a product that supports creative onboarding as easily. But you can still experiment with style: If you use walkthroughs or modals, experiment with how much they look like the regular modals that appear in your product.

On one hand, they could look exactly like any other window that pops up in your product; however, this may cause confusion for users. If they think they're looking at an error message ant not a guide, for example, you may be harming more than helping them. Alternatively, style them slightly differently from your core product, giving them a style and voice that still feels on-brand, but not identical to the rest of your product. Your Product Designers will typically have opinions on what's the best approach.

Limit your scope

With great power comes great responsibility. When you have the power to build in-app adoption content, you may have the impulse to put *all* your learning content in there, or to build flows for every single feature.

Don't use in-app walkthroughs to introduce every single product component. If you're making an inventory of everything you users might think to do, you're going to end up with an overwhelming product experience and a lot of maintenance headaches each time you change your UI; focus on the areas you already know users have trouble with or miss.

You might also be tempted to do a lot of fancy behavioral targeting and personalization (for example, let's deliver messaging X to customers in vertical Y who have clicked button Z). My advice is that you should only do that if you:

Know *why* you're doing that level of customization, not just because it seems cool.

Have the resources to build it (which is why you shouldn't just do it because it seems cool).

Can maintain it into perpetuity. The fancier you get, the easier it is to break as your product updates and changes.

If you do want to add some customization or personalization, try things like having some dynamic fields (for instance, you could say "Hello, [NAME]" or "Customers in [VERTICAL] industry most often use this feature in this way."

Once you try to add more layers of customization, you're essentially building a product that requires inordinate levels of QA. So if you're just starting, start simple. Deliver the content that has the most chance of moving the needle on customer satisfaction, support contacts, or key feature adoption.

Listen to your UX Designer

Most Customer Education teams who implement In-Product Education do so with the blessing of (or in partnership with) their Product Management and Product Design teams. Many companies have a Product Designer or UX Researcher on staff in one of those departments, and often that person knows a lot more about how to craft an effective design—no matter how many "UX for Learning and Development" sessions you went to at a conference.

Partner with this person or department; learn from their experience. You're more likely to have buy-in from your product and design teams—not to mention a better final product.

You down with OPP? (Other People's Products)

One effective way to get inspiration for In-Product Education is to see what other products do well (or not well). Observe how other products use different in-product UI elements to communicate different things to the user. Pay attention to whether they pop up in front of other content, whether they're "pushed" or "pulled" by the user, whether they block the user from interacting with the content, and how much content you need to put in them.

One of my favorite sites for this is useronboard.com, where Sam Hulick (an onboarding UX expert) tears down the experience of onboarding in several popular products, critiquing them step by step.

KEEPING CONTENT AGILE

Software used to be developed in a linear process—the requirements were gathered, then it was designed, then coded and developed, and then QA'd and acceptance tested. After a months-long process, it would be released to the customers, who would complain because the software was delivered late and didn't meet their needs.

This linear method is known as the "waterfall" model, because the software would cascade down from the source to the destination.

Eventually, a rival to the waterfall appeared. Known as "Agile," it prioritized building and releasing components of the software in short stages (usually called "sprints"). Development doesn't happen in succession, so the software components can be built in parallel. Using Agile methodologies, customers have more opportunities to see progress, and the team has more of an opportunity to re-scope the work as it progresses. Unlike waterfall development, Agile teams embrace change and continuous improvement.

Instead of placing the emphasis on a linear sequence of events, Agile instead focuses on routine and visualization as a way to manage development projects. Regular "stand-up" meetings and "sprint reviews" are used for collaboration and coordination. Progress is visualized and tracked in small chunks, instead of one large project plan.

For software companies, where products change frequently and Customer Education output is high, it only makes sense to learn from our peers in the engineering world.

ADDIE and SAM

Traditionally, Instructional Design followed its own type of waterfall model, called ADDIE. ADDIE is a linear design and development framework, which sees a project through the following stages:

Analysis: An Instructional Designer does all the upfront analysis necessary to scope the project. What is the problem? What is the desired outcome? How will this project change performance? Who are the subject matter experts and what do they know? What will the blockers to the project be? And so on.

Design: Now, the Instructional Designer proposes an instructional solution, like a classroom training or e-learning course. In a series of documents, they flesh out the design of the course, including what will be in each of the modules and what the assessment plan will be for each. The customer signs off on the design, which can't be changed after this point.

Development: The course is developed (sometimes by a different person than the Instructional Designer, like an Educational Content Developer). Slide decks and handouts are created, video components are shot and edited, and e-learning is developed.

Implementation: The customer finally gets to see the end result. A pilot course is delivered, or the e-learning is uploaded to the LMS. Very little can be changed at this point because the development work is done. Any future work will require a new project. Hope you got it right!

Evaluation: Based on the results of the pilot, the course gets rolled out more broadly. The course is evaluated based on how engaged learners were, how well they did on the assessments, and hopefully whether they applied the skills they learned.

And after a months-long process, the course would be released to the customers, who would complain because it was delivered late and didn't meet their needs. Where's a sad trombone when you need one?

For years, ADDIE was just the way you did instructional design (or at least the way you claimed you did instructional design), but as development became less costly and quicker, the flaws in ADDIE became clear. So just like Agile usurped the software throne from waterfall, ADDIE also found itself against the wall when the revolution came.

Most notably, Michael Allen, an e-learning pioneer and CEO of the training company Allen Interactions, proposed a successor to ADDIE: the Successive Approximation Model. That's right, say hello to SAM.

While SAM still includes analysis (called the "Preparation Phase"), it's not nearly as comprehensive as ADDIE's—with the intent being to get started on the project, and to be comfortable in the face of imperfect information.

Next, the project is planned and designed in an iterative manner. Each design is prototyped loosely (perhaps with a script, a storyboard, a wireframe, or some other rough-draft content) and put in front of the customer for evaluation. The same goes for development: After the design is approved, each component can be developed, implemented, and evaluated in a successive manner, with an "Alpha" release, a "Beta" release, and so on as feedback continues to roll in.

One of the failures of ADDIE is the amount of time that elapses before a customer sees your work, so it's possible for Instructional Designers to produce content that doesn't match your current product. If it doesn't resonate with customers, developing the content was not time well-spent.

In software, the concept of MVP (Minimum Viable Product) refers to the first working version of a product that can be deployed to customers. Instead of being perfect, it's got *just enough* to meet early customer needs. From the MVP, you continue to get feedback from customers, test different approaches, and iterate based on the data you have.

We Customer Education types are often perfectionists, so we must learn to embrace the MVP as a way of sharing content with our customers before we think it's entirely ready. Note that MVP doesn't mean "I forgot to QA it and released it with a ton of bugs"—your customers shouldn't replace your job of quality controlling your own content. If you find yourself overcorrecting from ADDIE and releasing incredibly buggy products, then consider changing your approach to a "MVPP" (Minimum Viable Product you're Proud of).

When you're developing content—especially in large projects such as multi-stage academy courses or certification programs—you'll almost certainly benefit by piloting it with customers whom you trust and who are eager to experiment with you. By showing them designs and prototypes throughout your development cycle, you can get feedback before it's too late, and use it to iterate to perfection.

Yes you Kanban

One element of agile development that can prove useful for Customer Education teams is the Kanban board—a way of visualizing a workflow using cards on a board.

In a project, you would write each component (whether that's a course, lesson, article, video, bug fix, or customization task) on a card. The cards can be color-coded to represent different types of work. Place that card on a whiteboard divided into different sections or lanes. In Customer Education, those sections may be:

Backlog: things you know you want to do but haven't been able to prioritize yet.

On Deck: things you're about to do in the next period of time, but haven't started yet.

In Progress - Plan (or Design): things you're mapping out.

In Progress - Doing: things you're working on.

Review (or Testing): things that have been created and are now being reviewed by someone else.

Done: things that are done. Celebrate!

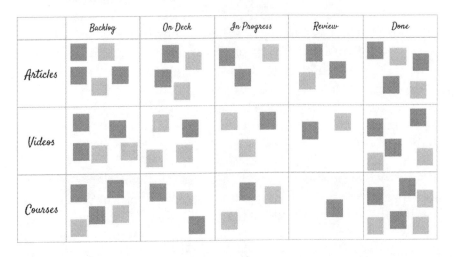

Example of a Kanban board for Customer Education.

Depending on what you're using your board for, you may need different stages. For example, if you're using your board purely to track e-learning, then your board may map to the different stages of the Successive Approximation Model. If you're using it for articles, then maybe it's simply a Doing - Review - Done model. If you're tracking them all on the same board, then more generic categories that encompass different types of work may help.

Because the different pieces of work are clearly displayed on cards, it's harder for work to hide in a project plan, where it gets forgotten without a Project Manager to run around and harangue people. Instead, you conduct regular standup meetings with your team in front of the board where you review the work that's in progress.

Generally, with a Kanban board, you want to observe three rules:

Limit work in progress: Whether you measure this in terms of the team's capacity, or each team member's capacity, you want to limit the amount of work that's "In Progress" (active work like design and development). This way, you know that the team member working on the progress has limited distractions and can focus on finishing what's in progress. Some teams even gamify WIP limits by visualizing them with lego blocks.

Finish before you start: When walking through the Kanban board in a stand-up meeting, it's important to start from the right-side of the board, pulling work that is nearly complete into "Done" status. This is what frees up a spot for you to introduce new work into the "In Progress" lanes. Only at the end should you pull new work from "On Deck" into an "In Progress" stage.

Have a system for what moves from "Backlog" to "On Deck": For a while, my team at Optimizely would just continuously pull new work from the backlog as it became available. This led to a sense of endless work without structure, and it didn't give us an opportunity to debate what was most important to put on deck based on our priorities. We eventually moved to bi-weekly sprint review meetings where we would celebrate all that we had accomplished and decide as a team what work was most important to place on deck for the next two weeks. High-urgency items could be added as needed, but with the Kanban board in place, it was easier to communicate what other work those urgent items would displace.

Both Optimizely and Checkr use an agile methodology to keep track of inputs and outputs and visualize activity and progress through a Kanban board. Optimizely's Education team would do stand-ups several times a week to keep track of what's in progress and where potential blockers lie. Checkr's cross-functional documentation team meets bi-weekly to review the status of work.

In both cases, we experimented with physical boards as well as digital boards, which many project management software tools provide. If you're debating the digital vs. physical board, consider a few tips:

> **Your best option is the one you actually use.** Instead of getting caught in a debate about what's ideal, I'd recommend making a quicker decision and commit to revisit it later. If the board's not getting used, who cares if people thought it was the ideal solution? For example, a digital solution might give you better tracking on how long a card stays in each stage, so you can do analytics on it later, but that same system may make it hard to create and move cards. That's not going to help you build a habit around Kanban.

> **Physical is better for "in-your-face" reminders.** When your Kanban board is physical, it usually sits somewhere near your team. This makes it easy for the team to look at every morning and remember what's most important to work on. It also makes it easy for you to do stand-ups around the board, and to have the tactile feeling of moving cards around. Digital boards are easier to forget.

> **Digital is better for distributed teams.** If your team is centralized in one office, having the board in front of you is helpful, but what about distributed teams? If you have one or two remote members, you can have them virtually attend the stand-ups in front of the board with a webcam, but at a certain point, it's going to be easier to just put the board online where everyone can access it.

Build a habit around your Kanban board so that looking at it, and using it to prioritize, becomes second nature. Like any new habit, it will feel unnatural at first, but it becomes a valuable way to manage work.

MEET YOUR METRICS

MEET YOUR METRICS

Customer Education metrics aren't easy. In a few critical ways, it's harder to measure the effectiveness of Customer Education than to measure traditional internal L&D. Why? Your learners aren't right there in the building with you, and it's and it's harder to actually see what changes take place after the training. So early on in your Customer Education journey, it's necessary to gain trust and sponsorship from your executives, then start proving the efficacy of your programs.

Executives increasingly care about the results that Customer Education departments yield. LEO Learning noted in its annual report of emerging learning trends that between 2017 and 2018, education teams saw a 71% increase in "executive pressure to measure learning's impact."

Just like product development or brand marketing, Customer Education is a "big bet," a high-effort but high-value investment that will pay off later. Once you *do* get your department up and running, and you're able to see the impact it provides, the rewards can be huge. You'll be able to see how Customer Education influences your customer growth and retention rates, support ratios, marketing impact, and more.

Yet in both the 2017 and 2018 LEO surveys, learner satisfaction ranked as the number-one way to measure the department's success, above ROI, performance improvement, or organizational impact. Customer Education leaders have to get better at showing the impact of their programs, beyond just how happy customers are with it.

As you're setting up your Customer Education strategy, you'll want to know whether the strategy is successful, so that you can show its impact to your broader team. You'll also want to know how to build on your strategy and improve it over time, to be sure you're headed in the right direction.

To do this, you'll need to look for effective **value metrics** that show the overall value of your Customer Education function. These are the "storytelling" metrics that you'll report out to the rest of your business to show your impact.

You'll also need **operational metrics** that give you more actionable insights into your individual programs. These aren't necessarily for reporting out to the business; they're metrics that you use to gauge the health of your programs, and to measure the success of individuals on your team.

You'll eventually need both types of metrics, but which do you tackle first? This section will discuss which metrics you can use for each category, and some of the tradeoffs of going after one or the other.

Operational metrics

Before you get to the success metrics for your overall strategy, you can often find "leading indicators" of success—earlier metrics that tell you how well your Customer Education activities are going. These operational metrics allow you to see if you are headed in the right direction and let you change course early, re-prioritizing or de-prioritizing initiatives as necessary.

Google Analytics is fine for answering some basic questions about your online content. For example:

Unique Visitors: How many people are visiting my site? Is my viewership growing or shrinking?

Sessions and Pageviews: When people visit my site, how much of it do they explore?

Audience: How many of the people visiting the site are new vs. returning? Have I created resources that people return to over time?

Acquisition: How do people get to my content? Are they coming in through search engines, links from my product, or other ways?

Behavior: Which pieces of content are most highly viewed? Are those the pieces I *want* people to see?

These are fine questions to answer using your analytics tool, especially if those are the only metrics you can access. But it would be a mistake to use these default metrics as your main goals; you have to know what you want to achieve, then find the appropriate and available metrics to measure your progress.

For example, if you're using Google Analytics, you probably won't be able to answer some key questions about the metrics it provides:

Is bounce rate good or bad? Does a high bounce rate mean that the customer found the right information and then left the site? Or did they leave because they got frustrated?

Is scroll depth good or bad? Does it mean that the customer engaged with the article and read the entire thing? Or did they have to search through the whole thing to find a specific piece of information?

How many pageviews is the right number of pageviews per session? Do I want people to view one page because it was the correct page? Or does a higher pageview count indicate that customers were engaged with our content?

Even for sites that don't offer help or learning content, these metrics can easily be vanity metrics. They might show a line going up and to the right, but what do they actually tell you about your content? What happens when the trend you've been happily showing to your company reverses, and you don't have an explanation?

As you'll see, looking at these metrics in a vacuum, especially without any other qualitative feedback, is a recipe for disaster.

Regardless of the specific metric you use, you generally want to show that your customers are finding what they want, when they want it. This will look a little different depending on what type of Customer Education you're doing, so I'll show you a few basic frameworks to put in place.

With each metric, try to get a baseline at the beginning, set an improvement goal for the next one or two quarters, and experiment fearlessly to move that metric in the right direction.

KNOWLEDGE BASE METRICS

With Knowledge Base platforms, you aim to help customers self-serve when they have questions. You want them to get a clear and helpful answer before they need to contact your Support team. So, success hinges on the *discoverability* of the content, and the *value* customers derive from it.

Discoverability

How many customers are finding a particular piece of content? Which content is being used the most? The simplest way to determine this: pageviews. Once you know which content is most highly viewed, you can make sure that the content is well-written, up-to-date, and helpful.

For highly viewed content, you look into the referral sources. How are people finding this content: organic searches, like Google? Referral links from your marketing site or your product? "Direct" links, which may come from your Support team or other sources?

You want to know which channels are driving the most traffic to your sites so that you can decide whether to amplify those channels, or change course and try to put more effort into other channels.

Whether customers find your content using organic search like Google or an internal search engine on your site, the customers' search terms can also give you a fuller picture of what customers are trying to find. Google Analytics, Webmaster Tools, and Search Console can give you this information. Some on-site search tools can identify which search terms yield zero results (although this feature can sometimes be useless, depending on how much content you have and how powerful your search tool is).

Typically there will be a cluster of basic terms that many customers search for. Make sure that these very common terms yield the right articles when a user searches. Also, audit those articles regularly to make sure that they're up to date and have high helpfulness ratings from users. If not, prioritize fixing them.

Then there's a "long tail" of queries, which you can either analyze manually (I promise you'll find some funny ones) or feed into a text parsing tool to see if there are any common phrases turning up. Sometimes the same phrases will appear in multiple queries, even if the exact queries are different. These long-tail queries can help paint a more vivid picture of what users are trying to find.

One pro tip here: Exclude your company IP addresses when you do this analysis, especially if your Support agents and CSMs use organic search to find articles. I bet you many of them do, even if you have an internal search tool.

Once you've identified your discoverability data, you can work closely with your Customer Success and Marketing teams to understand what people are searching for and create educational content geared toward that.

You can also work more closely with your product team to produce help content within your product. For example, at both Checkr and Optimizely, our most frequently discoverable articles were prominently linked from the product itself. When these corresponded to common support issues, we saw the number of customer contacts around those issues drop, because it became easier for customers to answer their own questions instead of getting frustrated, losing productivity, and contacting our Support team.

Now you'll be turning discoverability into an advantage, not an obstacle.

Value

When customers find content, how effective is it for them? If it's a support article, does it solve their problem? If it's a strategy or "best practice" article, does it help them implement a new idea? If it's an FAQ, does it A the Qs that are actually F?

Most Knowledge Base software comes equipped with an upvote/downvote button, so you can get at least a broad sense of customer sentiment toward your articles. If you want to get more sophisticated feedback, you can implement an embedded survey tool that allows you to ask deeper questions.

At Optimizely we used a survey widget to get a sense of whether content was helpful to customers. After asking "Was this article helpful?" we branched the survey to ask why the article was or wasn't helpful. For instance, a customer might find an article unhelpful because it's out of date and the product looks different now. It might be unhelpful because it's written unclearly. It might be unhelpful because the customer was searching for something entirely different.

To measure helpfulness, I recommend using a binary scale (upvote/downvote) or a 1 – 4 scale (which forces respondents not to sit on a "neutral" 3).

One upvote or downvote won't tell you much, but the trends will tell you much a lot more. Look for articles that receive high-volume positive or negative feedback to understand why, and make changes as needed. You can then use your upvote-downvote ratio overall as a measure of health. I call this the "Helpfulness Index," and I generally measure it as the number of upvotes over the total number of votes. You can also measure it as upvotes vs. downvotes—just be consistent about how you track it. Measure the Helpfulness Index and aim to improve it over time.

How do you analyze helpfulness if you're not already receiving a huge volume of upvotes or downvotes for customers? For one, your content probably isn't discoverable enough. But you can also audit content before it becomes a problem for customers.

In addition to the helpful/unhelpful indicator, we gave customers the option to provide a written response. Aside from a few responses where customers thought they were actually contacting our Support team, the free text responses gave us good insight into things we could quickly fix in each article.

Content Audits

An effective Customer Education program requires you to have a content strategy. Professional Content Strategists, who deal with high volumes of content in their jobs, must perform regular content audits. Kristina Halvorson, CEO of the Content Strategy firm Brain Traffic, recommends in her book *Content Strategy for the Web* that you catalog your existing content to inventory the title, URL, format, source (who created the content), metadata (like tags or keywords), traffic and usage metrics, time of last update, and language. This will give you an idea of how much content you have, where it can be found, and how useful or discoverable it is.

Don't just look at your Knowledge Base in a vacuum; look for other places where customers might find similar information. For example, try Google searching some common questions you hear from customers and prospects and see what comes up. Does your company have "FAQs" on your marketing site that provides information similar to what's in your Knowledge Base?

Partner with your Marketing team to audit your content and find gaps. For example, customers and prospects typically have questions that aren't really "feature documentation" topics, but are nonetheless common questions in the buying and onboarding process.

For Optimizely, those were questions like "How long does it take to run an A/B test?" "What are common test ideas for e-commerce companies?" and "How do I use Optimizely on a Single Page App?" At Checkr, we see questions like, "How long does the average background check take?" or "What are the legal requirements for background checks on W-2 employees vs. independent contractors?"

This is a great initiative for you to collaboratively focus on with your Marketing team. You may be able to create "marketing site" and "help site" versions of the same content to increase prospect and customer knowledge.

There's one more way to look at value: how often are your Support reps using a given article? If an article is commonly used in support tickets, it's probably generating value for customers (and it's almost certainly generating value for your Support team).

Many support ticketing systems use tags, which you can configure to analyze how often your Support agents reference help articles. This way, you can analyze which articles appear most often in support tickets, and which agents use them most frequently.

Sit with your Support teams, your CSMs, and your Sales-humans to find out what questions they're answering from customers and prospects on a repeated basis, or what customers are trying to accomplish with your product. Using that information, you'll be able to prioritize creating relevant content, and you can help customers access this information more easily.

Discoverability and Value in a Content Cycle

Once you're tracking discoverability and value, it becomes easier to categorize the content you have and take action based on your analysis. By collecting data and acting on it, you can create a content development cycle that lets you iterate and improve content over time.

Think of your content development cycle in two main phases: input collection and output creation.

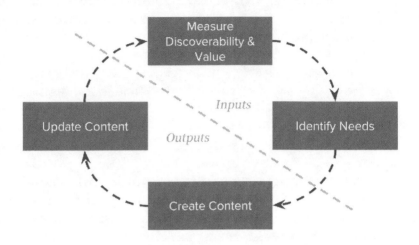

Inputs and outputs in a content cycle.

In the **input collection phase**, you gather metrics and identify the most pressing needs. Your inputs will include:

Gaps: feedback from Support agents and account managers on frequently asked questions and customer pain points that you *haven't* yet documented.

Discoverability: most-viewed help articles and common search terms that aren't documented properly. Avoid analysis paralysis—your focus here shouldn't be on collecting the *most* data, but the *most actionable* data.

Value: upvotes, downvotes, qualitative feedback from your customers, and how frequently the article is referenced in support tickets.

In the **output creation phase**, you act on the highest-priority opportunities. Your outputs are the pieces of content you create and include:

Knowledge Base articles and written content, which require a lower time investment to create. They're also easily indexed into organic search, so they may be easier to find.

Videos or **interactive modules** are better for showing on-screen processes or helping users think through more complex topics. If your video is going to be longer than about five minutes, it's probably not an appropriate medium for Help Center content.

Macros (canned responses) for your Support team to use as part, but not all, of their customer responses. These are best for explaining repetitive concepts that your rep would normally have to type out repeatedly.

As you author new content, continue to index the discoverability and value of each piece of content. Tracking these two metrics helps you determine whether a given article is worth updating vs. retiring, and gives you a "heatmap" for where you should be focusing the most attention.

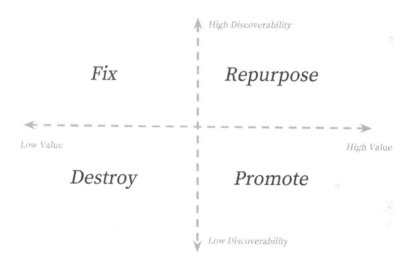

Taking action on content measurement

Discoverability and value are interesting indicators of health on their own, but the gaps between them create opportunities for improvement:

If content is *discoverable* but *not valuable*: Edit it for clarity, add images or video, and ensure it addresses to common feedback. Ask your Support reps what would better help the article solve the customer's problem.

If content is *valuable* but *not discoverable*: Try different approaches like changing the title or exposing it to customers in different ways, such as e-mail campaigns or in-product triggers. Try inserting terms that will help boost its SEO. Remember that organic search and in-product links are often the best drivers of traffic.

If content is already *both discoverable and valuable*: Great content can be repurposed. For example, this is probably content you want to highlight in your onboarding training. If the content isn't already in a video, it might be a prime candidate to become one. There's one other thing to think about when content is both discoverable and valuable—why are customers still looking for it? Consider whether there's a product issue. If customers keep looking for content on a certain troubleshooting issue, that's great feedback for your product team. Perhaps it's something they can fix.

If content is *neither discoverable nor valuable*: You have permission to destroy it. Just because someone thought it was a good idea to write an article about something two years ago, that doesn't oblige you to maintain that content now.

Over time, if you use a content cycle like the one I've described, you'll accumulate a healthy body of documentation, strategic best-practice articles, help content, FAQs, and more. Hopefully if you've been paying attention to your metrics, your content has become so helpful that it's a competitive advantage for your business, and customers use it to self-serve so often that it's not necessary for them to contact Support.

Some companies I've spoken to have fully embraced processes like Knowledge Centered Support (KCS), which allow individual Support agents to produce a high volume of content. After a certain point, the sheer volume of content ends up making it hard to find the content that's actually useful—both for agents and for customers. Ouch. Now, with each product update, each new feature release, and each new strategy framework you release, you need to continue updating your help and learning content. Do you have the team in place to sustain that?

This is the problem that many Customer Education and Documentation teams face, especially ones that have opened up documentation to their broader team through processes like KCS. This isn't something that companies always think about as they build up their documentation content. More content can equal more out-of-date content.

Respond to trends in data

Downvotes happen. If you're in the support content world, you've made your peace with the fact that you won't satisfy everyone 100% of the time. No matter how good your content is, sometimes someone still won't get what they need. So take downvotes for what they are: the gift of feedback. Sometimes the feedback is immediately implementable (like when customers catch typos), but most isn't. Whether it's an unclear comment, or no comment at all, many pieces of feedback are unhelpful in isolation but tremendously helpful in the aggregate.

You probably categorize your articles already: Most Knowledge Bases structure their content by product section or issue type. If you use additional tags in your Knowledge Base, you may also be able to tag articles by their function.

What does the article do?:

> Troubleshoot a *problem*?
> Answer a common *question*?
> Describe a process or *strategy*?
> Describe a *feature*?

What type of article is it?:

> Quick Start guide?
> User guide?
> Full feature document?
> Troubleshooting walkthrough?
> Release note?
> FAQ?

The more you can break down your overall helpfulness ratio by category, the better you can understand what types of articles are doing well or poorly.

From this data, you can form simple hypotheses and test them. What if you improved this highly viewed, highly downvoted article in a certain way? What if you combined these rarely viewed articles into one larger, master article? See what these improvements do not just for the individual article, but to the broader trends in your data.

Ask yourself where updates are essential

Many documentation teams waste time making updates that aren't essential. For example, if your product design team makes a minor change to the UI, does that trigger you to update all of your articles and videos that show the UI?

Obviously, in an ideal world, we'd like all documentation to perfectly mirror the UI that the customer sees. But thinking more broadly, many customers would probably choose to have your product innovate and iterate quickly than to have docs that 100% mirror the UI.

So ask yourself—does it really matter if we changed this font size, moved that logo, or changed the name of this column? Will it meaningfully improve our users' ability to get things done in the product? Or could we take the time that we're spending updating minor things to produce fundamentally more helpful content for our users? Our time is valuable because our customers' time is valuable.

Plan the work, and work the plan

You won't be able to do this discoverability and value work all at once, but you can start by focusing on SMART (specific, measurable, achievable, results-oriented, time-bound) goals. Start with an internal dashboard for your most-viewed content, most-upvoted content, top search terms, and other key metrics that help you focus your attention and set quarterly goals. For instance, try setting achievable quarterly goals like:

Create content for your top five search terms that don't have an associated article

Get your five most downvoted articles to net-positive status

Create video content for your five most popular articles and measure their engagement

With each of these goals, you should be able to measure the impact on discoverability or value. In turn, you should see progress against your key goal metrics over time.

TRAINING METRICS

For training—whether in a classroom, a virtual classroom, or a self-paced online academy—there's a generally accepted way to measure the operational soundness of a program.

Dating back to the 1950s, the Kirkpatrick Model, named after Donald Kirkpatrick, was the first four-level evaluation model created for learning. To this day, the Kirkpatrick Model still forms the basis of how many L&D professionals think about measuring learning effectiveness. The four levels, from most immediate to most long term are Reaction, Learning, Behavior, and Results.

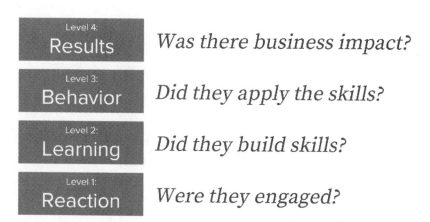

Level 4: Results	*Was there business impact?*
Level 3: Behavior	*Did they apply the skills?*
Level 2: Learning	*Did they build skills?*
Level 1: Reaction	*Were they engaged?*

The Kirkpatrick Model of training evaluation

Level One: Reaction

The first thing you generally want to know about a training is, "Did the customer like it?" While some training professionals measure this by the number of heads nodding minus the number of drool puddles emanating from the gaping maws of sleeping participants, the more common way to measure Reaction is through what training insiders call a "smile sheet."

The "smile sheet" is a post-training survey. Generally, it will ask a few simple questions about the quality of the content and the quality of the facilitator (if it was a facilitated training). It's important to separate these out because a fantastic Trainer can save the worst content in the world, and conversely, strong content can be tanked by a dull Trainer.

One thing to consider when developing a survey is whether you want a "neutral" option or not. In a four-point evaluation system, your ratings look something like this:

1 = Strongly Disagree
2 = Disagree
3 = Agree
4 = Strongly Agree

When you have five points, your ratings become:

1 = Strongly Disagree
2 = Disagree
3 = Neutral
4 = Agree
5 = Strongly Agree

For questions about the quality of the training, or the facilitator, it's often better to leave a "neutral" option in, because participants may not have a strong opinion.

Some companies also like to measure reaction using Net Promoter Scores (NPS), which asks "On a scale of 0 to 10, how likely are you to recommend this training to a friend or colleague?" If your organization widely uses NPS, you may consider using it for your training measurement as well. That said, I wouldn't recommend using the 0-10 scale for *every* question. NPS is mainly designed to measure customer loyalty and likelihood to promote your business.

Two other areas to gauge in the smile sheet are:

How *engaging* learners found the training—in other words, how interactive was it? Did they get opportunities to involve themselves and try things hands-on, or was it just a lecture?

How *relevant* the training was. Will they be able to apply the skills or subject matter in their everyday jobs?

Level Two: Learning

So they liked it, but did they learn anything? It's possible that you could see high satisfaction scores attributed to a morally bankrupt Trainer who, in exchange for high ratings, handed out gift certificates to Olive Garden so that all participants could treat themselves to unlimited soup, salad and breadsticks.

It's also possible that learners found a particular training entertaining because the Trainer was charismatic or the videos were funny, but without an opportunity to practice hands-on skills, they didn't actually learn anything.

Typically, learning is measured by a pre- and post-assessment, where you gauge the learners' knowledge, skills, and attitudes (KSAs) at both the beginning and at the end of the training, then measure the delta.

In reality, the pre-test commonly gets left out, but I think it's actually pretty powerful to include it if you can. Why? Learning research shows that when you start by presenting learners with tough challenges or questions that are hard to answer, they're more likely to be receptive to learning. This stands in contrast to the approach many training programs take, where we simply start with the easiest material because we're afraid of challenging our learners. As a result, we bore everyone in the session who nows the basics already.

When we measure KSAs before and after training, here's what we're looking for:

> **Knowledge:** Does the person now know the concepts that were trained?
>
> **Skill:** So what if they know it, can they *do* it? Can the person now do the thing that was trained?
>
> **Attitude:** Remember intrinsic motivation. They'll only do what you trained if they *want* to, so does the person believe that they'll now actually do the thing that was trained?

When many companies build certification programs for their products, they're often just doing a large-scale assessment of learning. They want to see whether a customer knows enough about how to operate the product, can successfully operate it, and actually wants to operate it.

Level Three: Behavior

So they learned something, but are they actually going to do it?

You might hear this referred to as "learning transfer"—in other words, how do I know that learners are going to take this stuff out of the classroom and transfer it into everyday use in their jobs?

Imagine for a moment that you and your team are the customers of a particular software product. Think about a piece of software you're supposed to be using all the time, like a CRM or Support ticketing software. Your team members are responsible for using the product effectively.

You see a report showing that your whole team attended a training session and got a passing grade on the certification exams. They also seemed to enjoy the course. The Trainer was a laugh-riot and handed out stickers.

But over the next few days, as you're meeting with your team and walking the floor, you notice that almost none of your team ever seems to have the software up on their screens. When they do, they seem to be clicking around aimlessly. They start coming to you and complaining about the new software, asking why they have to use it in the first place and saying it's too hard. And worst of all, customers and stakeholders are starting to complain because your team isn't doing what they need to do in the software.

Now, take your customer hat off and put on your education hat. Wasn't that a terrifying scenario? It seems like, even though they "got trained," and were "certified," the team in this scenario wasn't able to apply those skills on their job. This shows the risk inherent in treating training like a state. It doesn't quite matter if you, as a human, are "trained" or "untrained"—it matters if you changed your behavior.

When companies go whole-hog after measuring training attendance and certification achievements, but don't measure behavior change or outcomes, they open themselves up to risk. Once customers are trained, you have to determine whether they're *also* doing the things you expect them to. The skills you taught in training must now be applied on the job.

For software products, adoption metrics generally tell you whether customers are applying the skills you taught. Do customers use the software more post-training? During onboarding, time to first value or time to full ramp are helpful metrics to look at. We'll come back to these when we discuss value metrics.

Level Four: Results

Think of this one as the metric that helps to calibrate and validate the others. After you've successfully changed behavior, you need to be able to measure that the behavior change generated the outcomes that you wanted.

For a Customer Education team, that typically means that you're looking at whether the training caused a change in long-term product adoption, lead generation, customer retention, and account expansion.

We shouldn't be measuring the number of classroom hours delivered or the learners' satisfaction scores without also looking at the impact that Customer Education has in driving broader results for the customer.

Often, we treat learning transfer like the afterthought, choosing to pack our training agenda full of topics and deciding what to measure later. As you start to develop more content, consider how you can flip this. Start by thinking about what your learner is actually going to be doing after they've learned the content. Think about what tools you can provide them on the job to make it easier. Think about what they're going to be asking after the course is complete. And, if you want to measure the effectiveness of your program, think about how you'll measure learner performance after the course. This is the reason you want to design the education in the first place, and provide tools along the way that help customers actually get better at doing their jobs.

I'll discuss these metrics more in the later section on value metrics, but suffice it to say that collecting these metrics is *hard*. So hard, in fact, that many teams just don't do it.

Why are they so hard to collect and analyze? First of all, they usually require access to data housed in systems that don't talk to each other. For example, to know whether training engagement has any sort of correlation to renewal, you need for your training engagement data to live in the same system as your renewal metrics. So unless you have a system that's already porting all of your training data into your CRM, or exporting all of this data into your data warehouse, then your only option at first might be to do ad hoc analyses in a spreadsheet. For example, export a list sampling your customers who churned or renewed in the past year, and manually mark whether they have been trained so you can analyze the impact of training on renewal.

The other difficulty in collecting and analyzing the results of a training is that the further out you get from measuring the training itself, the harder it is to prove that any of the effect you're seeing is causal and not just correlative. For example, if you release a new feature and then do a training on it, how do you know that the uptick in customer adoption came from the training, and not the mere fact that you released the new feature?

To be fair, you likely won't be able to measure these types of results on day one, but it's still important to come in with a perspective on what results you are looking for and a plan for how you can reach the right depth of data analysis to measure your program performance. This is something you'll likely have to lobby for continually.

Kirkpatrick+

Since Kirkpatrick first developed his four-level model, others have adapted it and added new levels. While these adaptations have created a schism in the world of L&D orthodoxy, they can also be of benefit to you by giving you more measurement options. I call these additions "Kirkpatrick+."

Level 0: Attendance

The Kirkpatrick Model begins with an assumption that everyone is attending training. That's not always true, especially in Customer Education, as training often isn't mandatory for the customer. Level 0 gives you a measure of who participates in the training. Most webinar tools and Learning Management Systems will give you reporting on who has or hasn't attended a particular training.

Level 5: ROI

After Kirkpatrick released his original model, others came onto the scene to enhance it. Arguably the most notable training professional to build on the Kirkpatrick model was Jack Phillips, who is now the founder and CEO of the ROI Institute, Inc.

Phillips adds a fifth level, ROI, which takes the "Results" level and compares it to the cost of creating the program. He also recommends measuring impact throughout each of the previous four levels: in other words, taking continuous measurement and surveys to determine whether the change you're seeing is due to the training itself, or some other factor.

I'll come back to Phillips and his ROI model when I discuss value metrics.

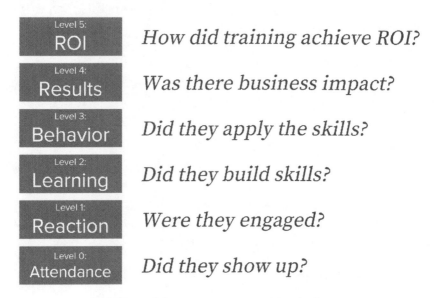

Kirkpatrick+ measurement techniques

Measuring Drop Off

One thing that's changed dramatically since Kirkpatrick first developed his four-level model is that, well, the Internet happened. And as training went online, it became easier to measure drop off. Drop off didn't really matter as a metric when trainings were all in-person, because what were you going to do—measure the number of people who just walked out in the middle of your class?

Today, though, it's not just customers rage-quitting your classroom training that you have to worry about. Drop off is real in the world of online learning, whether it's customers signing up to attend your training webinar and then dropping off in the middle, or customers starting a course and never returning to finish it.

Six years after the dawn of the modern MOOC (that's Massive Open Online Courses)—widely hailed in 2011 as the future of learning—MIT and Harvard University released a seemingly damning report showing that only 5.5% of people who enrolled in a MOOC actually finished it. Other similar studies from Udemy and Coursera reported average completion rates of 4%—and cited that on average, students only consume 30% of the material.

If you're doing virtual instructor-led training or self-paced online academies, make drop off one of your top operational metrics. To be clear, I'm not suggesting that learners *must* finish all of your courses. In a world that's becoming increasingly self-service, learner behavior is trending toward a notion of, "I'll sample a few courses when I need them," not "I must complete everything."

That said, by understanding where learners drop off during courses, you can identify lessons that are difficult to complete or potentially irrelevant. (Hopefully you'll get this feedback in your reaction surveys too.) And in completion percentage, you have a metric you can improve over time.

Here, you should be measuring:

Course Enrollments

Course Completions

Percentage of enrollments that lead to completions

Which individual lessons yield the highest drop off

COMMUNITY METRICS

Customer Communities help you scale your support efforts by allowing customers to answer one another's questions, and at their best they also enhance your brand's value by creating a common space where customers and prospects can talk about your industry.

Operational metrics for Communities depend heavily on what you consider your Community to be. For instance, some businesses define "Community" as their online Community forums. Others define "Community" as local in-person events where customers can connect with one another.

For an online Community, you'll want to look at a few categories of metrics.

Acquisition

Communities don't work if people can't find them, so you'll need to measure how good you are at acquiring new members. Which metrics help you figure out how you're attracting new members?

Total Sessions: Measure the raw number of sessions and pageviews to see if more people are visiting your Community each month.

Registrations: Measure how many new members sign up every month, as well as what percentage of your total Community they represent.

Traffic Source: Measure which sources drive the most traffic to your Community. Do you have the most visitors arriving from organic search? From marketing campaigns? From nurture emails?

Engagement

Once you attract new members to your Community, you need to keep them constantly engaged. After all, if new users show up and the Community is a one-horse town with tumbleweeds blowing through, they won't stick around. Try measuring things like:

Monthly Active Users: How many active users do you have each month? This can be defined as members who posted, responded, or performed another activity—not just how many people visited your site.

Reactivation: How many inactive users became active this month?

Deactivation: How many active users became inactive this month?

Posts and Replies: How many posts were published? How many replies?

Posts Per User: What's the average number of posts per user?

Response Time: What's the average first response time for a post? How many posts went more than 12 hours without a response?

Top Posts: Which posts got the most views? Which got the most responses?

Quality

You'll need to ensure that you maintain a level of quality in your Community—otherwise people will lose trust in it over time. Here, measure:

Accepted Solutions: What percentage of threads had an answer marked as "best" or "accepted solution"?

Likes: How many "likes" or upvotes are being given to posts?

Badges and Achievements: Which badges or achievements are your Community members earning over time?

Support Usefulness: Which Community threads are linked the most often in support tickets? Which agents link posts the most?

Satisfaction: Many Community platforms let you measure users' satisfaction with your Community, including whether they were able to find what they were looking for.

Advocacy

Communities aren't just useful for support deflection; they can also drive brand value by creating advocates in your customer and partner base. Many programs identify the top contributors and reward them for their participation. Try measuring:

Most Active Users: Which users post and respond most often?

Most Liked Users: Which users' posts receive the most likes or upvotes?

Most Accepted Users: Which users' solutions are most often accepted?

Most Badged Users: Which users have received the most badges or achievements?

IN-PRODUCT EDUCATION METRICS

Because In-Product Education is so closely tied to your product, you'll want to measure your In-Product Education similarly to how you measure your product adoption.

Reach

Start by understanding how many people are exposed to your In-Product Education. You'll want to break this down in a few ways:

Total Guide Views: How many people are exposed to in-product guides?

Views by Type: If you can classify your different guides, break down your total views by onboarding guides, support guides, upsell/notification guides, tooltips, or other guide types.

Views by Guide: Some guides will be more popular than others. This metric helps you determine how users find your guides. For example, low views of a certain guide may indicate that it's not displaying properly, or that users aren't going to the section of your product where the guide is.

Drop Off

Users typically have little patience for long, multi-step guides and tours within a product, so you should measure drop off to understand *where* users are dropping out of your guide. Ways to look at this include:

Completion Percentage: Which guides are completed most often? Longer guides will generally have lower completion rates.

Drop off by Step: For each guide, analyze the number of users who make it to each step. If you notice dramatic decreases in guide usage at certain steps, that may indicate that the step is irrelevant, confusing, or has a bug in functionality.

Activation and Conversion

In-Product Education is usually closely tied to another product-related metric. For example, onboarding guides are supposed to foster activation, free trial guides help with conversion to paid plans, and support cues should lead to ticket deflection. In each of these cases, be sure to measure the relationship between the consumption of In-Product Education and the outcome in user behavior. Try using Dave McClure's "pirate metrics," which track the customer lifecycle using the memorable acronym "AARRR":

Acquisition: Measure whether your new users engage with In-Product Education. You may be able to target In-Product Education based on *where* the new user came from.

Activation: Measure whether users had a successful first-time experience. When users complete your guides, are they more likely to return to your product for a second time?

Retention: Measure whether users continue to return to your product. Does guide consumption or completion predict increased usage of your product?

Referral: Measure whether users would refer others. Does guide consumption or completion correlate with higher NPS, satisfaction scores, or referrals?

Revenue: Measure whether your free trial users convert to paid plans after using In-Product Education. Similarly, measure whether users who actively engage with In-Product Educations are likely to renew or expand their contracts.

Your programs' operational metrics give you a good sense of what's working and not working. They also give your team good guidance on what they should be working on, as they highlight interesting themes, trends, and issues. I recommend holding a Monthly Program Review for each of your education programs to report on the operational metrics, analyze the data, and make decisions about what to do next.

But operational metrics don't tell you the whole story. Specifically, they miss the big picture of how Customer Education affects the rest of your business. For that, let's move on to value metrics.

Value metrics

I have a pet theory that SaaS businesses often don't invest in Customer Education departments because "learning" is not a clearly measurable outcome.

You can't put learning on a scoreboard (well, not in any meaningful sense). You can't easily award the manager whose team "did the most learning." There isn't really a comparable quantifiable metric in Customer Education to deals closed, pipeline generated, or net renewals. This obstacle makes it tougher for you to define and champion the ROI of your Customer Education strategy.

In the past, Education Services teams didn't have to deal so much with attribution metrics, or defining and championing the ROI of their strategy. They were businesses in their own rights, selling training, so they could rely on metrics like revenue, bookings, and margins. Now, Customer Education is more aligned with the practice of Customer Success. It's less important for many of these businesses to generate high margins on trainings than to ensure that accounts renew over time.

Danielle Campbell, Head of Americas Digital Learning Services at Adobe, notes the shift from Services to Success by saying: "These [traditional] metrics only provide a small window into the true health and value of a training business. The real proof is in the customer behavior. What are the outcomes of a trained customer?"

Christine Souza, whom you may remember from the section of this book on the customer journey, expands on this idea:

"We keep talking about how we need to speak the language of the business, but just because you take training activity metrics and start calling them 'Key Performance Indicators,' that's not going to cut it. We need to figure out what aligns meaningfully to the business."

When you think about the department-level success of Customer Education, I'd encourage you to think of it in a cross-disciplinary way:

Think like Customer Success. In CS, your activity metrics (like number of business reviews delivered, customer engagements) only matter if they deliver outcomes (adoption, renewal, and expansion). Customer Success generally uses Renewal, Churn, and Customer Lifetime Value (CLTV) as its goal posts, and I believe Customer Education should as well. The main difference is that Customer Education requires infrastructure work, so it's not as immediately measurable as an individual CSM's gross churn rate.

Think like Marketing. It's infamously difficult to measure marketing attribution. Although software is making it easier to measure the attribution that marketing campaigns have in digital channels, how do you really know whether a certain campaign led to a certain amount of sales-qualified leads? That doesn't stop Marketing teams from observing macro-level trends and experimenting with different approaches. In Customer Education, it may be even harder to measure the direct business impact, so an experimental approach is also beneficial before you can directly measure ROI.

Think like Product Management. The content development side of Customer Education is actually a lot like Product Management—after all, learning materials at their best are in fact products. Many Customer Education content teams take pages from the book of Agile product development, planning their capacity for content development in sprints, and measuring themselves on the delivery and quality of content.

Think like Internal Learning and Development. The more sophisticated L&D teams out there have turned away from measuring activity like training hours and number of courses developed. Instead, they try to measure improvements in job performance for their trainees. With Customer Education, look to the outcomes it generates for customers. Are they more enabled to do their jobs? If so, are they using your product more? Giving you higher CSAT scores? Contacting

Support less? You should be able to see and measure a behavior change.

What can we take from these related disciplines? Ultimately, we should aim to find high-level metrics that don't just describe the *activity* that we do, but what *business outcomes* our activity creates. At the same time, we should be able to describe our department health in terms of the products we deliver and the impact that those products have on the customer journey.

In a perfect world, you would be able to measure the exact impact your education programs had on every customer's health. If you have access to a data science team, then one day you may be able to conduct a regression analysis that finds the exact causal relationship between a customer's engagement with education materials, and their churn, retention, and expansion.

If you have a wealth of resources or your company's name rhymes with "moogle," then by all means, take this approach.

But for the rest of us, we're going to have to get creative about how we tell this story. An effective way to start is by finding a set of proxy metrics. In the next few sections, I'll walk through some approaches to measuring the value of Customer Education.

ROLLUP METRICS

First of all, even though you'll be doing of plenty of measurement on individual pieces of content, you'll want a few key "run-the-business" metrics to roll up to the rest of your business. These should be high-level summaries of your operational metrics that can communicate the health of your Customer Education business over time. I will discuss a few of the ones I feel are critical roll up metrics.

Engagement Rate

How is it measured? Customers engaged in education programs divided by total customer base.

What does it communicate? Maybe you've surmised by this point that I'm not a huge fan of activity metrics. It doesn't really matter how much you're doing if you can't show the value. But in this case, I do think it's important to show the rest of your business how often customers are adopting the programs you create, and whether that rate is rising or falling over time.

Helpfulness Index, Satisfaction, and Net Promoter Score

How is it measured? Helpfulness Index is the number of upvotes over the total number of votes to a question like "Was this article helpful?" Satisfaction is the average or median score for a post-training survey such as "Overall, how would you rate this training?" and Net Promoter Score asks "On a scale of 0 to 10, how likely are you to promote..." with the percentage of detractors (who rate 0 - 6) subtracted from the percentage of promoters (who rate 9 or 10).

What does it communicate? Earlier I described both Helpfulness Index and Satisfaction as operational metrics. The good news is that once you're measuring them, you can also use them as rollup metrics to show that the articles and courses you create are well-received by customers. Also, Net Promoter Score is more widely accepted as a leading indicator of customer loyalty.

Education Revenue and Margin

How is it measured? Revenue is the number of dollars you brought in (usually from selling education services or subscriptions), and margin is the percentage of profit you make. For example, if you sell a course for $2,000 in revenue and it takes $1,500 in development and delivery hours to create, you've made 25% margin on that course.

What does it communicate? For Customer Education functions who operate on P&L (Profit and Loss) statements, your revenue and margin communicate in part whether you've created ROI for your business. Many teams operate for net-zero margin—in other words, they aim to pay for themselves instead of generating additional revenue.

MEASURING RETURN ON INVESTMENT

Your Customer Education function creates Return on Investment (ROI) for your business, but ROI isn't always where you might think to look for it. If you can't show ROI, it's hard to justify future investments in your team.

Part of the struggle for Customer Education teams arises from being classified as a cost center in the business. In other words, you cost money to operate, but you don't directly add to the company's profit. What are your options as a Customer Education leader when you may not be able to invest in the people or software that you need, because you're a cost center?

1. Take your ball and go home

2. Start focusing maniacally on revenue-generating training services and subscriptions

3. Get better at defining how Customer Education creates ROI

I'm not a big fan of #1, and you probably aren't either, because then what are you going to do, find a new kickball team?

Many software companies focus on #2, in the form of revenue-generating services. They make strong investments in an Education Services P&L because it's dramatically easier to define ratios than ROI. Just take each Trainer, assign them a target utilization rate, and hire them (or add training partners) based on your forecasted demand. So now you have a small army of Trainers who are going on-site for paid trainings, and perhaps a network of training partners to accommodate additional demand.

Of course, you also need people to create your content. There's a solution for that, too: Either bake the content development cost into the margins of your paid training subscription, or charge a subscription price for your content, to recover your costs of development.

I'm being a little bit audacious here—none of this is easy or quick to build. I won't fault any company that's generating direct cost recovery on its training programs, or even healthy service margins. But this is simply not feasible for many early-stage companies, and things can get thorny. For example, you may find yourself:

Struggling to get Training Services attached to deals when it's seen as a minor transaction that should just be discounted or waived anyway.

Having to produce content (potentially of questionable quality) to keep up with subscription demand.

Lacking the bandwidth to produce content that helps the rest of your customer base adopt your product, because your content development time is focused on premium offerings and customizing content for individual trainings.

Even if you're running a strong Education Services business today, there may be a greater way to contribute to your business and your customers' overall health. Especially in SaaS, where constant adoption is key, a Customer Education team can do much more than simply pay for itself.

Calculating ROI

Put simply, when you're an early-stage company, creating direct ROI on your Customer Education efforts is probably less valuable than using your Customer Education efforts to fuel your company's growth and firm up Customer Lifetime Value.

In many cases, the value of having education content can't be quantified simply in training revenue generated; it creates additional value by reducing customer friction, increasing customer delight, and differentiating your company in the market through thought leadership.

To use a calculation, ROI is the difference between the benefit and the cost of the training, divided by the cost of the training.

So, for example, let's say you create a program that will save you

$100,000 in headcount costs for Customer Success and Support teams next year. It's expected to bring in another $20,000 when you monetize it. So now your dollar benefit is $120,000. You pay an Instructional Designer, Graphic Designer, and Trainer $50,000 in total to put the training program together.

So what do you end up with as an ROI? It's (120,000-50,000)/50,000. In other words, 70,000/35,000. That's 200% ROI!

Jack Phillips, whom you may recall from the last chapter from his work on measuring training ROI, admits that "by design, most programs do not warrant the five levels of ROI. Even in facilitator-led training, only 5-10 percent of programs should be measured at Level 5." Most training materials by nature won't be evaluated beyond Level 3, but strategic programs (and your training program as a whole) deserve higher-level measurements.

The example I used above brings the limitations of ROI as a measurement tool to light. It's hard to say definitively whether an individual program will bring in $120,000 in that example. More likely it's a collection of programs that achieve that result.

Additionally, a 200% ROI might not be believable to some executives, even if it's true. It's often better to talk about ROI in dollar terms than percentages for this reason.

ROI in Hour Buybacks

If your Customer Education strategy is successful, you'll have influenced many areas of the business. This influence can be quantified.

For example, are you measuring how many potential support cases are being deflected by your education content, thus saving support headcount? You can use this to calculate the support cost savings that came from your education efforts.

The metric for this is "Contact Rate" or "Customer Case Factor." Contact Rate is defined as the support tickets filed per a certain number of customers—for example, "We receive 500 support tickets a month for every 100 customers."

In terms of Customer Education, contact rate is a deflection metric—in other words, if your education content works, you should see fewer tickets and you can point to your content's impact on your Support team. If you can segment this data to show the accounts who have interacted with your education content, all the better. Chances are that trained customers will either have a lower contact rate overall, or that the types of questions they're asking are not basic, but more sophisticated questions that show a higher level of engagement with your product.

An ROI argument for cost savings in Support would look like this:

1. Calculate your customer contact rate (the number of tickets submitted monthly divided by the number of customers you have).

2. Calculate your Support team's hourly pay rate.

3. Project a percentage decrease in customer contact rate due to increased education efforts.

4. Then multiply that percentage decrease in tickets by the average hourly salary it would have taken to solve the tickets.

Voilà! You've shown where Customer Education can pay for itself. And this is before you've even mentioned that self-service generally increases customer satisfaction.

The other area where you're buying back time is from CSMs. If you don't have a Customer Education program, then it's usually up to CSMs to train customers ad hoc, one-by-one. Before we even get into the ROI calculation for this, there are some other pitfalls associated with ad hoc CSM training:

The trainings are usually inconsistent, so there's no way to know whether a customer was exposed to a certain topic, feature, or technique.

CSMs often don't know when a new member of the customer-side team starts, and they can't always deliver another training each time a new user starts.

Small customers often aren't offered CSM-led training altogether.

Once you start developing scalable training, you can use it as a standard part of your initial account onboarding, as well as progressive user onboarding. This will buy time back from your CSMs. Calculate it like this:

Take the number of hours each CSM spends preparing for and delivering an initial onboarding training.

Multiply that by the number of onboarding customers you expect to have in the next year.

Then calculate the average number of hours CSMs spend either on retraining for basic skills or new user onboarding in existing accounts.

Add both of these figures together, and multiply by your CSMs' average, fully loaded hourly cost.

Some businesses get touchy about the idea of taking facetime away from CSMs. You might bring in this buy back calculation and get the response, "Well, it's our strategy to have as much customer engagement as possible, so we don't want to take trainings away from the CSMs."

If your business isn't scalable and you only manage a few, large accounts, then that strategy may work. But allow me to offer a few counterpoints:

The less time CSMs spend delivering basic training, the more time they have to do deeper discovery with the customer and build stronger relationships. CSMs are best deployed toward strategic issues that deepen the account relationship, not transactional activities like delivering an onboarding slide deck.

CSM delivery isn't scalable, so some customers will get left in the lurch if you don't build scalable training. (And if you just decide to replay a recording of a CSM delivering the training as your "scalable onboarding" strategy, tell me if that moves your adoption numbers at all.)

Even large Enterprise customers often have an appetite for scalable resources in addition to custom, on-site training. Every business is different, but as businesses become more distributed, the idea that every large customer wants you to come on-site to deliver classroom training is becoming more perception than reality. Scalable resources are key for Train the Trainer programs, where you'll be rolling out to many teams within a large organization.

You'll often see a benefit in hiring a dedicated training professional. Typically, the Trainers who get the best engagement during trainings are the ones who know how to facilitate. They can make trainings engaging and interactive, more of a two-way dialogue than a presentation. You can try instructing all your CSMs to train customers in this manner, but for early-stage businesses where CSMs are already typically underwater chasing renewals and answering frantic customer questions, I've rarely seen this work.

Because Customer Education has a unique ability to reduce the hours spent conducting repetitive trainings and answering support tickets, I often refer to it as the "Scale Engine of Customer Success."

ROI in Behavior Change and Attribution

Pat Durante, President of the Computer Education Management Association (CEdMA) and Senior Director of Technical Enablement at Talend, says, "At the end of the day, no matter how large your training business, [training revenue] numbers are often a rounding error on the overall software revenue and the C-suite is not losing sleep over these numbers."

Instead of "easy" metrics that show activity, he argues, we should be measuring the impact that our Customer Education efforts have on metrics that the business really cares about—churn, retention, and expansion.

At Optimizely, we used a dashboard to continuously monitor the behavior of customers who did or didn't use our educational resources. We would look at the percentage of trained and untrained customers who:

Logged into our product

Created new projects

Achieved statistical significance (the true sign that you were getting value from Optimizely)

Filed support tickets

	% logged in	% created project	% stat. sig.	average # tickets/mo.
Trained Accounts	98%	94%	72%	62
Untrained Accounts	87%	84%	46%	23

An example of how to display training impact data. Numbers are examples only.

Within a given time period, we could look at the difference in behavior for our customers who used educational resources, and those who didn't. And as you may suspect, trained customers used the product more and filed fewer support tickets (especially basic ones that could have been answered easily). By showing the numbers side-by-side we were able to show the impact of education on customers.

Takeaway: Measure the percentage of trained vs. untrained customers who use your key product features, or who contact support.

But don't stop at product adoption and support tickets—look at longer-term business impact, as well. It would stand to reason if that educated customers use the product more, they also renew and expand more often.

We would do the same type of correlation analysis for customer churn, renewal, and expansion, looking at the percentage of:

Churned customers in the last 90 days who did or didn't use education

Renewed customers in the last 90 days who did or didn't use education

Expanded customers in the last 90 days who did or didn't use education

	% churned	% renewed	% expanded
Trained Accounts	5%	55%	93%
Untrained Accounts	95%	45%	7%

An example of how to display training impact on churn and renewal. Numbers are examples only.

Again, as you might expect, customers who used education made up a higher percentage of renewed and expanded customers, whereas churned customers showed very low engagement with education.

Takeaway: Measure the percentage of churned accounts (or accounts that partially churned, *i.e.* decreased their contract value) that were trained, vs. the number of renewed or expanded accounts that were trained.

Perhaps at this point, you're wondering, "How will I tell my executives that these results are actually because of education?

How can I prove that this is causation, not correlation?"

If you have enough data to show that education directly *caused* product adoption, support ticket reduction, time to first value, renewals, or expansion—and you can regress the data to remove all other potential factors—by all means, do that analysis!

Most teams don't have that rich data or resources to use. In general, you're not trying to prove that education directly caused every bit of the business impact, but that successful customers were by and large educated customers. If your most successful customers demand high-quality education resources, then you've gone a long way toward showing the role education plays in your organization.

One bonus tip: If you're already measuring the percentage of trained vs. untrained customers, and you know that trained customers renew and expand more, take those stats to your Sales, Customer Success, and Marketing teams. These numbers become good incentive to get more customers into training—or, if you sell training, to attach training to new deals and renewals.

ROI in NPS

Another area where Customer Education can create ROI for your business is by increasing customer satisfaction, which is a leading indicator of renewal. For businesses that prize Net Promoter Score as a key success metric, you can show how Customer Education directly increases NPS for customers.

You may be tempted not to release scalable education content because you're concerned that self-serve education programs will reduce customer touchpoints with your account and Support reps, who make every experience delightful. Tony Hsieh, of the online retailer Zappos, often said that the company's Customer Service reps were its best marketing channel by creating "Wow" experiences.

Education materials, when built correctly, are a way to broadcast how delightful your company is to work with. Aim to create materials that capture your team's personality and brand's voice. Dry, boring manuals are *so* 1990.

For an example, Wistia, a video hosting company, naturally has a well-produced series of live-action tutorials on effective video production and marketing. Each of their education videos features their team members showing off their personalities, and sometimes getting goofy. When you watch their videos, you don't just learn a topic—you also get to know the team you'll be working with, and you see that they're real humans with personalities.

It's not just about scaling the delight, however; it's also about serving customers in the way they want to be served. Many customers would rather have an answer *right now*. They don't care how delightful your support experience is—they don't even want to have to contact support!

Ideally, your education content should be available when and where the customer wants it, and it should be ridiculously easy to find. Often, this means putting well-written education content directly into your product, which in turn should drive traffic to your Knowledge Base and decrease support tickets that trickle down to your agents. But this is a two-way street: your team should be active in generating scalable content and sharing best practices, so that you can document them and make them discoverable.

FROM HERE TO ETERNITY

FROM HERE TO ETERNITY

There's a proverb that goes "The best time to plant a tree was 20 years ago; the second best time is now." If you don't have a Customer Education function yet, you're probably past the *optimal* time to have built it—so don't let that stop you.

At this point, you may be overwhelmed by the sheer amount of *stuff* you need to build. How do you get from having ad hoc, CSM-led trainings and a handful of inconsistent support articles to having all those built-out, engaging trainings, clear and concise documentation, a thriving user community, effective In-Product Education, meaningful certifications, and more?

Customer Education is a big bet: It's a high-effort, high-value proposition. It takes time to build. But you have to start somewhere.

Chance are that anything you build today will be better than nothing. If you operate under the assumption that anything you create today will need to be revised later, then you'll be able to learn from your early efforts and iterate from there.

That said, if you build your early strategy with a perspective, rather than just throwing spaghetti at the wall to see what sticks, you'll be immeasurably better set up for success. Strategy and values are essentially "free" resources. They take nothing more than the time necessary to think them up.

In this section, we'll walk through practical steps that you can take to move from ad hoc education to a defined and optimized Customer Education department.

There are plenty of maturity models that you can map to for this, including the Capability Maturity Model that I discussed in the customer journey chapters. There's also ServiceRocket's Enterprise Software Training maturity model (which runs from reacting, through performing and scaling, to optimizing),

Tagoras's Learning Business maturity model (which runs from static, through reactive and proactive, to innovative), and more examples out there in disciplines. No matter which maturity model you use or what the capabilities and steps are (you could use "failing, nailing, scaling, and sailing"—I won't charge for that idea!), it's important to know where you're going before you go there.

As you mature, you go from doing things ad hoc and reactively, to being able to repeat that process more than once. You repeat it several more times, and you can define and document it: Now you're performing. You start to define operational metrics that help you scale. Finally, you can start to optimize based on those metrics. When I see Customer Success teams think about their onboarding processes, they usually make one of two mistakes:

> They try to jump through the model too quickly, coming up with abstract quantitative metrics before they've really defined the process, or...

> They get a couple of steps up the maturity curve, and assume that they're done simply because they made their ad hoc process repeatable. But they never think about how to define, quantify, or optimize it.

For the sake of this section, we won't use a complicated maturity model. We'll keep it simple: first you crawl, then you walk, then you run.

Crawl

Kristen Swanson, Chief of Staff for the Customer Experience at Slack, has this to say about day one of your Customer Education journey: find the one "tricky wicket" for your clients and try to remove it.

You're not going to have a mature onboarding program overnight, but it starts with a vision and a willingness to get to the next level of execution. So even if you can't get to the top of the maturity curve in short order, ask what you can do to start progressing, and how it will benefit your broader business. Start working with other stakeholders in your business to align around the benefits of having a more consistent, scalable onboarding.

ESCAPE FROM AD-HOC-ATRAZ

In the "crawl" stage, most education in your business is done in an ad hoc fashion. CSMs deliver inconsistent onboarding trainings for customers—each usually making their own decks— and *maybe* retrain customers by request. Support agents write articles on an ad hoc basis, but there's no system to prioritize new content or ensure the quality of your content. Community probably doesn't exist outside of a few ad hoc user groups. Your other programs are nonexistent.

What you do next is critical. Whether you've been hired as the first Customer Education person to fix this, or you're in another role but trying to take initiative on Customer Education, your best opportunity is to start with one clear problem and fix it. You are not a giraffe—you're going to go for the low-hanging fruit first.

Instead of a long-term roadmap, start with a 30-60-90 day plan. Just like you would on a brand-new job, this plan is your opportunity to define what problem you'll solve and how you'll measure your progress.

Before you start running around fixing all the problems, do a quick gap analysis to figure out what the difference is between how things operate today and where you want them to be. For example, in your desired future state, ask questions like:

What would make customers less irate?

What could your CSMs be doing with increased bandwidth?

What could your Support team do with fewer basic-level questions because your customer base is more educated from day one?

How can your entire organization work together to increase the speed to first value and product adoption rate, so that you'll be set up for success when renewal time comes?

Write down what this future would look like in your organization. Whose life would be easier? What would this change look like in your organization after *just 90 days*?

Put names and faces on the problem if you can—in the early days of ad hoc education, you're not usually solving problems at scale. You're solving problems for individual humans with names and faces, with portfolios to manage, with contract values to consider.

Now, go back to today. You're going to find the gaps between your 90-day future and today. To do this, look at the gaps that are preventing your team from scaling. Specifically, look for the repetitive, low-value activities that your team performs.

Some examples of repetitive, low-value activities:

> What are your top support ticket questions? Could the answers to those be documented and distributed to customers instead of taking up Support reps' time?
>
> Do you perform the same onboarding training for all customers, and do you redo the training when the customer onboards new team members? Is this something that could be delivered to multiple customers at once?

Now, pick *one* problem to solve. You're not going to solve all of them at once. Because this is an experiment, one way to choose the right problem is to form a hypothesis that you can quickly test. For example:

"If we documented the top ten support issues in our online Knowledge Base, and linked to those instead of rewriting each response, we would see a reduction in ticket volume and handling time for each agent."

This hypothesis gives you a clearly scoped project to work on, and a clearly measurable result. It's not fancy, but it's a way to move in the right direction.

In fact, I strongly urge you not to get fancy at this point, unless you have a clear path to accomplish your fancy goals. Here are some ways I see people get fancy too early and end up not completing their projects:

Taking on too much content at once

Trying to develop content that's too polished (you're going to need to change it anyway!)

Doing anything that involves building in-product functionality or requires product/engineering work

Implementing new systems before you've tried out a quick-and-dirty version of the content

Doing anything that asks too much of customers on an ongoing basis (e.g. Community programs)

Anything that smells of translation, localization, or internationalization before you've designed core content

Trying to measure in too-sophisticated ways. For your first few experiments, you're better off looking at very simple metrics and getting qualitative feedback from Support reps, customers, and whoever else constitutes your audience.

These are all great ideas in the long term, but masochistic ideas for your first experiments. Don't think about this in terms of the final product. Think of this as an early prototype that will validate your direction and get feedback about how to proceed. To steal a term from the product development world, this is your "minimum viable product."

In your 30-60-90 plan, break down your experiment into smaller goals, for example:

30 days:

Meet with Brian, Jenna, and Sandra from the Support team to analyze the top ten support issues.

Shadow calls with each of them to understand the customers' issues.

Inventory the current Knowledge Base to determine the level of coverage for these issues.

60 days:

Write or revise five of the ten articles.

Work with the Support team to incorporate these articles into customer responses and measure satisfaction on those tickets.

Share the articles with Amber, Chris, and Tom from the mid-market CSM team to use in their new customer onboarding and ask for feedback.

90 days:

Complete writing or revision of all ten articles.

Follow up with the Support team to understand the impact on customer contact rate and handle time for those topics.

Follow up with the mid-market CSM team to understand the impact on the onboarding customer experience. Look into whether those onboarding customers filed support tickets on those issues.

By now, you've hopefully fixed a tricky wicket for your customers and made an impact on your business.

TEST, LEARN, ITERATE

Your first experiments should yield simple work products and simple metrics. In the support ticket example I gave above, most of the metrics were collected manually. They were probably managed in a spreadsheet. They solved a concrete problem in a simple way.

In the early days, you won't be able to show statistically significant results around your experiments; statistical significance usually requires thousands of participants to get right. You're not looking for statistically significant causation, so don't make the conversation about that. Make it about the result you were trying to achieve, why that result is important to the business, and what changed for customers and internal employees as a result of your experiment.

Because you knew what you were trying to achieve, you were able to tell a story around your efforts. And because this is an experiment, you're able to change courses and iterate if things aren't working. You're not aiming for perfection; you're aiming for feedback from internal and external customers who can help you iterate.

When Mark Kilens first started to experiment with industry-focused webinars at HubSpot, he reported that the way he initially measured success was:

> More than 1,000 people tuned in to the webinars with positive feedback. They were saying things like "Finally, landing pages make sense," and "Blogging doesn't seem that hard anymore."

You can use an experimental approach even if you don't have dedicated Customer Education team members.

For example, take the following hypothesis: "If we dedicated 50% of one of our Support agents' time for one month to writing Knowledge Base articles about any question we see more than five times, we can likely reduce inbound tickets about those topics." All you need to set this up and measure it is a way to tag tickets by category, a lightweight Knowledge Base platform, and an agent's time.

You can do the same thing, even if you do have support articles written: "If we created videos for our five most common support questions and placed them in their corresponding articles, we can decrease support tickets related to those topics." All you need to set up this one is a simple video tool that will run a few hundred dollars at most, and creating five simple videos is an achievable quarterly goal.

You won't see statistically significant results from these experiments, but you will start to see a directional pattern emerging. And, better yet, you'll foster a culture of testing, learning, and iteration that helps you keep innovating around the metrics that matter.

TEAM: NO ONE LEARNS UNTIL YOU DO

Starting any new team is hard. If you're the first Sales, Support, or Marketing person in your organization, you've got a long, hard road ahead of you.

Starting a team that people don't understand is especially hard. Many companies don't understand the need for Operations, Procurement, or Quality Assurance teams until they've felt the pain that comes from disorganization, bad contracts, and errors. The further away you are from the perception that you're directly adding value, the more it feels like an uphill climb.

Customer Education teams are somewhat special in this regard: Starting a new Customer Education team is hard because most people *think* they understand what education is. They've all read articles and gone to classes. Most people in your organization were formally educated for 13 to 17 years of their lives. They've been to bad trainings (and hopefully some good ones). When it comes to education, they're like Supreme Court Justice Potter Stewart in the *Jacobellis v. Ohio* obscenity case: "I know it when I see it."

As Customer Education leaders, we not only have to constantly prove our value—plenty of teams have to do that—but we also have to help our organizations understand why what they *think* we do isn't what we *actually* do. And that will only happen if we push ourselves and our teams to challenge what we know, and what we think we can do.

Embrace the Growth Mindset

For decades, Carol Dweck, a psychology professor at Stanford, studied what motivates us to grow, develop, and ultimately push past the boundaries of our "natural" abilities. What she found was a key difference in mindset.

Many of us have been conditioned to adopt a "fixed" mindset, where we believe our abilities and talents are fixed—we're born with them and can't change them much. We rely on our accomplishments and don't push ourselves further. When we fail at something, it's because we're simply not talented at it.

However, what she found was that when people adopted a "growth" mindset, where instead of protecting themselves from failure, they embraced it as a learning experience, they were able to push past their failures and build skills in areas where they believed they didn't have natural ability. The key to the growth mindset is a belief that your abilities aren't fixed, a curiosity about mistakes, and a willingness to learn from setbacks.

We have to believe this about our learners as well as ourselves.

If we don't encourage our customers to adopt a growth mindset, and instead we stroke their egos with easy multiple choice questions and vapid microlearning, we're not going to be good partners to their businesses. We're not going to help them with the change management that's critical to adopting new products and adapting in their markets.

If we don't challenge ourselves to learn from our failures, and in fact be curious about them, then we'll continue to play it safe with established ways of educating customers—many of which are just plain ineffective. I recommend Dweck's *Mindset* book to any new Customer Education professional.

Get curious, creative, and cross-disciplinary

Scientists trying to conduct research in space have a problem: they need to be able to get large pieces of research equipment into orbit, but they're limited to the size of the rocket that transports them. Often, these rockets must be narrow, so cramming equipment into them becomes difficult. Starting in the 1990s, engineers began to solve this problem in a new, unorthodox way—origami.

By taking the principles of origami, engineers were able to use the same folding techniques to increase the space efficiency of the materials. This insight has also been used for applications like car airbags, which also require large amounts of material to be compressed into a small space.

Similarly, it's a well-known anecdote that Apple's competitive advantage around usability and design stemmed from Steve Jobs' training in calligraphy. In his own words, "Creativity is just connecting things."

In their book *Innovator's DNA*, Clayton Christensen, Jeff Dyer, and Hal Gregersen make the case that a central skill for innovators is the ability to "associate," or apply ideas from one discipline to another: "The more diverse our experience and knowledge, the more connections the brain can make. Fresh inputs trigger new associations; for some, these lead to novel ideas."

What's going on here? Neural reuse theory: Your brain is transferring patterns from one area to another. So if you love improv comedy, you may be able to bring a "Yes, and..." approach to your virtual classroom. If you've studied film, that may give you stronger perspective on how you incorporate visual storytelling and compelling narratives into your training. If you taught in a K-12 classroom, you have a unique perspective on how to manage attention spans.

Taking a multi-disciplinary approach to Customer Education is a large part of how you can build a program that's innovative and differentiated. If you can out-learn your competitors, you can out-educate them.

Walk

YOUR FIRST FEW QUARTERS OF CUSTOMER EDUCATION

In a matter of months, you can run your first Customer Education experiments to show the potential value of your strategy. Now you can start to place slightly bigger bets on your Customer Education function. In the Walk stage, you'll be able to build content and programs that require a little more investment, but which will position you toward a strategy that generates scale, adoption, and brand differentiation.

At this point, armed with a few wins, newly minted Customer Education leaders often start asking precisely the wrong questions:

> Which tools should I use?
>
> Which systems should I buy?
>
> Should I do live or virtual training?
>
> Should I use audio, visual, or kinesthetic learning?
>
> How do I update all my content when my product changes?

I hear these questions nearly every time I do a talk about Customer Education. They are among the most frequently asked in our Customer Education community. And while you need to answer them at some point, let's talk about why these aren't the best questions to be asking when you're just getting started.

Tools and Systems

It's often said in photography that "the best camera is the one you have with you." It's not about the power of the tool that you're using—a fancy digital SLR camera can help you capture better photos as a professional photographer, but it won't capture a blink-and-you'll-miss-it moment like the camera phone in your pocket.

There aren't many blink-and-you'll-miss-it moments in Customer

Education, but the "best camera" analogy still applies here: It's not about which systems and tools you use, but about using whatever you have, and using it well. With a simple authoring tool, a decent microphone, and creativity, you can create education materials that move your business in the right direction.

Sometimes when I speak to Customer Education leaders who are tasked with building a team from scratch, they say, "I really want to build an academy for my users, but I can't get the budget for a Learning Management System approved." Good news—you don't need to, as long as you understand the tradeoffs.

An LMS is good for tracking learners' activity, but it's not the only way to publish content. If it's mission-critical to see exactly what customers are doing in your learning materials from day one, then you have a business case for an LMS. If you're like many early Customer Education teams, and you're trying to prototype your content in front of customers to see how they react to it, you can do it on a system you already have. Most businesses already have access to a Content Management System (CMS) or a Knowledge Base tool, both of which allow you to publish content to the web. Many early Customer Education teams opt to use these tools for piloting content, before bringing an LMS in.

Delivery Methods and Learning Styles

Live or virtual training? Self-paced or instructor-led e-learning? Virtual labs or In-Product Education? Videos or articles?

The "how should people learn?" question has endless permutations. As Customer Education professionals, we're endlessly bothered by issues of format.

One reason that I think we're so obsessed with this question is that it's a tangible one: Before we create education, we have to figure out where we're going to put it. What's the best way to educate? Live, online, self-paced, or what?

The answer to this question is, obnoxiously, another question:

What's the problem you're trying to solve?

Different delivery methods serve different needs:

>**Live classroom training** is best for teaching skills that require a lot of human interaction. You'll be able to set up your most complex activities, role plays, and scenarios for the least cost in a live classroom training. That said, it's the least scalable format available. To do live classroom training, you constantly need to be traveling to see your customers (or have them come to see you). Often you'll need to customize the curriculum, which takes time for discovery and content creation. Live training also requires a high level of logistics to schedule and deliver. If you're not planning to scale your training (or you plan to eventually build a business around live delivery), then maybe this is the way to go. Otherwise, I mostly recommend this as a way to pilot content and get direct customer feedback before you scale the content.

>**Virtual classroom training** lets you take the interactive component of live classroom training—where you have back-and-forth conversation with participants—and scale it to multiple time zones or regions without travel. For software training, especially, virtual classroom training can be a viable option when paired with screen sharing and virtual labs, where customers can get hands-on practice. While there's still logistics to scheduling these, and they require someone's time to customize and deliver them, they scale more than live classroom training.

>**Virtual public training** lets you train multiple customers at once, usually with a public posted catalog. When an executive tells you to "start doing webinars," this is probably what they're actually asking you to do. If you have a large customer base—especially one that keeps adding new team members—this is a viable option because you're more likely to get healthy attendee numbers. Nothing is more depressing than teaching to groups of two or three every week, and those dismal numbers call the ROI of public trainings into question. If your product must be highly customized for each customers, you may not be able to get much mileage out of

public training, unless you can make your curriculum general and conceptual enough while still meeting your learners' needs.

Self-paced e-learning lets you train a virtually unlimited number of customers at once, but it requires the most upfront work to produce. Instead of having a facilitator lead interactivity, you'll need to build videos and e-learning modules to handle the engagement for you. So while it's the most scalable, you probably don't want to go full-throttle into this unless you've already validated your curriculum.

Written content like articles (or even written academy lessons) are quick to produce and extremely scalable, which makes them a good way to validate content, but you can only ask customers to go through so much written content before they get bored and leave. Eventually you'll want to supplement your written content with other formats.

Each delivery method has its own strengths and weaknesses, meaning that there's no *best* one to start with. But depending on the resources you have to produce and deliver content, the number of customers you need to train, the number of regions they're in, and the level of customization needed to train them properly, you'll be able to choose the first method or two that's right for your program.

The other reason that people are obsessed with delivery methods is that we've heard enough about learning styles over the years that if we don't get the "visual, auditory, reading, or kinesthetic" question right, we're worried that we'll lose our learners.

Put simply, most of the science around "learning styles" is unvalidated. Most people aren't inherently visual learners—they learn visually when the thing they learn is visual. Same goes with kinesthetic learning—people learn kinesthetically when the skill they're learning requires hands-on work. Reading works well when the goal is just to *know* a concept, as in a reference article, but it doesn't work as well when you want the learner to *do* something.

Instead of building multiple versions of your content to appeal to different learning styles, aim to choose the best way to communicate the concept—and avoid blatant mismatching. For example, if you're teaching an in-product workflow, hearing someone talk about the workflow (which is commonly what happens on a training call) won't be as valuable as seeing it in action or getting a chance to practice doing it.

Dealing with updates

Once Customer Education teams have a little content under their belts, many leaders have a sobering moment: *How am I gonna update all this stuff?*

It's maybe the most common question I hear from new Customer Education professionals. After all, products change, and in startups they change *often* (and often without notice).

If you remember from the chapter on video creation, I suggested a few tactics, and those hold true here as well:

> Create a threshold for how much change is necessary for an update. Knowing that products are constantly updated, you probably won't live in a world where your education content 100% reflects the current interface of your product. But major changes should trigger you to revise content, and you should also have a system of auditing content after a certain time period to make sure that the UI is up-to-date.
>
> Don't document your product as much. Content developers and documentarians get obsessed with documenting every nook and cranny of the product, but in doing so, they create more work for themselves and overwhelm customers. Start by creating content about the parts of your product that customers actually need help with. And when you *do* write about your product, don't write about the color or location of certain elements, as those change most frequently. That way, when they do change, you'll be able to swap out an image quickly without rewriting anything.
>
> Instead of focusing on your product's UI, focus on concepts. For example, at Optimizely, we created documentation and

courses on the experimentation process, which didn't change nearly as often as our product UI. Even when discussing our product, we would often do it in terms of a six-step process. We'd describe the six features you used, and while the product screenshots went out of date, the diagrams and other materials showing the process itself stayed fresh.

At this point, you'll also want to make better friends with your Product Management and Product Marketing teams. Because they own the release schedule and process, they can give you a heads-up about what will change and where. You may even be able to get updated education listed as a pre-launch requirement. Now, instead of being caught off guard when the product changes and you have to scramble to re-do everything, you'll be a partner in the process.

CREATING YOUR TWO-YEAR ROADMAP

After you've run your experiments as part of your 30-60-90 day plan, you should have some quick wins under your belt and a better story to tell about how Customer Education helps your business.

From these early wins, it's time to map out a vision for bigger wins. If you can map out the themes and goals for your next few years, you'll likely have an easier time communicating your vision for Customer Education to the business, as well as your priorities. If you're not talking about *why* you're doing what you're doing, you're just telling people what activities you're doing. It's hard to grow your team when all you're talking about is *what* you're doing.

At both Optimizely and Checkr, I started to carry around a two-year vision slide deck that I could share with executives and others in the company as needed. Here's the format I recommend for that type of deck:

Here's the grand vision. Start with an aspirational statement like "We will be the leader in education for Project Management" or "We will enable 1,000,000 people to become our users." Some Big Hairy Audacious Goal that you'll need to work towards.

Here's what happens if we achieve that vision. What does that future look like? Share some vision for what the future state looks like. What will customers be able to do that they have a hard time doing now? How many new skilled workers will be in the market? How will this create efficiencies in the business?

And here's what achieving the vision does for the business. At this point, I usually like to insert a slide that talks about the mechanics of Customer Education—how it drives adoption, ticket deflection, scale, revenue, competitive differentiation, and so on throughout the customer lifecycle. This is to help people who are unfamiliar with Customer Education understand what it does for the business, and why it's not just about "doing trainings."

Look at other Customer Education departments that drive their businesses. Now, I have a few slides handy about other state-of-the-art Customer Education teams and what they do well. People often want to know, "who in the industry is doing this well, and what are they doing?"

Our customers are asking for it—they need it. If you've talked to customers about your plans, or piloted with any of them, add their logos and their feedback. This can either be pain points they've had or praise for the pilots you've already shared with them. Bonus points if the customers you have here are ones your business really cares about.

If we don't get there, our competitors will. If you have competitive data about which Customer Education programs your competitors do or don't have (and what level of quality they're at), add a table that shows that comparison.

So where are we today? Now that you've shown what Customer Education looks like done well, why it matters to customers, and how close the competitors are, it's time to go back to the team's reality. I devote a couple of slides to sharing the team's recent achievements and metrics, as well as to the challenges or opportunities we have in front of us.

Don't shy away from making this a little scary—if there's a large gap between where you are and where you need to go, say so.

How do we get from here to there? This is the roadmap slide. Map out your proposed projects for the next four quarters. In the speaker notes, add why these projects are important and what they achieve for the business. I also like to add a line to this slide showing which projects we're saying "not now" to. With this line in place, we can have a conversation about prioritization.

And beyond... After the next four quarters, things may get hazy. So you may want to roadmap out the next year in fiscal halves instead of quarters. Here, you can include more aspirational projects as well—things that would create business and customer impact, but that will take more work to achieve.

Here's how we do it. You either have the resources to achieve your plan, or you don't. If you're going to need additional people or resources to make your plan happen, you can use the end of your roadmap to show the different levels of investment and what kinds of results they would yield.

In the appendix, keep any other ROI calculations you've done, other compelling customer quotes, other examples of great Customer Education programs, and answers to common questions you expect to be asked. There's no rush like being able to answer a question with, "I'm glad you asked. Let me show you on this slide..."

You can see that having a vision and a roadmap helps you prioritize and sort out what's important. It also helps you tell your story and have those conversations with other stakeholders in your organization. Maybe you won't use the exact format I have above, but I recommend using something close to it.

The format I use above is loosely based on *The Challenger Sale* by Brent Adamson, Matthew Dixon, and Nicholas Toman of the Corporate Executive Board. It's a narrative that piques interest and establishes business relevance, then reframes the problem. Using a combination of data and emotional impact, you can then propose an alternative path forward—with your proposed solution as the way to get there.

So for Customer Education, that story might sound something like:

> **The Warmer:** We've said that we're going to triple our revenue next year. I believe that by empowering our customers to use our product, we can accelerate our progress toward that goal. In fact, here's what I think our customer experience could look like to support it. [You spend a moment describing your vision for education.]
>
> **The Reframe:** We've thought of the solution to this problem as hiring Account Executives and Customer Success Managers. While we should do that, we're currently devoting the majority of their time just to keeping customers afloat. And as we know, we can't hit our targets without significant expansion in our current customer base.
>
> **Rational Drowning:** If we can't keep our customers long enough for their LTV to outweigh our costs to acquire and retain them, we won't achieve our goal. And according to research, the number-one cause of customer churn is poor onboarding. I've interviewed several of our customers and surveyed our competitors to see how well we're doing, and I think we have room for improvement.
>
> **Emotional Impact:** In fact, look at this quote from our point of contact at ClientCo. She feels like her team is stunted in their ability to grow with us because we have to reach out to them every time they onboard their new team members. She also feels like she can't have productive conversations with our CSM and Product teams because all her time is spent onboarding new team members.
>
> **A New Way:** So what if we can scale our customers' onboarding and growth in a way that buys our CSMs time back to do what they do best—build those relationships and encourage renewal? That would be a better path to LTV, wouldn't it? By investing in Customer Education, we can drive our revenue goals with a healthy level of scale.

Your Solution: So here's what I propose... [and now a hatch in the ceiling opens up as dollar bills start raining down on you!]

TEAM: FINDING GOOD PARTNERS AND LETTING THEM RUN

When you first start as a Customer Education team of one, you're a generalist. You create the content, you deliver it to customers, and you implement and manage the systems in your stack.

As you start to build out your team, though, you need to find people that you can trust as partners. Your team simply isn't big enough for people who want to take orders but not partner with you. When you start looking for new people to join your team, though, where do you look?

You'll generally need people who can fulfill four major needs:

Content: To produce articles and docs, you need clear and concise writers. To produce courses, you need people who can design and develop those courses. In either case, you need people who can get the knowledge out of the expert's head and turn it into something that's effective for learners.

Delivery: If you're going to train customers live or virtually, you need someone who's going to engage learners—someone who can get learners actively involved in the training, sharing and teaching more than they're passively learning.

Systems & Operations: As your Customer Education stack grows, you need someone who can take ownership of the different systems. At first, this may be someone who simply administrates your LMS, handling user enrollments, course uploading and scheduling, and reporting. But as time goes on, you'll need someone who can skillfully manage integrations and custom development as well, working with multiple supplier relationships and complex projects.

Community: If you build a Community during this phase, you'll need someone who can moderate the online forums, schedule and plan local events, and continue to grow the Community and its users over time.

Eventually these will all be separate roles—and as time goes on they'll get even more specialized—but what do you do before "eventually"? Do you hire more generalists, or do you hire specialists who are really good at one of these areas? This is a question without a clear solution, but let's explore some perspectives.

Option 1: More generalists

One approach is to find more people who do what you do—utility players who can switch between content development, delivery, and systems. Jesse Evans, writing about the growth of Box's Education team, took the strong stance of "Kill the Specialists and Hire the Actors."

In just a few years, Box reached 900 live sessions a year and 80,000 learners with a team of five generalists who could both create content and deliver it. Not only does this make everyone more adaptable (and able to fill in for each other's training schedules), but it also make sure that the people writing the content also stay close to the customer. To quote Jesse:

> Live instruction experience is critical for curriculum-builders because it forces them to be accountable for everything they say- effectively poll testing every piece of a course. A content builder whose only feedback comes from post-class surveys (or passing comments from the instructors) rarely gets any insight beyond reactions to the course as a whole—which is hard to connect to individual pieces. Building for a population you never interact with is also like guessing someone's weight before you've met them. Neither is going to make you very popular.

So what was that about actors? Box's team came largely from backgrounds like test prep (think: SAT, GMAT, GRE, and so on) and acting, placing the emphasis on people who could above all create a world-class experience for customers.

Above all, when looking for generalists, you should prioritize people who are versatile and can learn quickly. They may not have done everything you're going to ask them to do on this job, but they should be able to pick up the different skills with gusto, even if they favor one area over the others. Eventually, that area could become their job specialization.

Option 2: Hire specialists

On the other hand, you could go the route that Sherry Quinn and her team at Atlassian University took. Scaling to an audience tens of thousands deep, similar to Box, Atlassian took a different approach to building a team. Sherry focused primarily on hiring seasoned content professionals, with backgrounds in e-learning development and instructional design. This team was able to repurpose conference-based trainings into virtual instruction, and eventually even into interactive e-learning.

Roughly half of Atlassian University's team handles content development, and roughly the other half focuses on operations, systems, and instructor management (although there are no actual instructors on the team, because instruction is handled by Atlassian's certified partners). The team also has a leader focused purely on certification programs.

Sherry's team still needs to be versatile, but their core competency is content development and instructional design.

So what makes a great Customer Educator?

Box and Atlassian show two paths forward—two teams serving tens of thousands of users in just a few years, both operating lean and at scale. One hired generalists; one hired specialists.

Which worked better?

Both teams hired based on the types of programs they wanted to run—Box's strategy more oriented toward delivery and Atlassian's more oriented toward content and systems. Your two-year plan should inform where you want your team to focus. In the early days, you'll likely need people who can act as generalists, bouncing more capably between content and delivery; as time goes on, roles naturally begin to specialize, even if there is still cross-pollination.

My take on the "generalist vs. specialist" debate is that no matter what the specific responsibilities of the role are, it's important to find people who have a few traits that we saw both in Box's actors and test prep people *and* Atlassian's seasoned Instructional Designers:

> **Curious:** Customer Educators are, above all, learners. An innovative Customer Education strategy requires a willingness (or even enthusiasm) to explore complex new information and to challenge the way things have been done. I find that the best Customer Education professionals are curious, seeking out additional knowledge and context to improve their craft and their products.
>
> **Consultative:** Whether you design, develop, deliver, or run systems, Customer Educators deal constantly with many stakeholders and lots of information. They're also consultative, able to ask the right questions to get to the heart of the matter, and to push back on requests that don't make sense.
>
> **Creative & Innovative:** Great Customer Educators value creative learning experiences, and they use that creativity to engage learners through stories, analogies, frameworks, activities, and other out-of-the-box solutions. When they're able to point that creativity toward innovative practices to get better results, they're especially strong.
>
> **Adaptable:** Things change quickly—especially in young companies. Customer Educators must be able to prioritize on the fly, balance projects, and communicate clearly about what the most important thing is.
>
> **Action-Oriented and Practical:** Many learning professionals come from academic backgrounds, where instructional design is more of a theory than a practice. Many students graduate from Master's programs in Instructional Design without actually creating hands-on products or doing any e-learning development. Yet others come from large corporations where instructional design and content development

are completely different roles. While Customer Education professionals should still be intentional and consultative about how they approach work, they should also be able and willing to *do* the work.

Intentional: At the same time as a learning professional must be action-oriented, I also think it's important that they are purposeful and intentional about what they do. I often ask my team not just to freely state their positions and opinions, but *why* they believe what they believe. Being able to analyze the thought process behind a decision can sometimes feel frustrating in the moment, but it provides opportunities to become more intentional and learn from those decisions.

Whether the people I hire are relatively new to the field or experienced professionals, these are the types of attributes that I look for. In many cases, if you find someone who has these traits, they can learn the practical skills quickly and synthesize a large amount of subject matter to get to the core of the matter.

What's not on this list?

Knowledgeable: Some organizations insist that they're going to find experts in their field to develop and deliver education. Great in theory; often terrible in practice. It's really hard for experts to remember how they learned something, so their content and delivery end up being a "sage on the sage"-style knowledge dump.

Tactical: Often the first Customer Education person at a company is a CSM or Support person who just ended up in a position of teaching the content back. This is the "You've been a customer service rep for a while—why don't you train the other reps now?" Similar to how it's not always a good idea to promote your top-performing Sales-human into Sales management, there's no guarantee that just because a person ended up in an education position, they can develop the right skills to do it well.

Smart: Smart people fail all the time if they can't translate that intelligence into prioritization and decision-making. I prefer to look for "processing power" or "intellectual horsepower"—their ability to think quickly and synthesize information to make good decisions and good products. Moreover, I believe that intellectual curiosity is more important than pure intelligence. If a smart person can't admit they're wrong and change their position, then that's going to be difficult.

It's a little scary to hire people who may not have the exact domain expertise or title that you're looking for. You have to dive more deeply into who they are as a person, and you'll be using your instincts more.

As time goes on, your instincts generally improve—they're honed by subconscious data collection, just like conducting thousands of hours of deliberate practice. On the other hand, we're all susceptible to unconscious bias, so simply hiring people that we like or believe in means that we might be hiring people who are like us. I recommend a couple of tactics to keep this impulse in check:

> **Gut-check your gut.** When your gut is telling you that you like or dislike someone, take a step back to figure out why. Ask yourself in each case how similar or different the person is, compared to you and your existing team. What's their background like? Their unique skills and "superpowers"? Are they adding diversity or just fitting in?
>
> **Behavioral interviews.** Behavioral interview questions are questions that ask about specific situations—"Tell me about a time..." or "How would you handle this situation?" questions. Using behavioral interview questions, you can often get a sense of someone's competencies and attributes, even if they haven't done the exact type of work you're hiring for. These can point at achievements *and* at failures that the candidate learned from. For example, "Tell me about a time when you had too many projects to handle at once, and what you did," will tell you a lot about the candidate's adaptability, project management skills, *and* vulnerability.

Multiply your team

In the previous chapter, I discussed the importance of taking a growth mindset and embracing your own failures instead of trying to protect your own ego.

This concept becomes exponentially more important when you're leading a team. Now, having to protect your own talents and intelligence isn't just harmful to your own career: it's harmful to theirs.

In their book *Multipliers*, Liz Wiseman (who created Oracle University) and Greg McKeown (who also authored a book called *Essentialism* which I won't discuss here, but I highly recommend) confront the notion of leaders who are smart, but intentionally or unintentionally stifle everyone around them. "Their focus on their own intelligence and their resolve to be the smartest person in the room had a diminishing effect on everyone else," Wiseman writes. "For them to look smart, other people had to end up looking dumb."

On the other hand, she worked with some leaders who "applied their intelligence to amplify the smarts and capability of people around them. People got smarter and better in their presence."

Wiseman and McKeown point out five disciplines that separate multipliers from diminishers:

Talent Magnet: Multipliers know how to attract the best talent and optimize their potential instead of simply building empires of warm bodies.

Liberator: Multipliers create an environment of healthy intensity that demands people's best thinking and work, without dominating people and stifling their bold ideas.

Challenger: Multipliers provide opportunities for people to stretch and undertake challenges, instead of try to prove what they, themselves, know.

Debate Maker: Multipliers debate decisions early with the broad team before coming to a common direction, instead of tossing it around with a small inner circle.

Investor: Multipliers invest ownership and accountability in their teams, instead of micromanaging.

It seems to me that once you've learned to master the growth mindset for yourself, you're better equipped to multiply your team. Just as participants learn more when they can put themselves in the role of the teacher, your team can become more capable if you empower them. For Customer Education leaders, this should be intuitive, but it's difficult to break your own bad habits.

As leaders, we're not going to be everyone's best friends (even when we are close with our teams), but we do need to develop a strong team identity and make sure that our team members know we care about them and their growth, while giving constant feedback that helps them grow and instills accountability to results.

Part of that is giving your team space to do their best work. If you're always the one speaking up, or speaking on their behalf, or coming up with the ideas, then they're not going to be fully engaged.

If you're a high performer-turned-manager, make sure you're not squashing your team. Instead, be realistic about where you're diminishing your team, even unintentionally, and strive to multiply them instead.

Run

INTO THE FUTURE

By this point, you've built your two-year roadmap and brought several of your programs to market. You've gotten good feedback from customers, and you've made a dent in some key business problems. You've even hired a small team to build and improve on the programs so you can drive *more* value for your business.

Great—you've already made it further than the companies who neglect Customer Education until it's too late.

Where do you go from here? You developed a two-year strategy, but now your Customer Education function can start to become a true competitive differentiator for your business.

Building signal strength

Most Customer Education leaders that I met are relatively humble, intellectually honest people. This incidentally makes us terrible at marketing our own programs. We assume, whether we'll admit it or not, that good programs should speak for themselves. We don't present data if it's not 100% attributable to our work. And as a result, we don't sit at the table with the right decision-makers to grow our scope over time.

Some organizations are trickier to navigate than others, and some have just-plain-bad cultures. But I also can't help but think that some of this pain is self-inflicted. We don't do a good job telling a concise, powerful story about what we do.

If you have a vision—and that vision explains what you're going to do to grow the business, differentiate from the competition, save costs, make customers happy, etc.—then you have a powerful story to tell about how your team doesn't just "do trainings" or "write articles"—you drive the business forward.

To quote Terry Vyas, VP and GM of Education Services and Communities at Blackbaud, "Customer Education professionals need to have pride and swagger for the impact we provide... we scale better, and we provide a high return for the overall business."

The reason I started this book with a tour of Customer Education through the customer journey is to show the impact we can provide. If you execute well, you're seeing metrics change and getting good quotes from customers and internal stakeholders. Make sure everyone else in your business sees those metrics and hears those quotes.

It's on us to show that impact through operational and value metrics, through customer feedback, through business efficiencies, and even through strategic storytelling. And as we show that impact, we can transform our two-year visions into bolder, longer-term visions. While the projects in your roadmap will change, your ultimate vision shouldn't change as often. I believe that's how you take your strategy to the level that we saw in the examples from Hubspot, Salesforce, Box, and Atlassian.

We have a lot of perfectionists in our field, and it's important for us to realize that an imperfect-yet-powerful story now is going to be more helpful than keeping it to ourselves until we have perfect information.

EMBRACING TRENDS AND AVOIDING FADS

Go to a learning-industry conference and you'll see at least a handful of sessions devoted to "Is _____ the future of education?"

For a while, it was mobile learning. Then it was gamification. Then it was xAPI. Then it was microlearning. Around the time Pokemon Go came out, it was augmented reality. Now it's artificial intelligence and virtual reality. I've even seen sessions on how the blockchain will affect learners.

It's really hard to distinguish trends from fads. It's also really hard to distinguish which trends will affect you next year vs. the ones that are still a decade away.

For example, I believe that virtual reality will, at some point, change the way we learn. If we can cheaply and quickly build virtual environments for our learners to help them practice job-related tasks, then we'll be able to build immersive learning environments that actually help people learn better. But how many years away are "cheaply" and "quickly"? Will VR help customers learn to use software better than a live lab does? Does VR apply to reference materials like Knowledge Bases?

Unless you know how they're going to affect you in the next few years, and how you'll be able to devote resources to embracing them, then you're potentially better off just stuffing them in your "shiny things" folder and waiting for more concrete news.

If you see a trend emerging and think it might be the future of Customer Education, ask yourself:

> How long will it be until it's available to a company of my size?
>
> How many businesses have embraced the trend—or is it still mostly an academic exercise?
>
> What resources would it take for me to embrace this trend?
>
> If I embrace the trend, what will it actually do for my customers (or is it just cool)?
>
> Do I care about this trend because I see value in it, or am I just protecting myself from getting yelled at if I missed the trend?
>
> If this trend does actually become reality in the next year or two, and I don't embrace it, what's the cost?
>
> Am I really, really sure that this is not a fad?

When you go to conferences and hear about trends, you're generally hearing about it from researchers (who are necessarily a few years ahead of the curve) or from very early adopters. Don't get me wrong: I think there's value in being innovative and adopting certain technologies early, but the pattern I see most often is people who are both late adopters *and* distracted by fads.

Trends don't replace a vision or a strategy. Instead, use emerging technologies as necessary to support your vision and strategy, and pay attention to the ones that are becoming more affordable and accessible for businesses.

PRICING AND SERVICES

While every Customer Education function will have a different mix of programs and services, one question that most education teams encounter is: *Are we gonna make customers pay for this?*

In a startup, selling Education Services probably doesn't matter as much. When you're in hyper-growth mode, selling services is less interesting and necessary than acquiring, renewing, and expanding customers. Pre-IPO, you actually may not want to generate too much services margin, as investors try to keep service revenue capped compared to subscription revenue.

That said, the history of Customer Education actually lies in the Education Services world. In the past, Customer Education teams were nearly universally situated within the Professional Services organization. They were focused on delivering live, custom trainings to customers during their software implementation. Getting margin on their services was the holy grail.

The Technology Services Industry Association (TSIA) reports that as recently as 2010, 60% of Education Services teams' primary objective was to generate revenue. Just five years later, that number was only 29%, competing with CSAT and adoption. I'd imagine it's continued to decline since then, as more companies realize the value of Customer Education to drive adoption and renewal at scale.

That said, even if generating high margins on training services is no longer the primary reason that Customer Education exists, many teams are still expected to pay for themselves. By selling training services and courses, they can recoup the cost to hire employees and buy systems.

Fee or free?

The first decision you'll need to make is what your department's financial goal is (or maybe that's been decided for you already). Are you aiming for cost recovery? A percentage of margin? Or are you a cost center that drives product adoption and renewal?

Once you've decided this, you can think about your portfolio of education services. Chances are that some will be free and others will be paid.

First, a note on wording: I'm saying "free" here to represent "offerings that don't cost an additional amount," but you often don't want to say "free" to a customer. "Free" can subconsciously communicate a lack of value. Instead, consider saying "included with your subscription"—or even putting a price tag on the service, then discounting it to zero.

Let's walk through the pros and cons of free—or "included"—and fee:

The Pros of "Free"

More customers will be able to use free education, so your numbers will be higher.

You don't need to figure out the accounting or sales practices for free education—there's no revenue and no SOWs to develop.

Free offerings can be used earlier in the sales process, before the customer is fully committed to paying you for training.

The Cons of "Free"

If something doesn't have a price tag on it, it's perceived to be of lesser value. Even if you get more enrollments, you may see less completion.

Your department won't pay for itself if all education is free.

For intensive services, like custom on-site training and change management services, you will quickly run out of capacity—the demand will outweigh your supply of Trainers and Consultants.

The Pros of "Fee"

If you're spending money to customize content, travel, and deliver training, then you almost certainly want someone to pay for that.

Attaching a fee to education helps you have conversations with customers around trade-offs instead of just doing everything they ask.

Customers will often pay for services that they perceive as high-value—for example, certifications and other industry-focused courses that help with their continuing education and development.

The Cons of "Fee"

Your Sales team will often want to discount training, even to zero dollars, which doesn't help with your cost recovery. Training simply isn't the biggest line item in their deals.

Becoming too focused on training revenue may mean you lose sight of supporting product adoption and customer renewal.

If customers are paying for content (like e-learning), then you'll be under pressure to keep creating more training, sometimes for the sake of adding to your library instead of responding to actual needs. You'll also typically get more complaints from customers, since their expectations are higher.

If you do go the fee-based route, keep in mind that there's a tension between your need to recover operating costs and other teams' desire to give away training as part of the deal. Many Customer Education professionals try to flip this conversation by charging a premium for training (especially custom training) so that it creates a healthy margin and operates as a premium product instead of a loss leader. Then they create other free or less-expensive offerings for customers who don't want to pay.

Now, your Sales team will be having conversations with the customer about options, instead of just throwing education into the deal because the customer pushed them around. When you have a catalog with defined price points, you can consult with the customer more capably. Otherwise the conversation goes like this:

Customer: What kind of onboarding training do I get?

Sales-human: Our team will come out and train your entire team for two days, for the low, low price of $5,000 plus travel and expenses.

Customer: Why am I paying you $5,000? I'm already paying for your expensive software license. Don't you want me to be successful?

Sales-human: You drive a hard bargain. [Runs back and asks you to discount the training to $0 while saying this is a "strategic deal."]

Instead, with different tiered offerings, you can offer less costly programs to the customers who don't need the most resource-intensive customized on-site training. You're going to have some customers who say, "On-site training is important to me, and I have $50,000 that says so." Others are going to say, "Well, I guess it's more important that my team gets up and running quickly. They're also in ten different offices. I guess virtual training makes more sense."

Many Education Services teams end up with a model that looks something like this:

Free (or "Included"): Basic-level e-learning and public virtual classes, Knowledge Base resources, community forums.

Tier 1 (under $500): Intermediate or advanced public virtual classes, basic-level certification exams, training roadshow classes, premium e-learning subscriptions.

Tier 2 (hundreds to thousands): Private virtual classes, on-site public training classes.

Tier 3 ($10,000+): Custom on-site training, typically priced per day of delivery and for hours of content customization; additional services such as change management, Train the Trainer, or coaching.

More Education Services teams are also embracing subscription services, where customers can buy seats for more advanced content in the LMS, usually including premium e-learning and virtual classrooms. In 2017, 55% of the teams surveyed by TSIA had a subscription offer in their current portfolio, and those subscriptions accounted for 13% of their education revenue.

Offering training as a subscription, instead of as a service, also aligns closer with the Software-as-a-Service business model that today's tech companies use. In fact, roughly half of the teams surveyed included the education package subscription as part of the larger software subscription.

That said, when you create subscription services, you also create an expectation that there will constantly be new or updated content (or else why would the customer renew their subscription?), so be prepared to meet the demand for new content.

TEAM: BUILDING YOUR TRIBE

As your team grows, the culture you create matters. At this point in your team's evolution, you'll typically have several smaller social groups in your company—and even in your Customer Education function. The Content Developers will be cranking away on docs and e-learning, the Trainers will be on-site with clients, the technologists will be on calls with suppliers, and you'll be in meetings all day.

How do you keep your team aligned and focused on the vision, instead of getting distracted or demotivated? The way you lead can determine whether your team is mid-90's Pixar or mid-00's Dunder-Mifflin (that's the company from *The Office*—if you haven't watched it, no, you don't want to be on that team).

In their book *Tribal Leadership*, Dave Logan, John King, and Halee Fischer-Wright study the characteristics of "tribes" within organizations—typically teams between 20 and 150 people. Depending on how far along you are, this may describe your broader business unit, or your education team may be a tribe all its own!

Any given tribe in an organization can operate at different stages with different attitudes, ranging from "life sucks" to "life is great." But the key stages, according to the authors, are stages three and four—moving from "I'm great" to "we're great."

In their research, they found that roughly half of all workplace tribes operate with an "I'm great (and you're not)" mentality.

Individuals compete with each other, jockeying for power and status, ultimately leaving someone else demotivated and on the bottom. Because most teams operate at this stage, it's statistically likely that if you don't do anything else, your team will work like this too.

So how do you move from "I'm great" to "we're great"? One comment they make about "I'm great" cultures cuts particularly deep: "The gravity that holds people at Stage Three is the addictive 'hit' they get from winning, beating others, being the smartest and most successful."

In their estimation, it's "a language and a pattern of behavior; it is not a permanent state like 'tall' or 'short.'"

Doesn't this sound like another theory we've discussed in this book? This is the same chasm that separates multipliers from diminishers—it's the growth mindset. Instead of protecting our own egos and competing with one another, we need to form a culture that unites us and motivates us to outperform our competitors.

How do you move your Customer Education team to the "we're great" stage? While the *Tribal Leadership* book recommends several useful strategies, including:

> Change your dyadic (two-person) relationships to triads (three people). Don't make yourself the hub of information and everyone else the spokes; connect people to each other too.
>
> Watch your language—are you speaking in terms of "I" or "we"?
>
> Hire for diversity—including diversity of experience and thought. Don't just hire people with your same personality type and strengths.

In your Customer Education team, you can accomplish this by setting a common goal for the team and providing opportunities for different members of your team to collaborate on challenging projects together.

A CULTURE OF EDUCATION

A couple years into leading the Customer Education team at Optimizely, I was supposed to speak at an all-hands presentation about our team's initiatives.

It was an early-morning meeting, and people looked like they might just as well melt into the floor without a strong cup of coffee. On a whim, my inner facilitator came out—I had to do *something* to get people interacting.

So I started, "I know many new people have started since we last presented on Customer Education, and not everyone knows who's on our team. Could I have the educators in the room raise their hands?"

I held my hand up to demonstrate. The members of my team slowly raised their hands to follow—I was probably embarrassing them. Maybe this was a bad idea.

But I left my hand raised. "Are those all the educators, then?" I asked.

Our VP of Customer Success was the first to get it. He caught my eye with a look of recognition, then held his hand up, too. Slowly, others in the room started to raise their hands. It was dawning on them. I wanted *all* the educators to raise their hands.

Once every hand in the room was up, I said, "That's right. We are *all* educators."

We Are All Educators became a bit of a catchphrase. We even made shirts at one point and gave them to people who contributed to education materials. But the phrase itself was less important than what it symbolized: the fact that we had gone from a company of smart people who didn't have *time* to get all that knowledge out of their heads to a culture that valued education.

I've spent much of this book suggesting that we can't rely on our CSMs, Support reps, and others to run ad hoc Customer Education activities. But even so, they are all educators. They have essential roles to play in helping customers find value in your product and grow in their industries.

Customer Education is not only the secret scale engine for your customers' success, but a way of thinking more deeply about your customer relationships. When you create a culture of education in your business, you bring everyone into the mission of helping customers grow, develop, and become more successful. Often, that means you'll need to be the #1 Customer Education Evangelist at your company. But I hope you find the experience as rewarding as I have; a culture of Customer Education is something to foster.

ABOUT THE AUTHOR

Adam Avramescu is a Customer Education leader with over 10 years of experience working with software companies across finance, marketing, HR, and other industries. Since starting his career as an instructional designer working with organizations ranging from Fortune 500 companies to higher-education and nonprofits, he has built and grown Customer Education programs for companies such as Optimizely, Kasasa, and Checkr.

In 2014, he started the Bay Area Customer Education Meetup, which currently has around 800 members. He also co-hosts the podcast CELab: The Customer Education Laboratory, and is active in speaking and writing about the role of Customer Education for modern technology companies.

Made in the USA
Middletown, DE
12 February 2024

49592970R00182